10/6

Fulham Public Libraries

CENTRAL LIBRARY
598, FULHAM ROAD, S.W.6
TELEPHONE RENOWN 1127-28

Please return this book to the Library from which it was borrowed on or before the latest date below ; otherwise a fine of ONE PENNY for the first week or portion of a week, plus TWOPENCE for each succeeding week or portion of a week overdue will be charged. It is regretted that no reminder can be sent if the book is retained overdue.

21. FEB. 1961	18. DEC. 1961		
-6. MAR. 1961	16. JAN. 1962		
28 MAR 1961	13. FEB. 1962		
-6. APR. 1961			
	27. FEB. 1962		
18. APR. 1961	20. MAR. 1962		
-4. MAY. 1961			
20. MAY. 1961	10. APR 1962		
-2. JUN. 1961			
	-8. MAY. 1962		
12. JUN. 1961	17. MAY 1962		
14 AUG. 1961			
-9. SEP 1961			
-5. OCT. 1961			
21. OCT. 1961			
-6. NOV. 1961			
-9. DEC. 1961			

ELEMENTARY
BOOK-KEEPING

BY

R. GLYNNE WILLIAMS,
F.C.I.S.

C60/19700

657.2 WILy

INSTITUTE FREEMAN, INSTITUTE OF CHARTERED ACCOUNTANTS; "ALLAN COOK
FOR" FREEMAN, LIVERPOOL SOCIETY OF CHARTERED ACCOUNTANTS;
AUTHOR OF "ELEMENTS OF AUDITING" AND "INCOME TAX, SUR-TAX
AND PROFITS TAX, ETC.", AND JOINT AUTHOR OF "THE ELEMENTS
OF COSTING, ETC."

NINTH EDITION

THE DONINGTON PRESS,   THE GREGG PUBLISHING CO., LTD.
ST. PETER'S STREET,   GREGG HOUSE, RUSSELL SQUARE,
ST. ALBANS.   LONDON, W.C.1.

PREFACE

THE object of this book is to enable those wholly unacquainted
with the subject to obtain a sound knowledge and understanding
of the theory of double entry book-keeping.

While the book is intended primarily for examination can-
didates, care has been taken to enlarge upon and explain the
principles of the subject in such a manner as to demonstrate
clearly their application in practice.

The author has included at the end of each chapter a number
of carefully graded exercises. These are intended to enable the
student to obtain that practice which is so essential to success
in the subject. Detailed solutions to the arithmetical exercises
are set out at the end of the book so that students may have
no difficulty in checking their own solutions and locating any
differences in their work.

In compiling the volume, the author has kept prominently
in mind the requirements of the professional preliminary examinations and those of the elementary examinations of the Institute
of Book-keepers, the Royal Society of Arts and the London
Chamber of Commerce.

R. G. W.

LONDON,
    May, 1952.

CONTENTS

CHAPTER I

THEORETICAL BOOK-KEEPING

The subject of Book-keeping may be regarded in two entirely different ways. On the one hand it may be looked upon as a dry uninteresting subject wholly concerned with the figures and accounts which are the unseen and unlovely skeleton of business. On the other hand, and far more reasonably, it may be deemed to have a romance of its own, which well repays all time and thought devoted to its investigation.

Book-keeping, *i.e.*, the art of keeping books of account, is present in some form in every business the whole world over. It is the humble handmaiden of the small country-town tradesman, with his few elementary books and antiquated methods, and it is the highly-esteemed and comfortably-housed servant of the wealthy City merchant. It is a far cry from the white trader in the South Sea Islands to the great industrial combine with its palatial offices in London ; yet each makes use of book-keeping, although in one case it may consist of a single nearly indecipherable hand-written volume and in the other a veritable battery of ledgers, card indexes and loose-leaf systems written up by means of intricate mechanical appliances.

The very achievements of book-keeping are romantic. The great bank, with its branches and agencies spreading to the far corners of the earth, has need of book-keeping before it can give the world, by means of a balance sheet, any idea of its resources. In fact, to go a step further, the complex operations of a modern bank would not have been possible at all without the sound principles of book-keeping upon which it relies. Obviously, a concern cannot carry out many intricate transactions involving millions of pounds unless it possesses an extremely reliable and accurate method of keeping a systematic record of its dealings.

The Meaning and Object of Book-keeping.

All business transactions ultimately resolve themselves into acts relating to buying and selling, or borrowing and lending, and they always deal with money and goods, or, sometimes, with services, such as those rendered by sales assistants and members of the clerical staff. It can easily be understood that unless the

1

trader keeps a careful record of his buying and selling transactions, he will have no reliable knowledge of his progress, *i.e.*, as to whether he is gaining or losing on his transactions, or of the monetary value of his business, or of the debts owing to him or by him. If his business transactions become numerous, the absence of a regular and systematic record must soon result in hopeless confusion.

This explains, in simple terms, the absolute necessity for a system of book-keeping and the important part such system has attained in modern business.

The following definition should now be quite clear :—

> Book-keeping is "the art of permanently recording the monetary (*i.e.*, money) aspect of business transactions in a systematic manner."

Book-keeping is essentially a practical subject, the purpose of which is to aid the conduct of business transactions, *i.e.*, book-keeping was made for business and not business for book-keeping. This is an extremely important fact, and the reader must realize from the very commencement that although the fundamental principles of book-keeping remain the same, the methods of applying those principles in practice must be sufficiently elastic to be capable of application to any particular type of business.

The object of book-keeping is to supply accurate information as to :—

(*a*) The separate amounts owed by the business and to whom ;
(*b*) The separate amounts owed to the business and by whom ;
(*c*) The total amounts owed by and to the business ;
(*d*) The value of all property and possessions of the business ;
(*e*) The gains and losses of the business, in detail and in total ; and
(*f*) The amount of capital invested in the business or the amount of the deficiency if the business is insolvent.

The modern system of book-keeping supplies this information in a remarkably simple yet efficient manner, and enables the owner of a business to ascertain the actual financial position of the business at any given date.

The Theory of Double Entry.

All business transactions resolve themselves, ultimately, into acts of buying and selling goods and services payment for which is, or is to be, made in cash or value of some kind. In short, every business transaction, as distinct from a gift, is an exchange of values. Thus, when a man buys goods he exchanges money for goods, and when he sells goods he exchanges goods for money.

Therefore every business transaction has two entirely distinct effects on the accounts of *each* of the parties, for each of them gives a certain amount of something and receives an equal amount of something else. For example, when a greengrocer buys a box of apples for ten shillings, he gives cash on the one hand and receives goods of the same value on the other ; at the same time the wholesaler from whom he buys finds himself with less goods but more cash. It will be seen that from the point of view of either of them the transaction has a twofold aspect, and it must therefore be recorded twice in the books of both buyer and seller.

This idea of the twofold aspect of every transaction lies at the very root of the " Double Entry " system of book-keeping—the one almost universally adopted by business men—and it must be thoroughly and completely understood before any further progress with the subject is possible.

The conclusions already arrived at may be summarized as follows :—

(*a*) Every business transaction is a *purchase* or a *sale* ;

(*b*) A purchase or a sale is an *exchange* ; and

(*c*) An exchange is a *gain* and a *loss* of equal amount, and therefore every business transaction has *two separate aspects*, a gain and a loss of equal amount.

The Meaning of Debit and Credit.

In book-keeping terms the twofold aspect of every transaction may be expressed by the axiom :—

For every debit there must be a corresponding credit, and for every credit a corresponding debit.

It is first necessary to obtain a clear idea of the meaning of these two important terms *debit* and *credit*. If Smith says "I am indebted to Jones for his kindness," he means that he owes Jones, or he is in debt to Jones, for the favour Jones has done him. He has received a good turn from Jones and he is therefore a debtor to Jones to that extent. If, later, he is able to do Jones a good turn, Jones will be a debtor to him for the benefit received. The net result will then be that the indebtedness of the one will be cancelled by the indebtedness of the other, and the two friends will have repaid their obligations to each other. In other words, the debt Smith owed *to* Jones was balanced by the debt Smith was owed *by* Jones.

This simple illustration, though it concerns matters which cannot be expressed in terms of money, may be applied quite easily to those transactions which are capable of being measured in terms of pounds, shillings and pence, with which book-keeping

is concerned. For example, if Bates, a furniture dealer, sells a dining-room suite, worth £20, to Thompson, one of his customers who keeps an account with him, the result of the transaction is that Thompson becomes his debtor for £20. At the end of the month Thompson pays the £20 to Bates. The action of handing over £20 in cash, if it is considered alone without reference to anything that has happened previously, has the effect of making Thompson a creditor of Bates to that extent.

Let us consider how Bates would record the foregoing transactions. In the first place the sale of the furniture must be recorded in such a way as to show that Thompson is a debtor of Bates. An account in the name of Thompson is therefore opened and an entry made on the left-hand or debit side. It should be noted at this stage that every account has two sides, a debit and a credit side, the debit side by universal custom being on the left. Thompson's account will therefore appear as follows :—

THOMPSON'S ACCOUNT

Dr.				Cr.
19.....		£		
June 3.	To Goods	20		

Thus one aspect of the transaction, the receiving of value by Thompson, has now been recorded. In order to complete the record it is necessary to make some entry to reflect the " giving " aspect of the transaction. The goods have been taken from stock, or in other words, the stock of furniture has given value to the extent of £20, so that if the Stock of Furniture Account (or Goods Account, as it may be alternatively termed) is credited with that amount the record will be completed and so far as this transaction is concerned the Stock of Furniture Account will appear as follows :—

STOCK OF FURNITURE ACCOUNT

Dr.				Cr.
		19.....		£
		June 3.	By Thompson	20

Applying this principle to the subsequent settlement of the debt, it follows that when Thompson gives £20 to Bates the latter will record the fact by a credit to the giver in his account and a debit to the receiving account, which in this case will be the Cash Account, thus :—

THOMPSON'S ACCOUNT

Dr.   Cr.

		£
	19.....	
	June 30. By Cash	20

CASH ACCOUNT

Dr.   Cr.

		£	
19.....			
June 30.	To Thompson	20	

It will be seen that Thompson's account was debited when he received a benefit and credited when he yielded up some benefit in return. In the same way the Cash and Stock of Goods Accounts of the business are debited with amounts coming in, *i.e.*, benefits received, and credited with amounts going out, *i.e.*, benefits yielded up.

It has been pointed out that the principle of double entry arises from the fact that every business transaction has two aspects, a gain and a loss of equal amount, represented by a debit and a corresponding credit. The reader may find some difficulty in understanding in what manner the first transaction results in a gain, as far as Bates is concerned, as it actually appears as though he loses furniture to the value of £20. The correct explanation is not that Thompson gains goods to the same value ; the transaction must be considered from the point of view of Bates alone. It is, furthermore, incorrect to state that Bates gains £20 in cash, as at the date of this transaction no actual cash is received by him. It is always essential in this subject to concentrate solely and entirely upon *one transaction at a time*, and to forget for the moment every other transaction that has gone before or that may follow after.

In what manner, therefore, does Bates gain ? The correct explanation is that *he gains a debt due to him*, as Thompson becomes his debtor to the extent of £20. This conception is extremely important and must be clearly grasped. For purposes of illustration the case of a man buying a postal order for twenty shillings may be considered. He has lost £1 in cash ; but in what way has he gained ? He has gained a debt, owing to him by the Post Office, and he can turn this debt into money again by presenting the postal order for payment.

In the same way Bates has gained a debt, which, although not a material thing to be seen and handled, is nevertheless fully valuable and can be turned into cash later. When Thompson pays his account, Bates gains cash to the extent of £20 and loses a debt owing to him for the same amount. A glance at the account

which records Bates's dealings with Thompson will illustrate the foregoing explanations, and it will be observed that, as the two sides balance, there is now no debt owing by Thompson to Bates.

The foregoing entries are all made in the books of Bates. Thompson will make similar entries to the above (but on the *reverse* sides) in his own books, as for every transaction there are two entries (a complete debit and credit) in each party's books.

Cash Transactions.

There is one other kind of transaction which may well be explained at this stage, and that is where cash is paid for goods at the time of the actual purchase, as for example, if Thompson had paid Bates £20 in cash when he was actually in the shop making the purchase. Strictly speaking the position is the same as before, in that Bates first loses furniture and gains a debt, and at practically the same moment gains cash and loses the same debt. It would, however, be merely a waste of time and involve an unnecessary duplication of work to make two entries in Thompson's account, the first debiting him and the second crediting him with the same amount, thereby cancelling his debt. Therefore, in such a case, the personal aspect of the transaction, *i.e.*, Thompson, is ignored and the transaction is regarded as being an exchange of goods for cash. The necessary entries to be made by Bates are merely a debit to cash, because it has received £20, and a credit to stock of furniture, because it has lost furniture to the value of £20. The actual effect of the transaction divided into its two separate parts is as follows :—

1st TRANSACTION.	2nd TRANSACTION.
Debit Thompson with £20.	*Debit* Cash with £20.
Credit Stock of Furniture with £20.	*Credit* Thompson with £20.

It will be observed that the two entries in Thompson's account cancel each other and that there remain two entries, which are, strictly speaking, the only entries necessary to record a cash transaction, *viz.* :—

Debit Cash with £20.
Credit Stock of Furniture with £20.

Books of Account.

It has been assumed for purposes of simplification that the transactions between Bates and Thompson were entered by the former directly into the accounts concerned. In actual practice, however, all transactions will be passed through two books of account, *viz.* :—

(*a*) The Ledger ; and
(*b*) The Journal.

The Ledger.

Theoretically, the one essential and fundamental book is the *Ledger*, which consists of a number of separate *accounts* kept in a classified form.

> *An account is a statement in which are recorded all the transactions of one specific class which have taken place during a given period.*

Thus, in the previous example, Thompson's Account is a statement of all the transactions between Bates and Thompson ; the Cash Account deals with all transactions affecting Bates's cash ; and the Stock of Furniture Account is one in which are entered all the transactions which increase or decrease the stock of furniture.

In book-keeping an account consists of a page or *folio* of the ledger, down the centre of which a line is ruled to separate the two classes of entry, *i.e.*, debits and credits. There is a cash column on the right and a date column on the left of each of the two halves of the page. The columns headed Journal Folio are used for the insertion of page references to the book in which the original detailed entry is to be found. (Conversely, a " Ledger Folio " column is provided in the Journal (see ruling on page 9) for inserting against each transaction the page on which it is entered in the Ledger.) The extreme left-hand side of each account is headed *Dr.* which is an abbreviation of *debtor*, and the extreme right-hand side is headed *Cr.* which signifies *creditor*. The ledger is thus ruled as follows :—

SPECIMEN LEDGER ACCOUNT RULING

Dr.   Cr.

Date.	Particulars.	Journal Folio.	Amount.	Date.	Particulars.	Journal Folio.	Amount.
19.....			£ s. d.	19.....			£ s. d.

It is customary to prefix the word " To " before all debit entries and the word " By " before all credit entries indicating that the account is a debtor *to* or a creditor *by* the specified account respectively. A helpful rule to remember in making entries in ledger accounts is that the name of an account should not appear as an entry in that account, but that the name of the account in which the corresponding entry is made should be inserted. For example, entries in the Cash Account should *not* be described as " To Cash " or " By Cash," but as, say, " To Thompson " or " By Smith," these being the names of the debtor and creditor

paying or receiving the cash. Similarly, entries in the Goods Account will refer to the supplier or customer concerned (where the goods are bought or sold on credit terms) or to cash (where they are bought or sold for cash). Furthermore, the expressions "Received," "Paid," "Bought" or "Sold" need not appear in the entries in the ledger as the significance of the transaction is indicated automatically by the side of the ledger account on which it appears, e.g., an entry on the debit side of the Cash Account in respect of an amount received from Thompson is worded "To Thompson" and not "To Cash Received from Thompson," as unless it represented cash received it would not appear on the debit side of the Cash Account. Similarly, when cash is received or paid on account of a debt due to or by a trader, the expression "on account" need not appear as the fact that the receipt or payment is on account of the debt due will be evident from an inspection of the account of the customer or supplier.

The Journal.

The Ledger, therefore, contains the accounts in which are shown in a summarized and classified form the debits and credits which arise from the various transactions. From the point of view of the individual accounts, the ledger is the only book necessary to record fully all the transactions in accordance with the essential principles of the double entry system of book-keeping. If, however, no other book were kept, there would be no record of all the business transacted in the date order in which it occurred. Thus, to return to the case of Bates, the furniture dealer, he would have in his ledger a record of all the transactions with Thompson over a given period, and similarly of all those with each of his other customers, and with cash and with his stock of furniture, but he would nowhere have a complete record of *all* the transactions which took place on any one day or other period, in the order in which they occurred.

It is for this reason that the *Journal*, or book of first entry, is used in addition to the Ledger. The root meaning of the term is a *daily* book, or *day by day* book. Thus, it is a record of all business transactions set down, in the order in which they occur, so as to show clearly in one entry both aspects of each transaction.

In the ledger any particular account will show only one aspect of each transaction, the double entry being completed in another account. By showing both aspects of the transaction in one entry the Journal ensures the maintenance of the double entry principle in the ledger.

The ruling of the Journal is quite simple; it is divided by vertical lines into five columns, to record in respect of each item the date, the particulars of the two accounts affected, the ledger

folio reference, and two £ s. d. columns for the debit and credit amounts respectively. The account to be debited is always entered before the account to be credited, the latter being shown slightly more to the right-hand side on the next succeeding line. The abbreviation " *Dr.*" is shown after the debit entry, while the word " To " is prefixed to the credit entry. The credit entry is then followed by a *narration,* or explanation of the nature of the transaction. The narration is an essential part of the entry and should commence with the word " Being."

Thus the transactions of Bates referred to above would be recorded in his Journal in the following manner :—

JOURNAL

Date.	Particulars and Narration.	Ledger Folio.	Debit Column.	Credit Column.
			£ s. d.	£ s. d.
19..... June 3	Thompson . . . . . . *Dr.* To Stock of Furniture . . . . *Being sale of one dining-room suite.*	51 5	20 0 0	20 0 0
June 30	Cash . . . . *Dr.* To Thompson . . . . . . *Being payment of his account for furniture supplied.*	1 51	20 0 0	20 0 0

In actual practice, of course, these two entries would be separated by the record of the large number of transactions which would have taken place during the period between 3rd and 30th June, and the above entries might actually be many pages apart.

The conclusions arrived at in connection with the books of account may now be summarized as follows :—

(a) There are *two* fundamental books of account, the Journal and the Ledger ;

(b) The Journal records both sides of each transaction, *in the date order* in which the transactions occur ;

(c) The Ledger records transactions after they have been *arranged in groups* according to the special nature of each ; and

(d) All transactions must first be recorded in the Journal, from which the necessary postings are made to the Ledger.

It will be shown at a later stage that in practice the Journal

is usually sub-divided into a number of separate books and that the Ledger is similarly divided into a number of separate volumes. These sub-divisions of the two essential books, however, will not affect the main principles which have just been stated and explained, for such principles are fundamental and form the basis of the modern system of book-keeping. It is imperative, therefore, that the reader should be thoroughly conversant with all the book-keeping rules already mentioned before any further progress is made with the theory of the subject.

Kinds of Accounts.

As it is the object of book-keeping to record the two sides of every transaction that takes place, it follows that there must be an account for every person, every item of property and every type of expenditure incurred and income received. Obviously, therefore, accounts must be of many and various kinds, and a division of them into broad classes will be an advantage.

There are two main classes of ledger accounts :—

(a) *Personal Accounts ;* and
(b) *Impersonal Accounts.*

PERSONAL ACCOUNTS are those which record dealings with persons, including, of course, a trader's dealings with partnerships and companies. Thus the account which Bates opened in the name of his customer Thompson is a personal account.

IMPERSONAL ACCOUNTS consist of all ledger accounts other than those that record dealings with persons. Impersonal accounts are usually further sub-divided into two classes, *viz.* :—

(a) *Nominal Accounts ;* and
(b) *Real Accounts.*

NOMINAL ACCOUNTS are those which record items of profits and gains (*e.g.*, interest and commission received), and expenses and losses (*e.g.*, wages, rent, discount allowed).

REAL ACCOUNTS are accounts which record dealings in material things, *i.e.*, property, articles or commodities.

A simple method of distinguishing between the two kinds of impersonal accounts is to consider real accounts as being those dealing with *material* things, whereas nominal accounts are those concerning *intangible* things such as services. The accounts which Bates could open in his books would include those for recording his dealings with his cash, his stock in trade, his shop fittings, and possibly his shop buildings, if he owned the business premises. These specific accounts all concern visible material things and therefore are classified as real accounts.

Nominal Accounts.

Every transaction of an impersonal nature does not involve dealing in material things, so that it may not be possible to record the transaction in a Real Account. Thus a third kind of account—a Nominal Account, as it is termed—becomes necessary. It is obvious that in carrying on business, in addition to the purchase of assets and the buying and selling of goods, certain expenses are incurred and these must of necessity be recorded in two accounts. Our trader Bates, for example, will employ assistants who will be paid wages in return for their services.

In theory, a personal account might be opened for each assistant and when his wages were paid cash account would be credited as the " giving account " and the employee's personal account debited as the " receiving account." The employee is not, however, a debtor of the business, as the wages are paid for services rendered. The rendering of services itself requires a double entry, viz., a credit to the employee's personal account (as he has given the services) and a debit to a Wages Account, which is a Nominal Account recording the receipt of a service, just as a Real Account records the receipt of goods or property.

It will be appreciated that all these entries can be made at the time the wages are paid, but as the debit and credit in the personal account balance each other, it is usual to dispense with such entries and merely record the impersonal aspect. By so doing a great amount of time and labour is saved, particularly in a business where a large number of workmen are employed, as the total wages paid can be recorded weekly by one credit to the cash account and one debit to the wages account. Similarly, other services received can be and are usually recorded by crediting the cash account and debiting the appropriate expense account, the personal aspect being ignored. Conversely, services rendered by the business may be recorded by a debit to cash account and a credit to the appropriate nominal account, e.g., Commission Received Account.

The following are a few typical examples of Nominal Accounts, together with an explanation of the services which they represent:—

NAME OF ACCOUNT.	SERVICES GIVEN OR RECEIVED.
Wages.	Labour by assistants or work-people in shop or factory.
Rent.	Loan of property by landlord.
Insurance.	Right of indemnity in case of loss.
Discount.	Prompt payment of a debt.
Interest.	Loan of money or capital.

Capital Account.

There is one account which it is not easy to classify because it partakes of the nature of two different classes, and that is the Capital Account of the proprietor of the business.   In this account are recorded all transactions between the proprietor himself and the actual business.   It must always be borne in mind that book-keeping records only the transactions effected *by the business* itself and *on behalf of the business*, and not the transactions of the proprietor in a private capacity.

When Bates sold furniture for cash, the books of the business record the fact that there was an exchange between the goods section and the cash section of the business, and therefore Bates himself, as a private individual, is not really considered in this connection.

If this fact is clearly grasped, it will at once become evident that in the first instance Bates, when considered apart from the business, must have loaned a certain amount of money to the business to enable it to commence trading.   Therefore, the business owes Bates this amount and it also owes him any profits which it has made as a result of trading.   Thus, there must be an account between the business and the proprietor to record what the business owes to him, and this account is known as the Capital Account.

In the sense that this account records the relations between the business and the proprietor it should be regarded as a *personal account*, and it should always be considered in this light.   It can, however, be argued that, as the Capital Account records the difference between the total amount owing to the business and the total amount owing by the business, it should be classed as a nominal account.   This latter view is inadvisable as it usually gives rise to confusion in the minds of students.

The success or otherwise of a business cannot be judged solely from fluctuations of the balance shown on the Capital Account. Successful trading will most likely result in an increased balance, and a decrease in the balance will very probably be due to losses, but fluctuations in the balance are also caused by extra capital being put into the business, or by cash being withdrawn by the trader for his personal use—quite apart from trading results.

Rules for Debiting and Crediting.

The primary and most elementary principles of the subject of book-keeping having been stated, it is now advisable to consider the rules governing the correct making of entries with a view to applying these theoretical principles to actual practical examples. Before doing so, however, it will be useful to review and tabulate the main principles and rules which have already been stated,

in order that there may be a sound foundation upon which to build. The principles given in the preceding pages may be summarized as follows :—

(a) *Every business transaction* is an exchange.

(b) *Every exchange* results in a gain and a loss of equal amount.

(c) Every *debit* must have its corresponding *credit*, and *vice versa*.

(d) A *debit* is an entry on the left-hand side of an account which makes that account a debtor, as far as the item debited is concerned. Conversely, a *credit* is an entry on the right-hand side of an account, making that account a creditor, as far as the item credited is concerned.

(e) *When cash is not paid at the time of the sale of goods,* the gain of the business, in return for the loss of goods, is the gain of a debt owing to the business. Conversely, when cash is not paid at the time of the purchase of goods, the loss of the business, in return for the gain of goods, is the debt owing by the business.

(f) *When a transaction involves nominal items,* the gain of the business, in return for the loss of cash, is the gain of a service done to the business ; or conversely, the loss of the business, in return for a gain of cash, is the loss of a service done by the business.

In addition to the above principles, the following rules as to the right attitude to be adopted in recording book-keeping transactions have been stated, *viz.* :—

(a) Concentrate upon one transaction at a time. When considering the resultant debit and credit, loss and gain, ignore entirely any prior or subsequent transactions.

(b) Consider the accounts as being entirely those of the business, as distinct from the owner, the business being responsible to the owner for the amount he has loaned to it and for subsequent profits.

(c) If the settlement for a transaction takes place at the same time as the transaction itself it is usual to ignore the personal aspect.

If the foregoing principles are thoroughly understood, the reader will not encounter much difficulty in connection with the practical rules which govern entries in the accounts. It has been

explained at some length that a man who receives anything from another is indebted to him, *i.e.*, is a debtor to him, for that amount, and conversely, the man who gives something is a creditor of the recipient.   Thus it may be said that a man is a debtor for what he receives, and a creditor for what he gives.

Therefore, translating *debit* as meaning " make a debtor of," a man is debited in respect of what he receives and is credited for what he gives.   The same procedure may be adopted in the case of any kind of account, whether personal or impersonal, and thus, the following fundamental rules may be stated :—

DEBIT RECEIVING ACCOUNT, *i.e.*, place on the left-hand or debtor side of an account any value that comes into that account ; and

CREDIT GIVING ACCOUNT, *i.e.*, place on the right-hand or creditor side of an account any value that goes out of that account.

These rules, and the explanation of them, are vitally important, for they are the foundation of all book-keeping from the most elementary to the most advanced stage.

Consider their application to the different classes of accounts :—

PERSONAL ACCOUNTS.   In this class of account the rules resolve themselves into the general rule " *Debit Receiver, Credit Giver.*" If a person *receives* cash, goods or property of any kind or services from a business, that person's account in the books of the business is *debited*.   If a person *gives* cash, goods or property of any kind or services to the business, then that person's account is *credited*. The application of the rules to personal accounts is, therefore, quite straightforward and no difficulty should be experienced.

REAL ACCOUNTS.   If cash is received the receiving account is obviously the cash account and consequently the cash account must be debited.   If cash is paid away the cash account gives value and consequently must be credited.   Similarly the goods account or any other real account will be debited with property received or coming into the business and credited with value going out.   The rule for real accounts might therefore be said to be " *debit value in ; credit value out.*"

NOMINAL ACCOUNTS.   As previously stated, these accounts record services received and given.   If, for example, Bates pays his landlord £50 for rent of premises this payment represents the value of services received by way of occupation of the landlord's property.   In theory, the landlord must be credited as the giver of the service and debited as the receiver of the cash, whilst cash account is credited as the giver of the cash and rent account is debited as the receiver of the service, but, as has been previously mentioned, it is customary when recording such expenses to ignore the personal aspect and simply credit cash and debit the appropriate expense or " service " account.   The application of the

general rule to nominal accounts can best be expressed as "*Debit Expenses ; Credit Gains.*"

It is extremely important that the rules as explained above be clearly understood, as they apply to all transactions and unless they can be applied readily constant difficulty will be experienced.

A Practical Example.

For the purpose of illustrating the application of the rules and of providing the student with a little practice in this respect the transactions of Bates, the furniture dealer, for the first month in which he was engaged in business will now be considered.

EXAMPLE

TRANSACTIONS OF ARNOLD BATES, TRADING AS "THE DIRECT FURNITURE STORE."

19........

(1) 1st January.   Arnold Bates commences business with a capital of £500.

(2) 2nd January.   He buys furniture from Wholesalers, Limited, for £400.

(3) 15th January.   He sells a bedstead for £5, and is paid cash by the customer.

(4) 16th January.   He sells a bedroom suite value £35 to B. Lawson.

(5) 30th January.   He pays his new assistant one week's wages, £2.

(6) 31st January.   He pays £200 on account to Wholesalers, Limited.

In the above example are six distinct transactions, each of which must be considered separately.

(1) *The commencement of business.* In this transaction, Bates, as a private individual, hands over £500 to the Direct Furniture Store, as a business. It has already been emphasized that the transactions must always be regarded as those of the business, as a separate concern, and not as those of the proprietor of that business. The proprietor must be considered as someone entirely distinct from the business, to whom the business owes what it receives from him and also what profits it makes.

The transaction, as far as the business is concerned, is that it *receives* £500 in cash, given to it by the proprietor, Bates. Cash Account (a real account) receives value and, therefore, must be *debited* with the £500. The personal account of the owner, *i.e.*, his Capital Account, gives value to the business, and must be *credited* accordingly. Therefore the entries will be :—

DEBIT Cash Account.

CREDIT Capital Account.

(2) *Purchase of furniture.* The business in this case exchanges furniture for a debt, *i.e.*, it *gains* £400 worth of furniture and it *loses* an outgoing debt. The Stock of Furniture Account (a real account) receives value in and therefore must be *debited* with the value received. Wholesalers, Limited, give a benefit to the business, and thus their personal account must be *credited* with the amount due to them for the furniture. Therefore the entries will be :—

DEBIT Stock of Furniture Account.
CREDIT Wholesalers, Limited.

(3) *Sale of furniture for cash.* In this transaction the exchange made by the business is easily distinguished, for it concerns two material things, furniture and cash. The Stock of Furniture Account gives value and thus must be *credited* with the value taken out. On the other hand, Cash Account receives value and must, therefore, be *debited*. Therefore the entries will be :—

DEBIT Cash Account.
CREDIT Stock of Furniture Account.

(4) *Sale of furniture on credit.* In this case the business loses furniture as in the previous transaction, and thus Stock of Furniture Account must be *credited*. The business does not, however, gain cash, as in the previous transaction, but an incoming debt, for the customer, Lawson, becomes liable for the amount of the goods, and is a debtor for what he receives. His personal account must therefore be *debited*. Thus the entries in this case will be :—

DEBIT B. Lawson.
CREDIT Stock of Furniture Account.

(5) *Payment of wages.* This is a case of an exchange of cash for services, and a nominal account is therefore involved. Cash goes out of the business, and therefore Cash Account must be *credited* because it loses the amount paid out. Wages Account (a nominal account), on the other hand, records the receipt of the service, *i.e.*, it is the receiving account and must, therefore, be *debited*. Thus the entries will be :—

DEBIT Wages Account.
CREDIT Cash Account.

(6) *Payment to creditor.* Wholesalers, Limited, is a creditor of the business, because it is owed money by the business, in respect of the furniture purchased. In this transaction a payment is made on account, thus a portion of the debt is extinguished. Therefore, as Wholesalers, Limited, receive £200 and as they receive a benefit to that extent they must be *debited* while, as in the previous transaction, Cash Account has again lost value

and therefore requires to be *credited*. Thus the entries will be :—

DEBIT Wholesalers, Limited.
CREDIT Cash Account.

Entries in the Journal.

Having explained the meaning and reasons for each entry, it will not now be a difficult matter to enter up the Journal. As already explained (see page 8), it is usual to enter the names of the two accounts affected in the particulars column, the account to be debited being given first and the account to be credited on the next succeeding line, and to give below each entry a short explanatory description of the transaction, known as the *narration*. The abbreviation "Dr." is given after the name of the first account in each entry.

JOURNAL OF THE DIRECT FURNITURE STORE

Folio 1.

			Dr.			Cr.		
			£	s.	d.	£	s.	d.
19.....								
Jan. 1	Cash Account . . . . Dr.	1	500	0	0			
	To Capital Account of A. Bates	2				500	0	0
	Being amount of cash introduced by him.							
„ 2	Stock of Furniture Account Dr.	3	400	0	0			
	To Wholesalers, Limited .	4				400	0	0
	Being purchase of furniture.							
„ 15	Cash Account . . . . Dr.	1	5	0	0			
	To Stock of Furniture Account	3				5	0	0
	Being sale of bedstead for cash.							
„ 16	B. Lawson . . . . . Dr.	5	35	0	0			
	To Stock of Furniture Account	3				35	0	0
	Being sale of bedroom suite.							
„ 30	Wages Account . . . . Dr.	6	2	0	0			
	To Cash Account	1				2	0	0
	Being payment of wages for week.							
„ 31	Wholesalers, Limited . . Dr.	4	200	0	0			
	To Cash Account	1				200	0	0
	Being part payment of their account for furniture supplied.							
	Total . . .	£	1,142	0	0	1,142	0	0

Ledger Entries.

It is now possible to make the entries in the various ledger accounts. It should be noted that each account would, in practice, occupy a separate page or folio in the ledger, the pages of which are numbered consecutively. In this example, the accounts themselves are numbered, to facilitate reference. The nature of the transaction is usually indicated by inserting, in the particulars column, the name of the *other* account affected by the double entry.

The above Journal items will be entered in the Ledger thus :—

Account No. 1.

Dr.   CASH ACCOUNT   *Cr.*

19.....			£	s.	d.	19.....			£	s.	d.
Jan. 1	To Capital .	J1	500	0	0	Jan. 30	By Wages .	J1	2	0	0
„ 15	„ Stock of					„ 31	„ Whole-				
	Furniture	J1	5	0	0		salers, Ltd.	J1	200	0	0

Account No. 2.

Dr.   CAPITAL ACCOUNT OF A. BATES   *Cr.*

						19.....			£	s.	d.
						Jan. 1	By Cash . .	J1	500	0	0

Account No. 3.

Dr.   STOCK OF FURNITURE ACCOUNT   *Cr.*

19.....			£	s.	d.	19.....			£	s.	d.
Jan. 2	To Wholesalers,					Jan. 15	By Cash . .	J1	5	0	0
	Limited .	J1	400	0	0	„ 16	„ B. Lawson	J1	35	0	0

Account No. 4.

Dr.   WHOLESALERS, LIMITED   *Cr.*

19.....			£	s.	d.	19.....			£	s.	d.
Jan. 31	To Cash . .	J1	200	0	0	Jan. 2	By Stock of				
							Furniture .	J1	400	0	0

Dr.   B. LAWSON   Cr.

19..... Jan. 16	To Stock of Furniture .	J1	£ s. d. 35 0 0			

Dr.   WAGES ACCOUNT   Cr.

19..... Jan. 30	To Cash . .	J1	£ s. d. 2 0 0			

It will be noticed that debit entries have the prefix " To " and credit entries the prefix " By." These must be read in conjunction with the headings " Dr." and " Cr.," which stand for " Debtor " and " Creditor " respectively. Thus the entry on the left-hand side of the Wages Account indicates that Wages Account is " debtor to " the business on account of wages paid out of cash, while the credit entry in Capital Account indicates that the account is a " creditor by " the payment into the business of cash.

Ledger Balances.

In the foregoing example it will be noticed that the total of the entries on the debit side of, say, the Cash Account, does not exactly equal the total of the entries on the credit side, i.e., the two sides of the account do not balance. In the case mentioned, the total of the debit side is £505 and that of the credit side is £202, the difference being a surplus of £303 on the debit side. This difference is known as the *balance* of the account, and as the debit total exceeds the credit total it is said to be a *debit balance*. Conversely, an account is said to show a *credit balance* when the total of the credit items exceeds that of the debit items.

Balancing an account sometimes presents a little difficulty to beginners because the balance is first shown on the side opposite to that expected, i.e., a *debit* balance first appears on the *credit* side. A moment's thought, however, will show that if the total debit items exceed the total credit items the difference between the two sides must be placed on the credit side in order to make the totals of the two sides equal.

Thus in the case of the Cash Account mentioned above, the difference of £303 will first require to be shown on the *credit* side (although it is a debit balance) in order to make both totals amount

to the total of the greater side, *i.e.*, £505. The balance is then brought down to the opposite side, *i.e.*, the correct side, thus completing the double entry, and will represent the commencing point of the account for the succeeding period.

The following example shows the Cash Account after the correct balance has been inserted :—

Dr.   CASH ACCOUNT   *Cr.*

19.....			£	s.	d.	19.....			£	s.	d.
Jan. 1	To Capital .	J1	500	0	0	Jan. 30	By Wages .	J1	2	0	0
„ 15	„ Stock of					„ 31	„ Whole-				
	Furniture	J1	5	0	0		salers,				
							Ltd.	J1	200	0	0
						„ 31	„ Balance .	c/d	303	0	0
			£505	0	0				£505	0	0
Jan. 31	To Balance	b/d	303	0	0						

Accounts should always be balanced in this manner so that they may present a finished appearance. When, however, a single entry appears in a ledger account there is no need to balance off the account, as the nature of the balance is apparent at a glance.

The balance brought down on the ledger account may be dated for the last day of the current accounting period or for the first day of the succeeding accounting period. Thus the debit balance shown above may be dated " Jan. 31 " or " Feb. 1." The former method is recommended and has been adopted in this work, although there is no objection to the adoption of either method, provided one method only is adopted throughout.

It should be noted that when inserting balances in practice the abbreviations " c/d " and " b/d " are used to represent " carried down " and " brought down " respectively. Similarly, it is usual when carrying forward totals from the foot of one page to the head of the next to use the abbreviations " c/f " and " b/f " to represent " carried forward " and " brought forward " respectively.

The Trial Balance.

It now remains to explain the method of checking the accuracy of ledger postings, which is known as taking out a Trial Balance. This operation is based on the elementary and fundamental rule of book-keeping that every debit has a corresponding credit of the same amount and every credit a corresponding debit of the same amount. If, therefore, every transaction is recorded in the

books by means of (a) a debit entry in one account, and (b) a credit entry for the same amount in another account, it follows that if at any time the total of all the entries on the debit side of all the accounts is obtained, and likewise the sum total of all the credit entries in the accounts, these two grand totals should be equal. If the two totals do not agree, it indicates that there is some error or errors in the posting or in the additions of the accounts, which requires to be located before the books will balance correctly.

A Trial Balance consists of a summary of all the debit postings and of all the credit postings which appear in the accounts, to enable the accuracy of the book-keeping records to be tested. In actual practice, however, it is usual to make a list of the various debit balances and credit balances, and to omit the actual total debits and total credits. A little consideration will show that exactly the same effect is obtained if the above Cash Account is shown as a debit of £303 only as if it is given as a debit of £505 and a credit of £202.

It must be remembered that the balance of a ledger account represents the net result of the combined postings in that account.

The following Trial Balance of the accounts given in the above example is set out to show the totals of the debit and credit postings in addition to the balances of the accounts. It should be noted that both in practice and in working out exercises for examination purposes, only the *balances* of the ledger accounts need be given.

THE DIRECT FURNITURE STORE
Trial Balance at 31st January, 19.....

Ledger Folio.	Name of Account.	Total Postings. Dr.	Total Postings. Cr.	Balances. Dr.	Balances. Cr.
		£ s. d.	£ s. d.	£ s. d.	£ s. d.
1	Cash	505 0 0	202 0 0	303 0 0	
2	Capital . . .		500 0 0		500 0 0
3	Stock of Furniture	400 0 0	40 0 0	360 0 0	
4	Wholesalers, Limited. . .	200 0 0	400 0 0		200 0 0
5	B. Lawson . .	35 0 0		35 0 0	
6	Wages . . .	2 0 0		2 0 0	
		£ 1,142 0 0	£1,142 0 0	£700 0 0	£700 0 0

PUBLIC LIBRARIES

As, whichever method is adopted, the totals of the debit and the credit columns are equal, the arithmetical accuracy of the postings to the ledger accounts is proved, for every debit must have had a corresponding credit of the same amount, and *vice versa*. The agreement of the Trial Balance does not, however, prove that the various debits and credits have been posted to the correct *accounts*, but this is a matter which will be dealt with in a later chapter.

Summary of Double Entry.

At this stage the reader should appreciate that the three essentials in book-keeping by double entry are as follows :—

1. Every payment or delivery involves a receipt, and *vice versa*.

2. Every transaction in the separate accounts forming the series can be recorded both on the debit side of one account and on the credit side of another. Thus the account debited is always that to which something is given or added, and may therefore be regarded as the " receiving " account, while the account credited may be regarded as the " paying " account, being always that from which something is taken.

3. The total of all the items recorded on the debit side of all the accounts added together must always be equal to the total of the items similarly recorded on the credit side. Similarly, the total of all the debit balances of the accounts added together must always be equal to the total of all the credit balances of the accounts added together.

EXERCISE 1

A. What is Book-keeping ?

B. What are the objects of Book-keeping ?

C. Explain the theory of Double Entry Book-keeping, and the uses of the terms debit and credit.

D. Explain the uses of the Journal and Ledger.

E. How are the records in the Ledger classified ? Give an example of each kind of account.

F. Enter up the following items in the Journal and Ledger of J. Brown :—
   19.....
   Feb. 2. Sold goods to H. Scott, £30 5s.
   „ 14. Received cash on account from H. Scott, £25.
   „ 25. Sold goods to B. Farr and received cash for same, £12 12s.
   „ 27. Sold goods to H. Scott, £9 17s.
   „ 28. Received balance owing by H. Scott.

G. Make out G. Ridge's Account in your Ledger in respect of the following dealings during March, 19.....

			£	s.	d.
March	2.	Ridge buys goods from you.	20	15	9
„	8.	You receive cash from Ridge on account.	15	10	0
„	10.	You sell goods to Ridge.	16	17	4
„	31.	You buy goods from Ridge.	2	3	7

Bring down the balance on the account.

H. J. Temple, merchant, commenced business on 1st March, 19.... with a capital of £1,000 in cash. His transactions for the month of March were as follows :—

			£	s.	d.
March	2.	Bought goods for cash.	75	10	0
„	4.	Bought goods from M. Tower.	125	0	0
„	7.	Sold goods for cash.	30	0	0
„	8.	Paid M. Tower on account.	50	0	0
„	9.	Sold goods to J. Field.	113	7	6
„	10.	Paid carriage on goods.	4	3	6
„	10.	Paid wages.	5	5	0
„	12.	Sold goods to F. Lawn.	53	2	9
„	16.	Received cash from F. Lawn on account.	20	0	0
„	20.	Bought goods from H. Heat.	18	12	0
„	21.	Paid M. Tower balance of account.	75	0	0
„	25.	Paid rent.	9	0	0
„	30.	Paid wages.	7	15	0
„	31.	Bought goods at auction for cash.	33	10	0
„	31.	Sold goods to M. Lowe, and received £10 on account.	23	7	9

Enter the above transactions in the proper books and extract a Trial Balance as on 31st March, 19.....

J. The transactions of B. Neave, a wholesale draper, for the month of January 19..... were as follows :—

Jan. 1. Commenced business with cash, £1,570.
  „ 4. Bought of W. Sparrow, Cloth £100, Carpets £75.
  „ 5. Bought for cash, 40 rolls of Tweed at £10 10s. per roll.
  „ 7. Sold to J. Hignett, 4 Carpets at £5 15s. each.
  „ 9. Paid office expenses, wages £4, rent £2 and postages £1 2s. 6d.
  „ 9. Paid W. Sparrow £100 on account.
  „ 12. Received from J. Hignett cash in settlement of his account.
  „ 15. Sold Cloth for cash, £40.
  „ 22. Bought of S. Higham, 27 rolls of Velvet at £11 3s. per roll.
  „ 24. Sold to J. Dewar, 10 rolls of Tweed at £15 per roll.
  „ 30. Sold to J. Hignett, 12 rolls of Velvet at £14 7s. 6d. per roll.
  „ 31. Received from J. Dewar, £75 on account.
  „ 31. Paid S. Higham his account.

Open the necessary Ledger Accounts and post the above transactions thereto through the Journal. Bring down the balances on the Ledger and extract a Trial Balance as on 31st January, 19.....

CHAPTER II

THEORETICAL BOOK-KEEPING (*continued*)

In Chapter I an endeavour was made to give a broad idea of the fundamental principles of book-keeping, and to explain the elementary theory up to the extraction of a Trial Balance. In actual practice, however, the methods adopted require to be modified, and in this and succeeding chapters there will be introduced certain variations and developments which do not, however, affect the fundamental principles already stated.

It is considered advisable once again to state that successful progress in this subject depends entirely upon a sound knowledge of the rules given in Chapter I. It should be noted that these rules apply equally whether the journal is contained in one book or (as is more usual) is sub-divided into several separate books, or whether any other variations are introduced.

The Cash Book.

One of the first developments of the double entry system of book-keeping is the separation of the Cash Account from the remainder of the ledger.

It is obvious that in the majority of businesses the number of transactions involving the receipt or the payment of cash must out-number those of any other type of transaction. Furthermore, however many entries there may be in the Cash Account, only one clerk at a time (and that not all the time) can be employed in dealing with them if the account is included with all the other accounts in the ledger. If, therefore, the Cash Account is taken out of the ledger and bound up as a separate volume, this difficulty is removed, for one clerk, *i.e.*, the cashier, can then devote the whole of his time to the entry of cash transactions, while another is employed upon the remaining ledger accounts.

There is a further reason for the separation of the Cash Account, namely, that it is the account which requires to be most frequently balanced, in order that the cash in hand or at the bank at any given date may be ascertained and checked.

The cashier is responsible for all incoming and outgoing cash, and the only way in which he can check the accuracy of his work is by comparing the balance of the Cash Account with the amount of cash in hand or at the bank. Thus, for purposes of convenience

the Cash Account is recorded in a separate book known as the CASH BOOK, which is in the charge of the cashier.

The Cash Book is part of the ledger and must always be regarded as the Cash Account taken out of the ledger and bound up separately in order to facilitate the recording of cash transactions. It is particularly important that this should be remembered, because the Cash Book has also to be regarded as being, in a way, part of the journal.

As the Cash Book is separate and deals with all the cash items, it does not seem necessary to journalize the items individually, and useless duplication of labour is avoided by omitting all cash transactions from the journal.

Thus, in practice, every transaction which involves the receipt or the payment of cash is entered direct into the Cash Book, value which comes in (*receipts*) being debited, *i.e.*, entered on the left-hand side, in accordance with the fundamental rule, and value which goes out (*payments*) being credited, *i.e.*, entered on the right-hand side. The entries are then posted from the Cash Book to the respective accounts in the Ledger, items on the debit side of the Cash Book being posted to the *credit* side of the particular ledger account and *vice versa*, thereby completing the double entry.

For example, to return to the original transaction of Bates with Thompson referred to in Chapter I. When Thompson paid £20 to Bates, no entry would, in practice, be made in the journal, but the item would be entered at once on the *debit* side of the Cash Book, thus :—

Dr.			CASH BOOK			Cr.
Date.	Particulars.	Ledger Folio.	Amount Received.	Date.	Particulars.	Amount Paid.
19..... June 30	To Thompson		£ s. d. 20 0 0			£ s. d.

The ledger-keeper would then post the item to the *credit* side of Thompson's Account in the ledger, thereby giving effect to the rule that every debit must have a corresponding credit.

This separation of the Cash Account is an example of one of the cases of development from the elementary theory which were referred to at the commencement of this chapter. Yet a further development occurs when a specialized form of Cash Book is used with two or three cash columns on each side, as will be described at a later stage. For the present, however, attention should be confined to the simple form of Cash Book set out above.

Purchases and Sales Accounts.

The next development which requires to be considered is the sub-division of the account which records transactions in the goods or commodities dealt in by the business. In the elementary example given in Chapter I, this account was called the Stock of Furniture Account. It is sometimes referred to as the Goods Account, but whatever its name may be, its purpose is to record the dealings between the business and its stock of goods.

It will be remembered that in accordance with the fundamental rule, this account was debited with goods coming in, *i.e.*, goods purchased, and was credited with goods going out, *i.e.*, goods sold. Thus, in the example at the end of the previous chapter, the Stock of Furniture Account shows a debit item of £400 which represents goods purchased, and two credit items totalling £40 which represent goods sold.

In practice it is found much more convenient to open separate accounts to record goods purchased and goods sold respectively, as in this way more classified information is available. Thus, in the above example, it is just as easy to post the entries for goods purchased to one account and for goods sold to another as it is to post them to the two sides of one combined account. Therefore, in practice, the combined Goods Account is divided into the following separate accounts :—(*a*) Goods Purchased Account; (*b*) Goods Sold Account ; and (*c*) Stock Account.

The first of these accounts, generally termed the Purchases Account, is debited with the cost price of incoming goods, while the second account, known as the Sales Account, is credited with the sale price of outgoing goods. The purpose of the third account is to record the stock, or balance of goods on hand at the end of the accounting period. These accounts will be explained more fully in subsequent pages.

The double entry for purchases and sales may be summarized, at this stage, as follows :—

(1) CASH PURCHASE :   *Debit* Goods Purchased Account (or Purchases A/c.).

Credit Cash Account.

(2) CREDIT PURCHASE :   *Debit* Goods Purchased Account (or Purchases A/c.).

Credit Personal Account of Supplier.

(3) CASH SALE :   *Debit* Cash Account.

Credit Goods Sold Account (or Sales A/c.).

(4) CREDIT SALE :   *Debit* Personal Account of Customer.
                      Credit Goods Sold Account (or
                      Sales A/c.).

The Trading Account.

An endeavour has been made in the previous pages to state in detail the methods adopted to record transactions as incomings and outgoings or debits and credits. It will be noted, however, that no mention has been made of profits or losses on trading or of the steps to be taken in order to ascertain the exact position of a business at any given date. The ascertainment of profits or losses made by a business is one of the most important objects of book-keeping, and a general explanation of the procedure to be adopted to obtain this result will therefore be given at this stage, in order that the reader may be able to work elementary exercises as far as the preparation of the actual Balance Sheet.

Referring to the example at the end of Chapter I, it will be noted that although every debit has its corresponding credit of equal amount, there does not appear to be recorded any actual profit or loss resulting from trading.

A very simple example will probably be the most helpful illustration in this case, therefore it is proposed to reconsider the sale of the bedroom suite for £35 by Bates to Lawson. This particular suite was bought from Wholesalers, Limited amongst the £400 worth of furniture purchased at the commencement of business, and was priced at, say, £20. Bates therefore makes a profit of £15 because he sells for £35 an article which cost him £20. The reader will in all probability wonder why this profit is not shown in the accounts. The explanation of this apparent omission is that the Stock of Furniture Account has not been completed, as it is necessary to know the value of the goods remaining unsold in order to ascertain the amount of profit resulting from the trading transactions.

If Bates were to value all the stock of furniture in his shop on the 31st January at its cost price, he would find that it would come to, say, £376 10s. The balance of the Stock of Furniture Account, however, as shown in the ledger is £360 (£400 less £40). The difference of £16 10s. represents the profit Bates has made on his trading transactions for the period, and thus it will be seen that actually there is an idea of " gaining more than one gave," hidden beneath the figures of the accounts. In other words, Bates can add £16 10s. to his Stock of Furniture Account, and its balance will then agree with the actual value of the stock on hand. The explanation of the actual procedure to be adopted in practice will be deferred until a further example has been considered.

To take a still more simple example, suppose a boy with a business turn of mind buys ten apples at a halfpenny each, the

B

total cost therefore being 5d. If he sells four apples at a penny each, he still has six apples left which may be assumed to be worth what they cost him, *i.e.*, a halfpenny each, equalling a total value of 3d. Thus he has received 4d. for the apples he has sold and has apples to the value of 3d. still unsold, making a total of 7d. If the original cost of all the apples, 5*d.*, is deducted there is a profit shown of 2d.

This example may be shown in account form as follows :—

Dr.	TRADING ACCOUNT (*1st Period*).		Cr.
To Purchases	5d.	By Sales	4d.
(10 apples at ½d.)		(4 apples at 1d.)	
,, Profit	2d.	,, Stock at end	3d.
		(6 apples at ½d.)	
	7d.		7d.

From the above account it will be seen that the boy is left with a stock of six apples valued at 3d., and that he has made a profit of 2d., which will be required to be transferred to some other account. The succeeding period will commence with a stock of apples to the value of 3d., which the account must show as a *debit* balance as it represents value in.

Assuming that during this succeeding period the boy buys six more apples at a halfpenny each and is successful in selling eight apples at one penny each, he will, therefore, be left with four apples on hand to the value of 2d.

The Trading Account for this period will thus appear as follows :

Dr.	TRADING ACCOUNT (*2nd Period*).		Cr.
To Stock at beginning . .	3d.	By Sales	8d.
(6 apples at ½d.)		(8 apples at 1d.)	
,, Purchases	3d.	,, Stock at end	2d.
(6 apples at ½d.)		(4 apples at ½d.)	
,, Profit	4d.		
	10d.		10d.

Thus, in the second period, he has made a profit of 4d., which can easily be checked by a simple sum in mental arithmetic, without reference to these accounts. The result obtained from the above account may be given as a simple formula, *viz.* :—

PROFIT = [Sales + Closing Stock] *less* [Purchases + Commencing Stock].

This simple example, although so easily understood, is a perfect illustration of the Trading Account in actual practice. The value of the stock on hand at the beginning of the period is debited to

Stock Account.   At the end of the period this amount is transferred to Trading Account (*Credit* Stock Account, *Debit* Trading Account).   The total amounts of the Purchases and the Sales for the period are similarly transferred at the end of the period, the former being debited to Trading Account (*Credit* Purchases Account, *Debit* Trading Account), and the latter credited (*Debit* Sales Account, *Credit* Trading Account).   There is no necessity to carry the balance of an account down before transferring it to the Trading Account.

It then remains to ascertain the value of the stock on hand at the end of the period, and this ascertained amount is entered in the books by being debited to Stock Account and credited to Trading Account.   A debit balance therefore remains in the Stock Account, representing the value of the goods on hand at the end of the current period (and at the commencement of the succeeding period).   When the Trading Account is balanced, the amount by which the total of the debit side falls short of the total of the credit side, *i.e.*, the *credit* balance, will represent the *gross profit* for the period.

If the trader has been so unfortunate as to make a loss during the period, the position will be reversed, the total of the debit side will exceed that of the credit side, and the *debit* balance, or *gross loss*, will appear as an entry on the credit side of the Trading Account. Such a gross loss indicates that the trader has disposed of his goods below cost price.

The bringing into account of outstanding stocks in order to arrive at the true gross profit will perhaps be more fully appreciated if the matter is viewed in a different light.   At first sight it would appear that the sales less purchases will give the profit, but a little thought will make it clear that it is the COST OF GOODS SOLD rather than purchases which must be deducted from the sales to arrive at the profit.   The cost of goods sold must obviously be the opening stock plus purchases less closing stock, *i.e.*, in the second example on the previous page, 3d. + 3d. − 2d. = 4d.   If this figure is deducted from the sales (8d.) the result is 4d.—the amount of the profit.

The significance of the terms " gross profit " and " gross loss " is shown by the following simple formulæ :—

GROSS PROFIT : (Sales + Closing Stock) *less* (Purchases + Commencing Stock).

GROSS LOSS : (Purchases + Commencing Stock) *less* (Sales + Closing Stock).

In practice, certain other items may be debited to Trading Account, but, in order to avoid confusion, consideration of these will be deferred until later.

The Profit and Loss Account.

It will be noted from the preceding simple example that the boy made a small profit as a result of his business transactions. Furthermore, as he was in the fortunate position of having incurred no trading expenses, he personally gained to the full extent of the profit. A moment's reflection, however, will make it clear that this is not the case with the profit of £16 10s. which Bates made on his sales of furniture, for there are many expenses of trading which require to be deducted before it is possible to arrive at the net amount by which the trader personally gains. Wages must be paid, carriage deducted, and allowance made for heating, lighting and a score of other items.

It is to record these expenses of carrying on the business that the account known as the Profit and Loss Account is opened. This account collects together all the various items of gain or loss which have been made or incurred respectively during the trading period. The actual gross profit, or loss, on trading is also included in this account by a transfer from the Trading Account.

It was explained in Chapter I that nominal accounts are those which may be said to be responsible to the business for the services done to or by the business. Thus, when wages are paid in cash, Wages Account is debited because that account has received value in the form of services rendered to the business by the employees. All similar items of expense are now gathered together into a Profit and Loss Account, by means of transfer entries, and thus this one account takes over their responsibility, and itself becomes responsible to the business for all the services which have been received during the period. Similarly, any items of income, *i.e.*, in respect of services given by the business, are transferred to this account.

Therefore, in order to transfer the total amount of wages paid out during the period, Wages Account is *credited* and Profit and Loss Account is *debited*, for the latter becomes responsible to the business for the labour services received and thus receives value in. A similar procedure is adopted in the case of the balances of all other expense accounts.

The balances of income accounts, such as Interest Account, or Discount Received Account, are transferred to the *credit* of Profit and Loss Account, for the business becomes responsible to the latter for services which it has given out.

In order to transfer the gross profit or loss on trading the necessary entries are : in the case of a gross profit *debit* Trading Account and *credit* Profit and Loss Account : and in the case of a gross loss *debit* Profit and Loss Account and *credit* Trading Account.

Transfers of the type referred to above should be distinguished from entries in respect of trading transactions. They involve, it is true, a debit to one account and a credit to another account,

but they are more readily understood if the elementary rule of
debiting the "receiving" and crediting the "giving" account
is ignored and they are regarded as the cancellation of a balance
(or entry) in one account and its re-instatement in another account
on the same side as it originally appeared. For example, to
transfer a debit balance on Wages Account to Profit and Loss
Account involves a credit in the former account to cancel the
balance and a debit in the Profit and Loss Account, thus re-
instating the debit balance in that account.

When all the necessary transfers have been effected, the Profit
and Loss Account will show on the credit side the gross profit
(if any) on trading, together with any other income or gains, and
on the debit side the gross loss (if any) and any other expenses or
losses. This account may now be balanced in order to ascertain
the net result from the business transactions for the period. If the
total of the credit side exceeds that of the debit side the difference,
i.e., a *credit* balance, will represent the *net profit*, whereas if the total
of the debit side exceeds that of the credit side the difference, *i.e.*, a
debit balance, is the *net loss*, for the period covered by the account.

The result obtained by the Profit and Loss Account may be
expressed as follows :—

    (1) Where a gross profit is made :

        NET PROFIT = (Gross Profit + Gains) *less* (Losses +
        Expenses).

        NET LOSS = (Losses + Expenses) *less* (Gross Profit +
        Gains).

    (2) Where a gross loss is incurred :

        NET PROFIT = (Gains) *less* (Gross Loss + Losses +
        Expenses).

        NET LOSS = (Gross Loss + Losses + Expenses) *less* (Gains).

It is necessary at this stage to ascertain to whom this final
balance of the Profit and Loss Account belongs. It has already
been stated that book-keeping serves to record the transactions
of the business, not those of the owner, and that an account known
as the Capital Account shows the owner as a creditor of the
business for the amount he has put into it because the business
owes him that amount.

Obviously, therefore, when the business has collected into one
account a record of all the items of income and of outlay for a
given period, the net balance (if a profit) will represent the amount
it owes to the proprietor in respect of that period, as this amount
has been made as a result of trading with his money. Similarly,
if a loss has been made, the proprietor is responsible for it and
the net balance of the account will then represent the amount he
must be charged with by the business to cover the loss incurred.

The balance of the Profit and Loss Account is therefore trans-

ferred to the Capital Account, *i.e.*, it is placed *to the credit of the owner* if a *profit* has been made (*Debit* Profit and Loss Account, *Credit* Capital Account), and is placed *to his debit* if a *loss* has been incurred (*Debit* Capital Account, *Credit* Profit and Loss Account). To the extent that he does not withdraw a profit the trader can be regarded as having given the amount to the business just as if he had paid in further capital, and consequently he must be credited. On the other hand he has received a benefit to the extent that he has not made good any loss and the matter is regarded as if he had withdrawn capital. The Profit and Loss Account is thereby closed, for the transactions for the period have been disposed of, all losses and profits have been dealt with, and the financial result has been incorporated in the Capital Account of the proprietor.

The only balances then remaining in the books are those relating to real or personal accounts which represent property or debts belonging to, or owing by the business, as all the accounts which concern services given and received have been closed off.

A practical illustration of a completed Profit and Loss Account will be given later in this chapter, as it is first necessary to pursue the idea just mentioned to a further stage.

It should be noted that in the case of both the Trading Account and Profit and Loss Account the period to which the account relates should be included in the heading, *e.g.*, " Profit and Loss Account for the year ended 30th June, 19...."

The Balance Sheet.

As has just been explained, all the nominal accounts have been closed off, the gross profit or loss has been ascertained, and the net profit or loss has been arrived at and transferred to the Capital Account ; and therefore the time is now most opportune to ascertain exactly the financial position of the business. It will furthermore be found that the property (real) and debt (personal) accounts are the only ledger accounts that now show any balances.

A Balance Sheet is a *statement* of the exact financial position of a business at a given date, showing, in an orderly and classified manner, the *assets*, or property owned by the business, and the *liabilities*, or debts owing by the business.

In actual fact, the Balance Sheet is a list of the balances of all accounts which remain open after the Trading and Profit and Loss Accounts have been prepared, arranged in two columns with *debit* balances on the *right-hand side* and *credit* balances on the *left-hand side*.

It was stated when dealing with the Trial Balance, that as every debit has a corresponding credit, the total of all the debits must equal the total of all the credits in the accounts as a whole, or, in other words, that the total of all the debit balances must

exactly equal the total of all the credit balances. It follows, therefore, that, if the book-keeping has been carried out correctly, the two sides of the Balance Sheet must agree exactly, in just the same way as the two sides of the Trial Balance agree.

The Balance Sheet is headed with the date at which it is taken out (*e.g.*, " Balance Sheet as at 30th June, 19...."), and is divided into two parts by a vertical line, on the left-hand side of which are entered all the liabilities (*i.e.*, credit balances) and on the right-hand side all the assets (*i.e.*, debit balances). *Assets* are the property of the business, including debts which are owed to it, whereas *liabilities* are the debts due by the business, *e.g.*, to creditors. The credit balance (if any) on the Capital Account is included amongst the liabilities, for, as has already been explained, this represents the amount which the business owes to the owner.

It is important to realize clearly that the Balance Sheet, like the Trial Balance, does not form part of the books and accounts of the business. It is not an account, and no transfer can be made " to the Balance Sheet." In both cases one must imagine that the book-keeper takes a sheet of paper, and enters thereon, in debit and credit form, all the balances remaining open on the books. In the case of the Balance Sheet this is done after the balance on Profit and Loss Account has been transferred to Capital Account. The actual procedure is a little more formal than this, but the principle is the same, for a Balance Sheet, like a Trial Balance, is nothing more than a *statement* showing the balances of the various ledger accounts, although, of course, it performs a much more important function than the Trial Balance.

It is important to note that it is the practice in this country to show the various balances on the opposite side of the Balance Sheet to the side on which they appear in the books, *e.g.*, debit balances (assets) are shown on the right-hand side of the Balance Sheet. It must be emphasized, however, that the Balance Sheet is not an account, although its form is similar, and the words " To " and " By " should not, in strict theory, appear therein, although this rule is sometimes transgressed in practice.

In distinguishing between balances which appear in the Trading and Profit and Loss Accounts and those which appear in the Balance Sheet the following rules may be applied. If any value remains in the business to represent a debit balance (*e.g.*, the balance on Cash Account), such balance will appear as an asset in the Balance Sheet, whereas if no value remains (*e.g.*, the balance on Wages Account) the balance must be an expense to be transferred to the debit side of the Trading Account or Profit and Loss Account. With regard to credit balances, if the business is under an obligation to refund the value to an outside party (including the trader) (*e.g.*, the credit balance on

a Personal Account), then such balance will appear as a liability in the Balance Sheet, whereas if no such obligation remains (*e.g.*, the balance on Sales Account) the balance must be a profit or gain to be transferred to the credit side of the Trading Account or Profit and Loss Account.

The Trading and Profit and Loss Accounts may be distinguished from the Balance Sheet in that the former are intended to display a summary of the events which have made up the history of the period, whilst the latter is intended to display the facts which have resulted from those events. Thus the Trading and Profit and Loss Accounts are headed " for the..... ended .... 19....," whereas, the Balance Sheet is headed " as at .... 19...."

The foregoing explanation of the method adopted for closing off the books, preparing the Trading and Profit and Loss Accounts, and drawing up a Balance Sheet, will become very much clearer if we refer back to the transactions of Bates given in the preceding chapter and proceed to complete his accounts.

It will be necessary to repeat only the accounts which now replace the Stock of Furniture Account, *i.e.*, the Sales, Purchases and Stock Accounts, and to show the new nominal accounts and the Balance Sheet. In the Wages Account given in the example a credit entry should of course be made " By Profit and Loss Account " to transfer the item of £2 to the latter account. The period to be dealt with is the month of January; although in actual practice the accounts are usually closed off and a Balance Sheet prepared after the expiration of a period of, say, six or twelve months.

Dr.				PURCHASES ACCOUNT				Cr.
19..... Jan. 2	To Wholesalers, Ltd.	J1	£ s. d. 400 0 0	19..... Jan. 31	By Trading Account .	J1	£ s. d. 400 0 0	

Dr.				SALES ACCOUNT				Cr.
19..... Jan. 31	To Trading Account .	J1	£ s. d. 40 0 0	19..... Jan. 15 ,, 16	By Cash . ,, B. Lawson	J1 J1	£ s. d. 5 0 0 35 0 0	
			£40 0 0				£40 0 0	

Dr. STOCK ACCOUNT **Cr.**

19..... Jan. 31	To Trading Account	J1	£ s. d. 376 10 0	19.....			£ s. d.

TRADING ACCOUNT
Dr. For the Month of January, 19..... **Cr.**

| 19..... Jan. 31 " 31 | To Purchases " Balance, being Gross Profit transferred to Profit and Loss Account | J1 J1 | £ s. d. 400 0 0 16 10 0 | 19..... Jan. 31 " 31 | By Sales " Stock | J1 J1 | £ s. d. 40 0 0 376 10 0 |
| | | | £ 416 10 0 | | | | £ 416 10 0 |

PROFIT AND LOSS ACCOUNT
Dr. For the Month of January, 19..... **Cr.**

| 19..... Jan. 31 | To Wages " Balance, being Net Profit transferred to Capital Account | J1 J1 | £ s. d. 2 0 0 14 10 0 | 19..... Jan. 31 | By Gross Profit transferred from Trading Account | J1 | £ s. d. 16 10 0 |
| | | | £16 10 0 | | | | £16 10 0 |

Dr. CAPITAL ACCOUNT **Cr.**

19..... Jan. 31	To Balance	c/d	£ s. d. 514 10 0	19..... Jan. 1 " 31	By Cash " Net Profit transferred from Profit and Loss Account	J1 J1	£ s. d. 500 0 0 14 10 0
			£ 514 10 0				£ 514 10 0
				Jan. 31	By Balance	b/d	514 10 0

BALANCE SHEET

As at 31st January, 19.....

Liabilities.	£	s.	d.	Assets.	£	s.	d.
Creditor :—				Stock on			
Wholesalers,				hand . .	376	10	0
Ltd. . .	200	0	0	Debtor :—			
A. Bates—Cap-				B. Lawson	35	0	0
ital Account				Cash in hand	303	0	0
—Balance as							
at 1st Jan.,							
19..... :							
£500 0 0							
Add Net Profit							
for Month :							
£14 10 0	514	10	0				
	£ 714	10	0		£ 714	10	0

A Detailed Example.

The elementary theory of book-keeping has now been stated, and its various principles have been explained, including the taking out of a Trial Balance, the closing of the books and the preparation of the Trading and Profit and Loss Accounts, and the preparation of the Balance Sheet. If the reader has followed closely the explanations and examples given by way of illustration, he should by now have acquired a good working knowledge of an elementary system of keeping accounts, based upon the fundamental rules already stated.

It is obvious, however, that the system which has so far been explained is a very elementary one which would be inadequate in practice in the case of a business of any reasonable size. It must be remembered that there are a considerable number of developments, modifications and additional methods which have still to be dealt with, and added to the skeleton framework we have so far described. These developments will be considered in detail in the succeeding chapters.

In the meantime, it will no doubt be advisable to work out in complete detail the accounts of a business as far as the preparation of a Balance Sheet, and for this purpose it is proposed to revert to the transactions of Bates, trading as the Direct Furniture Store. It is essential that the reader should trace out the entries in the following example step by step.

EXAMPLE

Arnold Bates, the furniture dealer, whose commencement in business was recorded in Chapter I, has made considerable progress, and his position on 1st June, 19....., after a lapse of five years, is as follows :—

Assets.

Cash at Bank, £837. Debtors : J. Knowles, £120 ; H. Small, £42 ; L. Mawson, £98. Value of Stock of Furniture on hand, £1,148 ; Shop Fittings, £210.

Liabilities.

Creditors : Wholesalers, Limited, £441 ; Samson & Co., £338.

His transactions are as follows :—

19.....

(1)	June	1.	Purchased from Wholesalers, Limited, 20 Chairs at 10s. each.
(2)	,,	2.	Sold to H. Newson, 1 Dining Room Table for £15.
(3)	,,	4.	Paid Wholesalers, Limited, on account, £250.
(4)	,,	5.	Paid Carriage on goods, £3 15s.
(5)	,,	6.	Purchased from Samson & Co. :—

              50 Rugs at 15s. each.
              40 Carpets at £3 each.
              200 Door Mats at 2s. 6d. each.

(6)	,,	7.	Sold to H. Small, 1 Oak Sideboard at £17 10s.
(7)	,,	8.	Received cheque from J. Knowles, £120.
(8)	,,	8.	Paid Wages, £19.
(9)	,,	9.	Cash Sales for week, £178 5s.
(10)	,,	11.	Paid Rent, £89.
(11)	,,	12.	Received £59 on account from L. Mawson.
(12)	,,	13.	Sold to S. Parsons, 1 Bedroom Suite for £87 15s.
(13)	,,	14.	Paid Samson & Co. on account, £338.
(14)	,,	15.	Paid Wages, £19.
(15)	,,	15.	Purchased from Wholesalers, Limited :—

              10 Settees at £7 14s. each.
              50 Kitchen Tables at 10s. each.
              20 Bedsteads at £5 16s. each.

(16)	,,	15.	Received £59 10s. from H. Small.

Enter the above items in A. Bates's Journal, Cash Book and Ledger. Close the books on 15th June, and prepare Trial Balance, Trading and Profit and Loss Accounts and Balance Sheet as at that date.

The value of the stock of furniture on hand at 15th June was ascertained to be £1,457.

Opening Entries.

As has already been indicated, assets are represented by debit balances because they indicate value which has come in to their respective accounts, whereas liabilities are represented by credit balances because value has gone out of the particular accounts. The total of the debit balances must equal the total of the credit balances at any given date, and this rule, of course, applies equally

to the commencement of a period. Therefore, the total of the balances representing the assets given in the example as being in existence at 1st June must equal the total of the balances representing liabilities at the same date, in accordance with double entry principles.

It will be found, however, that the total of the assets given above is £2,455, whereas the total liabilities amount to only £779. The thoughtful reader will at once realize that the missing item is the balance of Capital Account, which must always equal the difference between the total assets and the total liabilities. Therefore, A. Bates's capital, amounting to £1,676, must be included in the opening Journal entry in order that the total debits and credits may balance.

In a case like this it would involve unnecessary duplication of work if every opening entry were made separately, and instead of this a combined entry is made as shown below, the debit entries being given first, followed by the credit entries. Where entries are combined in this way, it is necessary to open with " Sundries, *Dr.* To Sundries " as shown. This will be explained more fully in Chapter III.

Cash is included in the Journal entry in this case in order to give a complete record of the opening position and in order that the total debit items may equal the total credit items, but otherwise cash entries are made direct in the Cash Book and are not journalized.

JOURNAL

Folio No. 113.

			Dr.			Cr.		
19.....			£	s.	d.	£	s.	d.
June 1	Sundries. *Dr.*							
	To Sundries.							
	Cash	CB1	837	0	0			
	Sundry Debtors	Led						
	J. Knowles	2	120	0	0			
	H. Small	3	42	0	0			
	L. Mawson	4	98	0	0			
	Stock	9	1,148	0	0			
	Shop Fittings	10	210	0	0			
	Sundry Creditors :—							
	Wholesalers, Limited . . .	5				441	0	0
	Samson & Co.	6				338	0	0
	Capital Account	1				1,676	0	0
	Being assets, liabilities and capital as at this date.							
	Carried forward . .		£ 2,455	0	0	2,455	0	0

The Transactions Explained.

The following explanations will indicate the correct manner in which to record the transactions in order to comply with the fundamental rules of double entry which have already been stated :—

(1) This is a case of a purchase on credit. Goods Purchased, or Purchases Account, receives value and is debited, while the account of Wholesalers, Limited, gives value and is credited.

(2) This transaction is a sale on credit and thus is a reversal of (1). H. Newson receives value and is debited, while Goods Sold or Sales Account gives value and is credited.

(3) Cash Account loses £250 and Wholesalers, Limited, gain the same amount. Therefore the former account is credited, as it gives value, while the latter account is debited, as it receives value. " On account " indicates that only part of the debt is paid.

(4) Cash Account loses £3 15s., i.e., gives value, and is therefore credited. The account to be debited is Carriage Account, which records services done for the business by those who carry goods on behalf of the business ; thus, as a service is received (i.e., the service of carrying the goods) the nominal account must be debited.

(5) This transaction is dealt with in the same manner as (1). The details should be given in the Journal, but only one total amount passed through the books.

(6) This is similar to (2).

(7) Cash Account receives £120, and thus becomes responsible for it, i.e., is a debtor for it, and must be debited. J. Knowles gives value and must be credited.

(8) This is similar to (4). Cash Account loses value and must be credited. Wages Account receives services and thus is a debtor to that extent.

(9) The individual items dealt with during the week are passed through the books in one total. Cash Account receives value and is debited, while Goods Sold, i.e., Sales Account has given value and is credited. In practice Cash Sales are usually posted to a separate Cash Sales Account, but it will be in order here to include the item in the ordinary Sales Account.

(10) Another nominal account transaction. Cash Account is credited, while Rent Account is debited because it has received the service of the use of the shop, etc., for the period.

(11) See (7) above.

(12) See (2) above.

(13) See (3) above.

(14) See (8) above.

(15) See (1) and (5) above.

(16) See (7) above.

JOURNAL (*continued*)

Folio No. 114.

				Dr.			Cr.		
				£	s.	d.	£	s.	d.
	Brought forward			2,455	0	0	2,455	0	0
June 1	Purchases Account.	Dr.	11	10	0	0			
	To Wholesalers, Limited.		5				10	0	0
	Being purchase of 20 Chairs @ 10s. each.								
,, 2	H. Newson.	Dr.	7	15	0	0			
	To Sales Account.		12				15	0	0
	Being sale of 1 Dining Room Table.								
,, 6	Purchases Account.	Dr.	11	182	10	0			
	To Samson & Co.		6				182	10	0
	Being purchase of :— £ s. d.								
	50 *Rugs* @ 15s. each 37 10 0								
	40 *Carpets* @ £3 each 120 0 0								
	200 *Door Mats* @ 2s. 6d.								
	each 25 0 0								
	─────────								
	£182 10 0								
,, 7	H. Small.	Dr.	3	17	10	0			
	To Sales Account.		12				17	10	0
	Being sale of 1 Oak Sideboard.								
,, 13	S. Parsons.	Dr.	8	87	15	0			
	To Sales Account.		12				87	15	0
	Being Sale of 1 Bedroom Suite.								
,, 15	Purchases Account.	Dr.	11	218	0	0			
	To Wholesalers, Limited.		5				218	0	0
	Being purchase of :— £ s. d.								
	10 *Settees* @ £7 14s. each 77 0 0								
	50 *Kitchen Tables* @								
	10s. each. 25 0 0								
	20 *Bedsteads* @ £5 16s.								
	each. 116 0 0								
	─────────								
	£218 0 0								
			£	2,985	15	0	2,985	15	0

The first step is to enter the various items in the Journal, excluding those which concern cash (see previous page). The cash entries should then be recorded in the Cash Book, and this book should then be balanced. The ledger accounts will then require to be opened and the entries made therein from the Journal and Cash Book. Remember that debit entries are preceded by the word "To" and credit entries by the word "By," and that in the particulars column of the ledger there must be entered, against each item, the name of *the other account* affected by the double entry.

The accounts have then to be balanced and a Trial Balance prepared. If the totals of the Trial Balance agree, the closing transfers are made through the Journal, the Trading and Profit and Loss Accounts are prepared, and finally the Balance Sheet is drawn up.

CASH BOOK

Dr.			Receipts.						Payments.				Cr.	
Date.	Account.	Fo.	Amount.			Date.	Account.	Fo.	Amount.					
19.....			£	s.	d.	19.....		Led.	£	s.	d.			
June 1	To Balance.	J113	837	0	0	June 4	By Whole-salers,Ltd.	5	250	0	0			
„ 8	„ J. Knowles.	Led. 2	120	0	0	„ 5	„ Carriage.	13	3	15	0			
„ 9	„ Sales.	12	178	5	0	„ 8	„ Wages.	14	19	0	0			
„ 12	„ L. Mawson.	4	59	0	0	„ 11	„ Rent.	15	89	0	0			
„ 15	„ H. Small.	3	59	10	0	„ 14	„ Samson & Co.	6	338	0	0			
						„ 15	„ Wages.	14	19	0	0			
						„ 15	„ Balance.	c/d	535	0	0			
			£1,253	15	0				£1,253	15	0			
June 15	To Balance.	b/d	535	0	0									

LEDGER

Account No. 1.

Dr.			CAPITAL ACCOUNT							Cr.	
19.....			£	s.	d.	19.....			£	s.	d.
						June 1	By Balance.	J113	1,676	0	0

Account No. 2.

Dr.   J. KNOWLES   Cr.

19....			£	s.	d.	19.....			£	s.	d.
June 1	To Balance.	J113	120	0	0	June 8	By Cash.	CB1	120	0	0

Account No. 3.

Dr.   H. SMALL   Cr.

19.....			£	s.	d.	19.....			£	s.	d.
June 1	To Balance.	J113	42	0	0	June 15	By Cash.	CB1	59	10	0
,, 7	,, Sales.	J114	17	10	0						
		£	59	10	0			£	59	10	0

Account No. 4.

Dr.   L. MAWSON   Cr.

19.....			£	s.	d.	19.....			£	s.	d.
June 1	To Balance.	J113	98	0	0	June 12	By Cash.	CB1	59	0	0
						,, 15	,, Balance.	c/d	39	0	0
		£	98	0	0			£	98	0	0
June 15	To Balance.	b/d	39	0	0						

Account No. 5.

Dr.   WHOLESALERS, LIMITED   Cr.

19.....			£	s.	d.	19.....			£	s.	d.
June 4	To Cash.	CB1	250	0	0	June 1	By Balance.	J113	441	0	0
,, 15	,, Balance.	c/d	419	0	0	,, 1	,, Purchases.	J114	10	0	0
						,, 15	,, Purchases.	J114	218	0	0
		£	669	0	0			£	669	0	0
						June 15	By Balance.	b/d	419	0	0

Account No. 6.

Dr.   SAMSON & CO.   Cr.

19.....			£	s.	d.	19.....			£	s.	d.
June 14	To Cash.	CB1	338	0	0	June 1	By Balance.	J113	338	0	0
„ 15	„ Balance.	c/d	182	10	0	„ 6	„ Purchases.	J114	182	10	0
		£	520	10	0			£	520	10	0
						June 15	By Balance.	b/d	182	10	0

Account No. 7.

Dr.   H. NEWSON   Cr.

19.....			£	s.	d.	19.....			£	s.	d.
June 2	To Sales.	J114	15	0	0						

Account No. 8.

Dr.   S. PARSONS   Cr.

19.....			£	s.	d.	19.....			£	s.	d.
June 13	To Sales.	J114	87	15	0						

Account No. 9.

Dr.   STOCK ACCOUNT   Cr.

19.....			£	s.	d.	19.....			£	s.	d.
June 1	To Balance.	J113	1,148	0	0						

Account No. 10.

Dr.   SHOP FITTINGS   Cr.

19.....			£	s.	d.	19.....			£	s.	d.
June 1	To Balance.	J113	210	0	0						

Account No. 11.

Dr.   PURCHASES ACCOUNT   Cr.

19.....			£	s.	d.	19.....			£	s.	d.
June 1	To Wholesalers, Ltd.	J114	10	0	0						
„ 6	„ Samson & Co.	J114	182	10	0						
„ 15	„ Wholesalers, Ltd.	J114	218	0	0						

Account No. 12.

Dr.   SALES ACCOUNT   Cr.

19....			£	s.	d.	19.....			£	s.	d.
						June 2	By H. Newson.	J114	15	0	0
						„ 7	„ H. Small.	J114	17	10	0
						„ 9	„ Cash.	CB1	178	5	0
						„ 13	„ S. Parsons.	J114	87	15	0

Account No. 13.

Dr.   CARRIAGE ACCOUNT   Cr.

19.....			£	s.	d.	19.....			£	s.	d.
June 5	To Cash.	CB1	3	15	0						

Account No. 14.

Dr.   WAGES ACCOUNT   Cr.

19.....			£	s.	d.	19.....			£	s.	d.
June 8	To Cash.	CB1	19	0	0						
„ 15	„ Cash.	CB1	19	0	0						

Account No. 15.

Dr.   RENT ACCOUNT   Cr.

19.....			£	s.	d.	19.....			£	s.	d.
June 11	To Cash.	CB1	89	0	0						

As the Trial Balance (see below) agrees, the arithmetical accuracy of the postings is proved, and steps can now be taken to close the books and prepare the final accounts. The procedure to be adopted in order to prepare the final accounts has already been explained in detail, but it may be as well to summarize the various steps that should be taken :—

(a) Transfer the stock at the beginning of the period (*i.e.*, the balance of Stock Account) to Trading Account.

TRIAL BALANCE
As at 15th June, 19.....

Folio.	Name of Account.	Dr.			Cr.		
		£	s.	d.	£	s.	d.
1	Capital Account.				1,676	0	0
4	L. Mawson.	39	0	0			
5	Wholesalers, Ltd.				419	0	0
6	Samson & Co.				182	10	0
7	H. Newson.	15	0	0			
8	S. Parsons.	87	15	0			
9	Stock Account.	1,148	0	0			
10	Shop Fittings.	210	0	0			
11	Purchases Account.	410	10	0			
12	Sales Account.				298	10	0
13	Carriage Account.	3	15	0			
14	Wages Account.	38	0	0			
15	Rent Account.	89	0	0			
	Cash in hand.	535	0	0			
		£ 2,576	0	0	2,576	0	0

(b) Transfer the balances of Purchases and Sales Accounts to Trading Account.

(c) Credit Trading Account and debit Stock Account with the value of the stock at the end of the period. It is important to note that this figure, which is ascertained by making an inventory of the goods in stock, is not dealt with in any way until the final accounts are being prepared, and it therefore does not appear at all in the Trial Balance.

(d) Balance the Trading Account, and transfer the gross profit, or gross loss, to the Profit and Loss Account.

(e) Transfer the balances of all nominal accounts, *e.g.*, carriage, wages and rent, to the Profit and Loss Account.

The Journal entries for all the closing transfers would appear
as follows :—

JOURNAL

Folio No. 115.

			Dr.	Cr.
			£ s. d.	£ s. d.
	Brought forward		2,985 15 0	2,985 15 0
June 15	Trading Account . . . . . *Dr.*	16	1,148 0 0	
	To Stock Account.	9		1,148 0 0
	Being value of stock on 1st June, 19.....			
,, 15	Trading Account. . . . . *Dr.*	16	410 10 0	
	To Purchases Account.	11		410 10 0
	Being total purchases for the period.			
,, 15	Sales Account . . . . . *Dr.*	12	298 10 0	
	To Trading Account.	16		298 10 0
	Being total sales for the period.			
,, 15	Stock Account . . . . . *Dr.*	9	1,457 0 0	
	To Trading Account.	16		1,457 0 0
	Being value of stock on 15th June, 19...			
,, 15	Trading Account. . . . . *Dr.*	16	197 0 0	
	To Profit and Loss Account.	17		197 0 0
	Being gross profit for the period.			
,, 15	Profit and Loss Account . . *Dr.*	17	130 15 0	
	To Sundries.			
	Carriage Account.	13		3 15 0
	Wages Account.	14		38 0 0
	Rent Account.	15		89 0 0
	Being balances transferred.			
,, 15	Profit and Loss Account . . *Dr.*	17	66 5 0	
	To Capital Account.	1		66 5 0
	Being net profit for the period transferred.			
		£	6,693 15 0	6,693 15 0

(*f*) Balance the Profit and Loss Account and transfer the net profit, or net loss, to Capital Account.

(*g*) All accounts which still show balances must be classified and shown on their respective sides of the Balance Sheet, *e.g.*, shop fittings, cash at bank, etc.

From the above Journal entries the Trading and Profit and Loss Accounts can be prepared, *viz.* :—

TRADING ACCOUNT

Account No. 16.

Dr.　　　FOR THE PERIOD 1ST JUNE TO 15TH JUNE, 19.....　　　Cr.

19.....			£	s.	d.	19......			£	s.	d.
June 15	To Stock.	J115	1,148	0	0	June 15	By Sales.	J115	298	10	0
,, 15	,, Purchases.	J115	410	10	0	,, 15	,, Stock.	J115	1,457	0	0
,, 15	,, Balance, being Gross Profit transferred to Profit & Loss Account.	J115	197	0	0						
			£1,755	10	0				£1,755	10	0

PROFIT AND LOSS ACCOUNT

Account No. 17.

Dr.　　　FOR THE PERIOD 1ST JUNE TO 15TH JUNE, 19....　　　Cr.

19.....			£	s.	d.	19.....			£	s.	d.
June 15	To Wages.	J115	38	0	0	June 15	By Gross Profit transferred from Trading Account.	J115	197	0	0
,, 15	,, Carriage.	J115	3	15	0						
,, 15	,, Rent.	J115	89	0	0						
,, 15	,, Balance, being Net Profit transferred to Capital Account.	J115	66	5	0						
			£ 197	0	0				£ 197	0	0

It is unnecessary to repeat the various nominal accounts in order to show the closing entries. Purchases Account will be closed by an entry on the credit side " *By Trading Account* £410 10s." and similarly Sales Account by an entry on the debit side " *To Trading Account* £298 10s." Carriage, Wages and Rent Accounts will each be closed by an entry on the credit side " *By Profit and Loss Account,*" the amounts being £3 15s., £38 and £89 respectively. The adjusted Stock Account and Capital Account will finally appear as follows :—

STOCK ACCOUNT — Account No. 9.

Dr.   Cr.

19.....			£	s.	d.	19.....			£	s.	d.
June 1	To Balance.	J113	1,148	0	0	June 15	By Trading Account.	J115	1,148	0	0
June 15	To Trading Account.	J115	1,457	0	0						

CAPITAL ACCOUNT — Account No. 1.

Dr.   Cr.

19.....			£	s.	d.	19.....			£	s.	d.
June 15	To Balance.	c/d	1,742	5	0	June 1	By Balance.	J113	1,676	0	0
						„ 15	„ Profit & Loss Account.	J115	66	5	0
		£	1,742	5	0			£	1,742	5	0
						June 15	By Balance.	b/d	1,742	5	0

The transactions for the period have now been completely recorded in the books, the final accounts have been prepared, and the profit transferred to Capital Account. Before the transactions of the succeeding period are entered in the books, however, a list of all balances still remaining in the ledger is taken out, classified and arranged in the form of a Balance Sheet so as to show exactly the financial position of the business at the end of the period. The Balance Sheet in this case would appear as follows :—

THE DIRECT FURNITURE STORES
Balance Sheet
As at 15th June, 19.....

Liabilities.	£	s.	d.	Assets.	£	s.	d.
Sundry Creditors:—				Shop Fittings.	210	0	0
£ s. d.				Stock of Furniture.	1,457	0	0
Wholesalers,				Sundry Debtors:—			
Ltd. 419 0 0				£ s. d.			
Samson & Co. 182 10 0				L. Mawson. 39 0 0			
	601	10	0	H. Newson. 15 0 0			
A. Bates's Capital Account:				S. Parsons. 87 15 0			
£ s. d.					141	15	0
Balance as at				Cash in hand.	535	0	0
1st June. 1,676 0 0							
Add Net Profit							
for period. 66 5 0							
	1,742	5	0				
	£2,343	15	0		£2,343	15	0

Practical Work.

The reader has now been taken through the whole of the elementary theory of book-keeping and therefore should experience no difficulty in working any of the following simple exercises. The first essential is always to apply the main principles and fundamental rules already stated and explained, and to refer back constantly to the instructions as to procedure, which have been tabulated in the preceding pages, until the work becomes automatic.

EXERCISE 2

A. Where is the Cash Account usually kept ?   Explain why this method is adopted.

B. How is the Goods Account split up in practice, and what are the advantages of this method ?

C. Explain the uses of the Trading and Profit and Loss Accounts. How are these accounts prepared ?

D. What is a Balance Sheet ?   On which sides of the Balance Sheet are the debit and credit balances in the Ledger respectively shown ?

E. J. Castle is in business as a motor and cycle dealer. On 1st December, 19...., his assets and liabilities were as follows :—
Freehold Premises, £2,400 ; Motor and Cycle Stock, £3,200 ; Plant and Tools, £321 ; Sundry Debtors : R. Browne, £200 ; P. Premier, £128 ; E. Elswick, £100 ; Sundry Creditors : Rudge-Whitworth Co., Ltd., £428 ; Raleigh, Ltd., £814 ; Office Furniture, £100 ; Cash in hand, £1,528.
Record the necessary entries in the Journal as at 1st December.

F. M. Kent is in business as a jeweller, and on 1st January, 19...., his position
was as follows :—

Cash in hand, £223 7s. 9d. ; Fixtures and Fittings, £200 ; Stock, £1,450
14s. 4d. ; Sundry Debtors : R. Roberts, £86 5s. ; O. Jay, £86 3s. 8d. ;
Sundry Creditors : E. Polsen, £42 7s. 1d. ; R. Turtle, £90 15s. 8d. ;
M. Neil, £40 18s. 9d.

Open the necessary accounts to record the above particulars in Kent's
Ledger and post thereto, through the Journal and Cash Book, the following
transactions :—

19.....

Jan. 1. Sold, for cash, 3 brooches at £12 12s. each.

„ 2. Paid wages, £8 15s. 7d.

„ 3. Paid office expenses, £1 6s. 4d.

„ 4. Sold, on credit, to O. Jay, job lot silver matchboxes for
£36 5s., and 4 cigarette cases at £1 7s. 6d. each.

„ 5. Purchased, on credit, from E. Polsen, 25 wristlet watches at
16s. 3d. each, and half gross rolled gold tiepins at 13s. 11d.
per dozen.

„ 6. R. Roberts sent cash in settlement of his account.

„ 9. Paid wages, £7 18s. 4d.

„ 12. Paid £50 on account to R. Turtle.

„ 13. Purchased, for cash, 2½ dozen bead necklaces at 16s. 6d. per
dozen.

„ 18. Paid M. Neil's account.

Balance the Ledger and Cash Book as on 18th January, and extract a Trial
Balance.

G. G. Turner is in business as a grocer. His financial position on 1st April,
19..., was as follows :—

Cash in hand, £1,000 ; Stock, £2,050 ; Fixtures, £450 ; Motor Vans,
£625 ; Sundry Debtors : J. Beeton, £225 ; D. Hunt, £150 ; Sundry
Creditors : R. Ballard, £215 ; F. Shaw, £285.

Open the necessary accounts in the Ledger to record the above particulars,
and post thereto, through the Journal and Cash Book, the following
transactions :—

19.....

April 1. J. Beeton sent cash in settlement of his account.

„ 6. Paid rent, £100.

„ 8. Sold, on credit, to J. Beeton, goods value £144 12s. 6d.

„ 12. Received cash in settlement of his account from D. Hunt.

„ 15. Paid F. Shaw £150 on account.

„ 17. Paid for packing materials £7 7s. 6d.

„ 19. Purchased, on credit, from F. Shaw, goods value £123.

„ 21. Sold, on credit, to D. Hunt, goods value £15 7s. 8d.

„ 26. Purchased, for cash, goods value £27 10s.

„ 28. Paid from cash for new weighing machine, £40.

„ 30. Cash sales during month, £107 4s. 11d.

„ „ Paid following expenses for month :—Wages, £55 ; Postages,
£4 2s. 3d. ; Carriage, £3 7s. 9d.

The Stock on Hand at 30th April amounted to £2,100.

Prepare Trial Balance, Trading and Profit and Loss Accounts, and Balance
Sheet as at 30th April, 19.....

H. From the following Trial Balance, taken from the books of W. White, a general merchant, prepare Trading and Profit and Loss Accounts, and Balance Sheet as at 31st December, 19.....

Trial Balance—31st December, 19.....

	Dr. £	Cr. £
Stock at beginning of year.	326	
Purchases.	879	
Sales.		2,248
Salaries and wages.	596	
Office expenses.	98	
Carriage on sales.	87	
Rent and rates.	157	
Capital.		600
Creditors.		321
Debtors.	777	
Cash.	249	
	£3,169	£3,169

The stock on hand at the end of the year was valued at £295.

11. From the following Trial Balance, taken from the books of W. White, a general merchant, prepare Trading and Profit and Loss Accounts, and Balance Sheet as at 31st December, 19...

Trial Balance—31st December, 19...

Dr.   Cr.

Stock at beginning of year.   320

Office expenses.   93

Carriage on sales.   73

CHAPTER III

THE JOURNAL AND ITS DIVISIONS ; THE PRINCIPAL JOURNAL ; THE SALES DAY BOOK

The Journal, or book of first entry, has already been described, and the reader should by now be accustomed to its use for recording simple business transactions. It must, however, be obvious that while a single book of first entry may be used satisfactorily in a small business, it would prove hopelessly inadequate immediately the business expands, as it would be impossible for more than one clerk at a time to be engaged upon the work of journalizing.

Thus the elementary methods which have been described in the previous chapters will require to be modified to a very considerable extent in practice, and this development will now be considered in detail.

It is advisable, once again, to reiterate that the fundamental principles upon which the elementary methods are based hold good, and apply in every respect to the modern methods which are now to be described, these being nothing more than developments in the superstructure based on the same foundations.

There are two methods which could be adopted to cope with the difficulty of dealing with the increase in the number of transactions consequent upon the development and expansion of a business.

In the first place it would be possible to have two or more separate journals in use at the same time, each being under the control of a different clerk. By this method each day's transactions would be divided indiscriminately and recorded in one or other of the separate journals. This would no doubt prove a workable system, except that, with the continued expansion of the business, it would be a long and tedious process to refer back to any specific transaction on a certain day, as there would be no definite indication as to which of the separate journals contained the particular entry.

Apart from this objection, however, the foregoing method has not been adopted for the simple reason that there is a better and more efficient method available for recording the numerous and varied transactions of an average modern business. In practice, an alternative method is adopted by which the journal is split up into several separate sections. By this method the entries

are not made indiscriminately in the separate books, but the transactions are divided up into the classes into which they naturally fall, and a separate journal is kept for each particular class.

Thus, if the example worked out in the previous chapter is referred to it will be found that the journal entries may be divided into opening and closing entries and those in respect of purchases and sales. The opening and closing entries occur but once in any trading period, and thus can be ignored for the moment. On the other hand, as the principal functions of a business are the buying and selling of goods, entries relating to purchases and sales must be extremely frequent. Therefore it will be found that purchases and sales form two main classes to which separate journals are allocated.

There are other kinds of transactions to be explained at a later stage, which also fall into main classes, the transactions of each particular class being recorded in a separate journal. For example, the Returns Journals are used to record all those transactions which relate to goods returned to the seller by the purchaser as not being up to sample or as being of inferior quality or for any other reason. Furthermore, dealings in bills of exchange, to which a chapter will be devoted later, are recorded in separate Bill Books or Journals.

Advantages of Sub-dividing the Journal.

It is obvious that the most practicable method of recording journal entries is to divide the transactions of a business into their main classes and to reserve a separate journal for each particular class of transaction. This system, furthermore, has a number of advantages besides that of dividing the work of recording the transactions of a business among several clerks.

In the first place, each individual book-keeper is able to work with greater speed and accuracy if he concentrates his attention on one particular class of entry, e.g., where one clerk is engaged wholly on recording the sales of a business.

If the personal ledger accounts are sufficiently numerous to justify it, they may also be divided according to their nature, one ledger being devoted to customers' accounts, termed the Sales Ledger, and another to suppliers' accounts, termed the Purchases Ledger. The advantage of the division of the Journal will thus be still more apparent, for in this way one book-keeper will be able to post all the entries from the Sales Journal to the Sales Ledger, while another book-keeper posts those from the Purchases Journal to the Purchases Ledger (see page 138).

The most important advantage of the system, however, is to

be found in the great saving of time in posting the journal entries
to their respective nominal accounts in the Ledger. Referring again
to the example commencing on page 37, it will be found that in
posting the entries from the Journal to the Ledger it was necessary
to record three separate transactions in the Sales Account, and
similarly to record three separate entries in the Purchases Account.
Thus it will be obvious that if the transactions had been divided
into their respective classes and entered in the corresponding
separate journals, the individual postings could be made to the
personal accounts in the usual way, while the entries in the Sales
and the Purchases Accounts could be made periodically in total
in each case. Thus, the Journal entries would be :—

SALES JOURNAL

Date.	Particulars.	Ledger Folio.	Amount.
19.....			£ s. d.
June 2	H. Newson.	7	15 0 0
„ 7	H. Small.	3	17 10 0
„ 13	S. Parsons.	8	87 15 0
	Total credited to Sales Account.		£120 5 0

Therefore, in the above case the only entry necessary in the
Sales Account is a credit of £120 5s. at the end of the period,
whereas if no sub-division of the Journal is made, a separate entry
in the Sales Account will be necessary in respect of each Journal
entry. This simple example illustrates the main advantage of
sub-dividing the Journal, and in actual practice, when many
transactions are recorded daily, it will be found that great economy
in work is effected.

It is also advisable to note the manner in which the essential
principle of double entry is fully maintained. The personal
accounts of Newson, Small and Parsons are debited with the
individual amounts when the ledger is posted from the Sales
Journal ; thus the *total* amount *debited* is £120 5s. At the end
of the period, a similar amount is *credited* to Sales Account ; thus
the total debits eventually equal the total credits, thereby fulfilling
the fundamental rule of double entry.

In a similar manner it is usual to keep other Journals, each
of which is reserved for the recording of one particular class of
transactions. The entries in these subsidiary journals are posted
individually to the respective personal ledger accounts, and periodic-

ally, usually once a month, the *total* amount entered in each journal for the period is posted to the appropriate nominal account in the ledger.

The books that are generally used to record the main classes of transactions are :—

> (1) THE CASH BOOK—which records all the cash transactions. As has already been explained, this book fulfils the function of both a ledger and a journal.
>
> (2) THE SALES DAY BOOK—which records all the sales on credit. This book is sometimes called the Sales Journal or Sales Book.
>
> (3) THE PURCHASES BOOK—which records all the purchases on credit. This book is sometimes called the Purchases Journal or Bought Day Book.
>
> (4) THE RETURNS OUTWARDS BOOK—which records all goods purchased that are returned to the supplier by the business.
>
> (5) THE RETURNS INWARDS BOOK—which records all goods previously sold returned by the customer to the business.
>
> (6) THE BILL BOOKS—which record all transactions involving the giving or receiving of bills of exchange.

THE PRINCIPAL JOURNAL

In view of the fact that the main classes of trading transactions are to be recorded in subsidiary books, it now remains to consider what entries are passed through the principal journal, or, as it is sometimes called, the " journal proper." In practice it will be found that the only items remaining to be dealt with in the journal proper are those of an irregular or unusual nature.

There are certain types of transactions which cannot be recorded in any of the special journals mentioned above owing to the particular nature of such transactions. Furthermore, there is a greater necessity for these transactions to be passed through the journal proper, as their very unusual or irregular nature generally makes them of special importance. By recording these transactions in the principal journal, together with an explanatory narration in each case, a useful and detailed record is made. Transactions of a particular class may in certain businesses be so few in number as not to justify the keeping of a separate journal. For example, most firms have very few dealings with bills of exchange, so that the principal journal is useful for making the original records of such transactions.

In modern practice, it is a fundamental rule of book-keeping that *no entry must be made in the Ledger until it has first been passed through some book of original entry, i.e.*, the cash book, the principal journal, or one of the subsidiary journals. This rule must always be followed, even if the entry is merely the correction of a previous entry made to a wrong account in error. Thus there is a definite need for the principal journal in order to record the original entry in respect of every transaction that cannot be recorded in the other books of original entry.

Opening and closing entries are examples of entries where the principal journal is generally used, as there is no other subsidiary book in which they can be correctly recorded. It is very necessary, for purposes of future record and reference, that a complete statement of the various assets and liabilities with which a trader first commenced business should be set down in some convenient book. If this were not done, there would be no record of his commencing position, unless it were traced from the various ledger accounts, which would prove a very laborious process. This, of course, chiefly applies where an established business is taken over, since the only asset with which an entirely new business commences will be the cash capital brought in by the trader, subsequent purchases of assets and incurring of liabilities being recorded in the ordinary way.

Similarly, the various transfers, which require to be made when the books are closed at the end of the trading period, should also be recorded in some book of first entry. Examples of opening and closing entries have already been given in Chapter II.

The principal journal may also be used for making adjustments in respect of errors. For example, if a sale of goods to the value of £50 is debited to Arthur A. Smith instead of to Arthur E. Smith, when the error is discovered it should be corrected by means of an adjusting journal entry as follows :—

	Dr.	*Cr.*
Arthur E. Smith.	*Dr.* £50	
To Arthur A. Smith.		£50

Being correction of item debited in error to
Arthur A. Smith on .... 19....

There are other adjusting items for which the principal journal is used, such as the provision for depreciation, the writing off of a bad debt, the crediting of interest or commission, etc. These will be better understood by the reader at a later stage.

The uses of the principal journal may now be summarized as being to record :—

    (a) Opening entries at the commencement of business;

    (b) Closing entries in connection with the preparation of the Trading and Profit and Loss Accounts at the end of each trading period ;

(c) The adjustment of errors ; and

(d) All other transactions which cannot be recorded in the cash book or in one of the subsidiary journals.

Method of Entry.

The reader should by now be fully conversant with the use of the journal for simple entries, and it should hardly be necessary to state that the account to be debited is always given first, followed on the succeeding line by the account to be credited.

The *narration* is extremely important, as its purpose is to provide a concise yet adequate explanation of the transaction. If no narration were given, there would be nothing to indicate the nature of the transaction, as the mere names of the accounts concerned would generally be of little utility from the point of view of information. An explanatory narration will be found of great value when reference is made to an entry at a subsequent date.

It must be emphasized at this stage that a narration must always be included when an entry is made in the principal journal. The reader should accustom himself to this practical essential by adding narrations to all journal entries when working out book-keeping exercises. In every case the narration should give sufficient information, without unnecessary detail, to ensure that reference to it will adequately explain the entry.

Journal entries should be separated by a thin line ruled across the " Particulars " column after each narration.

The type of journal entry that has already been explained is known as a *simple entry*, *i.e.*, one in which only two accounts are affected. It sometimes happens, however, that more than two accounts are affected by one transaction, or that two transactions which both concern one account can be given together. In such cases the entry in the journal is known as a *compound* (or *composite*) *entry* and may take any one of the three following forms :—

(a) Several accounts to be debited and several others to be credited ; *or*

(b) Several accounts to be debited and one other to be credited ; *or*

(c) One account to be debited and several others to be credited.

The rule for setting out such entries is that the word " Sundries " must be given instead of the name of the account where more than one account is to be debited or credited, the *names* of the accounts being entered below. This type of entry will best be explained by a glance at the three entries set out below, which respectively illustrate cases (a), (b) and (c) just mentioned.

It is important to note that the main principle of double entry

must be maintained in each case, *i.e.*, the *total* amount to be debited must equal the *total* amount to be credited in respect of each particular entry. In the case of a compound journal entry, only one narration is required for each complete entry.

It should be remembered that it is always legitimate to combine two entries in the journal, provided that they both have one account in common and are concerned with a single transaction. Thus, if it is necessary to debit Depreciation Account and credit Buildings Account with £85 for depreciation and also to debit Depreciation Account and credit Machinery Account with £70 for depreciation, a combined entry can be made, as shown below under (*c*).

A compound journal entry, however, must not be made in order to combine two entries which are not related, or to record two entries where there is no common account to be debited in both cases (or credited in both cases). Similarly, a compound journal entry must not be used in respect of transactions on different dates.

The following are the specimen journal entries referred to :—

JOURNAL

		Dr.	Cr.
		£ s. d.	£ s. d.
(a)	Sundries . . . . Dr.		
	To Sundries.		
	Cash.	450 0 0	
	Stock.	540 0 0	
	Sundry Debtors.	142 0 0	
	Sundry Creditors.		200 0 0
	Capital Account.		932 0 0
	Being assets, liabilities and capital as at this date.		
(b)	Sundries . . . . Dr.		
	To Profit and Loss Account.		263 0 0
	Discount Received Account.	220 0 0	
	Bank Interest Account.	43 0 0	
	Being transfer of balances at close of period.		
(c)	Depreciation Account . . . . Dr.	155 0 0	
	To Sundries.		
	Buildings Account.		85 0 0
	Machinery Account.		70 0 0
	Being depreciation for the year written off, viz., Buildings—5 per cent. on £1,700 : Machinery—10 per cent. on £700.		
		£ 1,550 0 0	1,550 0 0

It should be noted that for book-keeping purposes it is considered incorrect to cross out or alter any entries that subsequently prove to be incorrect ; any adjusting entries should be passed through the Principal Journal.

THE SALES DAY BOOK

The sub-division of the journal has already been explained, and it will be clear that the most practical and economical method of dealing with a large number of sales is to enter them in a separate journal.   The entries are then posted individually to the debit of the personal account affected, while the equivalent credit entry is made periodically to the Sales Account in the Ledger for the total sales of that period.

The separate journal which is used for this purpose is the Sales Day Book.   The example given earlier in the present chapter is extremely elementary in ruling but it is sufficient to indicate the principle involved.   A more complicated ruling will be given shortly, but it is first necessary that the reader should have a general idea of what actually takes place when sales are dealt with in business.

Cash Sales.

It is frequently thought that a sale usually implies the simultaneous exchange of goods for cash, as is customary in the case of a retail shop.   This, of course, is not the case, and as far as book-keeping is concerned, cash sales occupy a less prominent position than credit sales, as there is no necessity to raise personal ledger accounts for each cash transaction.

At regular intervals, *i.e.*, daily or weekly, the cash in the till is counted and paid into the bank and an entry is made on the debit side of the Cash Book, " To Cash Sales."   This entry is then posted to the credit of a nominal account called *Cash Sales Account*, the balance of which is transferred to Trading Account at the end of the period in exactly the same way as in the case of the ordinary Sales Account.   Alternatively, only one Sales Account may be used and both cash and credit sales would then be posted to this account.

In practice, a Cash Sales Book is frequently kept in order to record the sales as they are effected and thus to check the amount of cash received therefor.   This book is merely kept for memorandum purposes and is not part of the double entry system, and it may be ignored by the reader when working exercises.

Credit Sales.

Credit sales, on the other hand, require to be recorded in full detail, and it is with this type of transaction that the Sales Day

Book is concerned. A credit sale may be said to be one where the ownership in goods passes from the seller to the purchaser at the date of sale, but where the payment in respect of such goods is deferred until some subsequent date.

When goods which have been ordered upon credit are dispatched, it is customary for the seller to send to the customer an *Invoice* giving full particulars of the transaction. An Invoice may be defined as a document containing a description of the goods sold, their quantity and price, with a note of the terms arranged. The Invoice also serves as an advice to the customer that the goods have been dispatched.

The following is a specimen form of commercial invoice in general use :—

INVOICE.

241, ROYAL COURT ROAD,
LONDON, S.W.1.

3rd October, 19.....

Messrs. Longley and Co.,
  7, *King Street,*
    Bristol.

Bought of **S. & J. Lewis.**

Terms 2½% Discount, Monthly Account.

				£	s.	d.	£	s.	d.
200	Bath Towels.	@	2/–	20	0	0			
120	Sheets.	@	16/6	99	0	0			
100	Witney Blankets.	@	38/9	193	15	0			
prs.			p. pr.						
				312	15	0			
	Less Trade Discount 33⅓%.			104	5	0			
							£208	10	0
	Carr. Pd.								
	Per G.W. Rly.								

In this case Longley and Co. have a retail draper's business in Bristol and have purchased various goods from Messrs. S. and J. Lewis, who are wholesale drapers. At the time when the order is executed and the goods dispatched, Messrs. Lewis' warehouseman or packer makes a memorandum of the goods dispatched in the *Goods Outwards Book,* and informs the office staff, who post to the purchaser an invoice in the above form. Thus the exact nature of the sale, the price, the total amount due, etc., are formally notified to the purchaser. In the event of there being any dispute regarding delivery, reference to the Goods Outwards Book will enable Messrs. Lewis to confirm the date and time of dispatch. It should be noted that this book is not part of the double entry system, but is merely used in order to retain a definite record of all goods

leaving the premises, thus providing the necessary particulars as regards quantities, etc., from which the invoices can be prepared.

A copy of the invoice is usually taken and from this the various details are entered in the Sales Day Book, so that the seller also may have an accurate record of the transaction. The terms of payment and the deduction of *trade discount* will be explained later in this chapter. The above transaction would be recorded, together with other similar transactions, in the Sales Day Book as follows :—

SALES DAY BOOK

Date	Particulars.	Ledger Folio.	Details.	Invoice Total.
			£ s. d.	£ s. d.
19.... Oct. 3	Longley & Co., 7, King Street, Bristol. 200 Bath Towels, @ 2/– each. 120 Sheets, @ 16/6 each. 100 prs. Witney Blankets, @ 38/9 per pair.		20 0 0 99 0 0 193 15 0	
			312 15 0	
	Less 33⅓% trade discount.		104 5 0	
				208 10 0
„ 5	James Hirst, 18, Norton Road, Shipley. 1,000 yards Jap Silk, @ 1/8 per yard. 60 pairs Silk Stockings, @ 3/8 per pair		83 6 8 11 0 0	
			94 6 8	
	Less 15% trade discount.		14 3 0	
				80 3 8
„ 6	Arthur Dunning, Limited, 7, Princess Arcade, Brighton. 6 doz. Ladies' Umbrellas @ 8/9 each.		31 10 0	
	Less 33⅓% trade discount.		10 10 0	
				21 0 0
	Total (*posted to the credit of Sales Account*)			£309 13 8

It will be noticed that a details column is provided for individual items, deductions, etc., so that the invoice total, representing the net figure to be debited to the personal account in each case, may be shown in one amount in the total column.* In practice, of

* In view of present legislation, it is advisable to incorporate an additional column in the Sales Day Book in order to record the amount of *Purchase Tax* chargeable to customers ; it is considered the book-keeping entries in connection with the tax are beyond the scope of a work on " Elementary Book-keeping."

course, the total of each page is carried forward to the succeeding page, until the end of the month (or other period adopted) when the total for the period is credited to the Sales Account.

It should be noted that only goods dealt in by the trader in the usual course of his business are recorded in the Sales Day Book. Thus, the sale on credit of part of the fixtures and fittings of the trader's business, would not usually be entered in the Sales Day Book, but in the Principal Journal.

The double entry for cash and credit sales may now be summarized as follows :—

CASH SALES :   *Debit* Cash Account.
                Credit Sales Account (or Cash Sales A/c.).
CREDIT SALES : *Debit* Customer's Account.

Credit Sales Account (in periodical total per Sales Day Book), and when cash is received in respect thereof—
Debit Cash Account.
Credit Customer's Account.

Trade Discount.

It will be noticed that both in the specimen form of invoice and also in the above ruling of the Sales Day Book deductions are made in respect of *trade discount*. This term may be defined as an allowance made by manufacturers or wholesale dealers to retailers or tradesmen, by way of a deduction from the list or catalogue price of goods supplied. At first sight there appears to be little purpose in charging a certain price and immediately deducting from it a considerable proportion as discount. There are, however, several substantial reasons for the adoption of this practice, and it is to be found in general use in the wholesale trade.

In many classes of business, the manufacturers or wholesalers prescribe the retail prices of their goods, *e.g.*, wireless sets and motor cars, and issue catalogues and price lists in which the retail prices of the articles are given, in order that the catalogue may be shown to prospective customers without disclosing the amount of the retailer's profit. The goods are then invoiced to the retailer at their list (*i.e.*, their retail) price, and the difference between wholesale and retail price is deducted under the name of trade discount. A memorandum, separate from the catalogue or price list, is given to the retailer in order to supply him with the necessary information as to the percentages to be deducted by way of trade discount from the list prices of the various classes of goods.

The wholesaler is thus enabled to vary the margin of profit as between different retailers, a good customer being granted a special rate for competitive purposes. Furthermore, if the manufacturer

finds it necessary to increase the price at which he sells to the retailer, he may reduce the margin allowed to retailers without affecting the retail prices. Extensive scrapping and reprinting of catalogues and price lists can thus be avoided.

It is obvious from the above that trade discount is merely a means of adjusting the actual selling price to the true wholesale price. From the point of view of book-keeping, therefore, the gross price and the amount of trade discount deducted are of no importance, and the only figure that requires to be entered in the books is the actual *net* price. Thus the trade discount is merely shown on the invoice and in the " Particulars " or " Details " column of the Sales Day Book, while the net amount is extended into the " Total " column and posted to the debit of the customer's personal account in the ledger.

Similarly, in the case of the books of the purchaser of the goods, *i.e.*, the retailer or tradesman, the *net* amount represents the cost and the liability and only this is posted to the debit of purchases account in total and to the credit of the seller's personal account in the ledger. The gross amount and the trade discount are merely noted, for purposes of reference, in the details column of the Purchases Day Book.

Cash Discount.

It is extremely important to distinguish carefully between trade discount and *cash discount*, as the two terms are not identical and are subject to different treatment in the books of account. The latter form of discount is a deduction from the actual net price paid to the seller by the purchaser, and is only allowed in certain circumstances, not unconditionally as in the case of trade discount. Cash discount may be said to be a percentage allowance which is made if an account is paid within a certain specified period ; thus, it actually amounts to a monetary inducement to customers to pay their accounts promptly. It is recorded in the books of account of both debtor and creditor and is not ignored as in the case of trade discount.

The item " $2\frac{1}{2}\%$ Discount " at the head of the invoice on page 60 refers to the cash discount which may be deducted if the account is paid within the specified period, and it bears no relation to the trade discount which has just been explained.

The entries for Cash Discount will be explained fully in Chapter V when the Cash Book is being considered.

The " Invoice Day Book " Method.

The method already described for recording entries in the Sales Day Book is that which should be adopted by the reader in working exercises or examples, but it may be useful to refer to a

modern method of recording sales transactions. This alternative method is one by which a carbon copy of the invoice is retained with a view to reducing the details given in the Sales Day Book itself. If the ruling given on page 61 is referred to, it will be noticed that the particulars entered therein in respect of the first transaction are identical with those given on the invoice itself. Thus it appears that there is an unnecessary duplication of the detail work, and therefore methods are adopted to avoid this duplication.

A convenient method that is adopted in practice is that by which only the name of the customer, the date, and the net total of the invoice are entered in the Sales Day Book, together with a reference number which identifies the carbon copy of the particular invoice. The marked carbon copies are filed in consecutive order so that it is a simple process to refer to any one of them if further details of any transaction are required. Thus each entry in the Sales Day Book is simplified by the omission of unnecessary details, and duplication of work is avoided, as the carbon copy is made automatically at the same time as the invoice itself.

An alternative method is the use of duplicate invoice books consisting of perforated invoice forms interleaved with blank sheets. Carbon copies of each invoice are made and the invoice is torn out and sent to the customer, the carbon copy being retained in the book. The Sales Day Book is then written up from the particulars given in the duplicate invoice book.

A further development of the above alternative method is to use the book of carbon copies of invoices as a Sales Day Book itself, the total being carried forward from page to page, and the postings being made direct from the copy invoices.

The Columnar Sales Book.

As business developed both in volume and in complexity, the need arose for some method of ascertaining the success or otherwise of the trading carried out in the various sections or departments of the business, as distinct from the total profit of the business as a whole. If no attempt is made to calculate the profit or loss incurred in respect of each department of a large business, it is possible for one department to be run at a constant loss which, however, will not be apparent because it is merged in the general results of the business.

It is often desired, therefore, to ascertain the results of the trading of each department or of each class of goods separately. This may be achieved by keeping a separate set of books for each department and analysing every transaction according to the particular department affected. This method is, however,

extremely cumbrous and involves unnecessary clerical labour, and the required result may be obtained, with greater economy and efficiency, by means of columnar day books. In place of the system by which one Sales Account and one Purchases Account is kept for all the sales and purchases of the business respectively, separate nominal accounts are opened for the trading transactions of *each* department. In this way a separate Trading Account

COLUMNAR SALES DAY BOOK

Date.	Particulars.	Sales Ledger Folio.	Details.	Invoice Total.	Drapery.	Costumes.	Fancy Goods.
			£ s. d.	£ s. d.	£ s. d.	£ s. d.	£ s. d.
19..... Oct. 3	Longley and Co., Bristol.						
	200 Bath Towels @ 2s. each.		20 0 0				
	120 Sheets @ 16s. 6d. each.		99 0 0				
	100 prs. Witney Blankets @ 38s. 9d. per pr.		193 15 0				
			312 15 0				
	Less 33⅓% trade discount.		104 5 0				
				208 10 0	208 10 0		
„ 5	James Hirst, Shipley.						
	1,000 yards Jap Silk @ 1s. 8d. per yard.		83 6 8				
	60 pairs Silk Stockings @ 3s. 8d. per pair.		11 0 0				
			94 6 8				
	Less 15% trade discount.		14 3 0				
				80 3 8	80 3 8		
„ 6	Arthur Dunning, Limited, Brighton.						
	6 dozen Ladies' Umbrellas @ 8s. 9d. each.		31 10 0				
	Less 33⅓% trade discount.		10 10 0				
				21 0 0			21 0 0
„ 6	Watkinson & Co., Luton.						
	3 dozen Ladies' Costumes @ 47s. 9d. each.		85 19 0				
	Less 15% trade discount.		12 17 10				
				73 1 2		73 1 2	
„ 7	Cash Drapers, Limited, Croydon.						
	60 Ladies' Fancy Handbags @ 9s. 6d. each.		28 10 0				
	Less 33⅓% trade discount.		9 10 0				
				19 0 0			19 0 0
				£401 14 10	288 13 8	73 1 2	40 0 0

This total must agree with the sum of the totals of the analysis columns.	Post this total to credit of Drapery Sales Account.	Post this total to credit of Costumes Sales Account.	Post this total to credit of Fancy Goods Sales Account.

can be prepared to show the gross profit or loss of each department, the figures afterwards being combined to show the results for the business as a whole.

To meet these requirements the entries in the Sales Day Book will have to be divided up according to their respective departments, and this result is achieved by the provision of additional (analysis) columns in the Day Book. One of these additional columns is allocated to each department, the name of which appears at the head of its respective analysis column. The entries are made as usual in the first five columns, as shown in the example already given, but each item is also extended into its appropriate analysis columns.

The sum of the totals of all the analysis columns will, of course, equal the total of the " Invoice Total " column, and thus the same effect is obtained, from the double entry point of view, if a number of departmental Sales Accounts are credited with various amounts, as if one Sales Account is credited with the total of all these amounts. A glance at the example on page 65 will illustrate this method.

It will be noticed that the first three entries are the same as those already given in the simpler form of Day Book but they are now analysed between the three departments in order to illustrate the principle of the columnar system.

Similar analysed day books will be necessary in the case of purchases, returns, etc., and these will be considered in Chapter IV.

Practical Work.

The reader should at this stage be feeling more conversant with the books and accounts of a business. Furthermore, if he has practised assiduously and constantly, he should be able to work exercises without being compelled to refer to the fundamental principles of practice or procedure given in these pages. If, however, a difficulty is experienced with any particular point, the text-book should be referred to and studied carefully until all doubts are dispelled.

A thorough grasp of the fundamental principles and a detailed knowledge of the reasons for all the rules of elementary procedure are essential for complete success in the subject of book-keeping.

Until the other sub-divisions of the Journal are explained, the ordinary form of journal should be used for recording all transactions other than those relating to sales, the latter, of course, being entered in the Sales Day Book.

EXERCISE 3

A. Why is it necessary to sub-divide the Journal ? What are the chief books into which it is divided ?

B. What are the uses of the Journal proper ?

C. What is the difference between a Cash Sale and a Credit Sale ? How is each recorded in the books ?

D. Describe the uses of the Columnar Sales Day Book.

E. G. Elliott is in business as a Wholesale Chemist. On 1st January, 19....., his position was as follows :—

	£	s.	d.
Trade Debtors—R. Bartley.	231	7	9
C. Crossley.	174	8	4
I. Cooks.	31	11	10
Trade Creditors—F. Larking.	477	16	0
H. Teal.	823	1	7
Cash in hand.	760	5	0
Stock on hand.	1,171	2	5
Fixtures and Fittings.	427	3	6
Freehold Buildings.	4,250	0	0
Motor Vehicles.	475	0	0

Ascertain G. Elliott's capital, and show the opening Journal entry recording the above particulars.

F. Write up the Sales Day Book of the Vaults Wine Co., Ltd., from the following particulars :—

19.....

Mar. 1. Sold to N. Carrow, 2 Hogsheads of Brandy @ £30 each, subject to 7½% trade discount.

„ 2. Sold to J. W. Watson, 5 dozen of Super Port @ 35/– per dozen, and 7½ dozen of Scotch Whisky @ 115/– per dozen, all subject to 5% trade discount.

„ 3. Sold to J. Robinson, 1 pipe of Port @ £52, net.

„ 5. Sold to C. Smith & Co., 4 dozen of Port @ 27/6 per dozen, 2 dozen of Rum @ 73s. 6d. per dozen, all subject to 5% trade discount.

„ 7. Sold to J. Johnson, 5 10-gallon casks of Cider @ 2s. 3d. per gallon, subject to 2½% trade discount.

G. G. Gregory deals in Carpets and Rugs. Enter the following transactions in his Sales Day Book.

19.....

July 2. Sold to B. Black, 24 Axminster Squares @ £6 10s. each net.

„ 3. Sold to W. White, 6 Turkey Rugs @ £3 each, less 10% trade discount.

July 10. Sold to P. Pink, 67 feet Stair Carpet @ 9s. per yard net.

,, 17. Sold to S. Salmon, 2 Brussels Squares @ £5 10s. each net, and 1 Axminster Square @ £4 less 5% trade discount.

,, 19. Sold to G. Green, 4 Brussels Squares @ £10 10s. each, less 7½% trade discount.

,, 27. Sold to S. Scarlet, 16 square yards of Felting @ 1s. 6d. per square yard, less 2½% trade discount.

H. From the following particulars write up the Sales Day Book (with analysis columns for Motor Cars, Motor Cycles and Accessories) of Automots Ltd., Motor Agents:—

19.....

Jan. 3. Sold to Wilson's Ltd., 1 Morris Cowley 4-seater, @ £182 10s. net.

,, 5. Sold to Wilson's Ltd., 1 Vulcanizing Outfit, @ £2 10s. net.

,, 7. Sold to Robinson & Co., 1 B.S.A. Motor Cycle Combination, @ £72 10s. less 10% trade discount.

,, 7. Sold to Clark's Motors, Ltd., 3 Morris Vans @ £157 10s. each, less 15% trade discount.

,, 9. Sold to Robinson & Co., 1 Lighting Set @ £3 15s. net.

,, 10. Sold to J. A. Parker, 4 Dunlop Tyres @ £2 2s. 6d. each net, and 4 Dunlop Tubes @ 17s. 6d. each net.

,, 12. Sold to Drafter's Ltd., 4 Douglas Motor Cycle (Tradesmen) Combinations @ £75 each net, 1 Singer 2-seater at £185 net and 1 dozen Lodge plugs @ 4s. 9d. each net.

J. Compile the Columnar Sales Day Book of L. Heam from the following particulars:—

19.....

June 1. Sold to A. Baker, 20 sacks Flour @ 24s. 6d. and 2 quarters Wheat @ 37s. 6d.

,, 3. Sold to B. Cashir, 37 bushels Oats @ 7s. 3d., 4 sacks Flour @ 23s. 7d. and 2 sacks Flour @ 22s. 3d.

,, 4. Sold to C. Dacre, 65 quarters Wheat @ 24s. 11d., 17 bushels Oats @ 6s. 2d., and 14 bushels Barley @ 17s. 3d.

,, 5. Sold to D. Euston, 22½ bushels Maize @ 12s. 3d., and 2 sacks Flour @ 23s.

,, 6. Sold to A. Baker, 17 sacks Flour @ 23s. 9d.

CHAPTER IV

PURCHASES BOOK; RETURNS BOOKS

THE PURCHASES BOOK

The Purchases Book, or as it is sometimes styled, the Purchases Journal, Bought Day Book, or Bought Invoice Book, is the subdivision of the Journal in which are recorded the purchase of goods on credit by the business. It is similar, in general form, to the Sales Day Book, therefore the greater part of the explanation given in the preceding chapter applies in the case of the Purchases Book.

Procedure with Purchases.

Cash purchases by a business are comparatively rare, and when they occur, they are treated in a similar way to Cash Sales, being debited to Cash Purchases (or Purchases) Account and credited in the Cash Book. Care must be taken, however, to see that cash purchases are correctly treated, as occasionally such articles as new office desks, etc., may be purchased for cash, in which case the amount must be debited to Office Furniture Account, or other asset account as the case may be, and not to Purchases Account. For this reason, the nature of cash purchases and sales must be clearly indicated in the Cash Book.

The sole function of the Purchases Book is to record goods purchased upon credit terms. In the first place, it should be noted that the position of a business as regards purchases is the reverse to that discussed in the preceding chapter in connection with sales. The purchase of goods involves the receipt of those goods by a business as opposed to the dispatch of goods by a business when a sale is effected. The invoice for the purchase is not prepared and sent out but is received, usually by post, from the seller.

The specimen invoice given in Chapter III may be taken as an example, but it must be remembered that the transaction is being regarded from the opposite point of view, i.e., from that of Messrs. Longley and Company, the *purchasers* of the goods described in the invoice.

The procedure adopted in the case of purchases, differs, of course, from the general procedure that is necessary in connection with sales. When the purchase invoice is received the first step is to compare it carefully with the copy of the original order to ensure that the goods correspond as regards quality, quantity and price with those ordered. The extensions and calculations require to be checked, the trade discount agreed, and the terms of payment noted.

69

When the goods are received particulars are entered, by the yard foreman or storekeeper, in a *Goods Inwards Book*. This is similar in general form to the Goods Outwards Book described in the preceding chapter. It is merely a memorandum book, and should not be regarded as a book of account. Its purpose is to provide a record, in case of dispute, of the particular goods received and of the actual date of receipt.

The details are then entered in the Purchases Book from the invoice as in the case of the Sales Day Book. The ordinary ruling of the Purchases Book is given below,* together with three specimen entries by Longley and Company. It will be noticed that the first entry is identical with that given in the Sales Book of Messrs. Lewis, but naturally the other two are different and refer to purchases by Longley's from other wholesalers or manufacturers.

PURCHASES BOOK

Date.	Particulars.	Ledger Folio.	Details.			Invoice Total.		
			£	s.	d.	£	s.	d.
19..... Oct. 4	S. and J. Lewis, 241, Royal Court Road, London.							
	200 Bath Towels @ 2s. each.		20	0	0			
	120 Sheets @ 16s. 6d. each.		99	0	0			
	100 prs. Witney Blankets @ 38s. 9d. per pair.		193	15	0			
			312	15	0			
	Less 33⅓% trade discount.		104	5	0			
						208	10	0
„ 5	Marsden & Co., 241, Holborn, London.							
	20 Dining Room Chairs @ 28s. each.		28	0	0			
	1 Sideboard @ £15.		15	0	0			
	1 Gate-leg Table @ £7 15s.		7	15	0			
			50	15	0			
	Less 20% trade discount.		10	3	0			
						40	12	0
„ 6	H. & H. Horton, 9, High Row, Axminster.							
	20 Carpets @ £5 17s. 6d. each.		117	10	0			
	5 Carpets @ £9 3s. 6d. each.		45	17	6			
						163	7	6
	Total (*posted to debit of Purchases Account*).					£412	9	6

* In view of present legislation, it is advisable to incorporate an additional column in the Purchases Book in order to record the amount of *Purchase Tax* payable to suppliers (see note on page 61).

Trade discount is dealt with by the purchaser in a similar way to the seller, *i.e.*, it is recorded in the " Particulars " and " Details " columns of the Purchases Book, but only the net purchase price is extended and posted to the creditor's personal account.

The double entry for cash and credit purchases may now be summarized as follows :—

CASH PURCHASES :   *Debit* Purchases Account (or Cash Purchases A/c.).

Credit Cash Account.

CREDIT PURCHASES : *Debit* Purchases Account (in periodical total per Purchases Book).

Credit Supplier's Account.

and when cash is paid in respect thereof— *Debit* Supplier's Account.

Credit Cash Account.

The " Invoice Purchases Book."

In actual practice it is usual to find that the " Invoice Book " method is adopted for recording purchases, in a manner similar to that explained in the previous chapter in connection with sales. In working out exercises, however, the reader is advised to adopt the ordinary method, the Purchases Book being ruled as in the above example.

In modern business the time expended on reproducing in the Purchases Book the details of each invoice is avoided by the expedient of filing the invoices in numerical order, and giving in the Purchases Book itself only the name of the seller, the net amount of the invoice and its reference number.   Each invoice is numbered consecutively on receipt, and as the corresponding number is recorded against each entry in the Purchases Book, it is a simple matter to refer to any particular invoice when details of any individual transaction are required at a later date.

It should be noted that this system can be more readily adapted to purchase transactions than to sales, as the original invoices remain in the office and therefore the necessity for carbon copies does not arise.

The Columnar Purchases Book.

The necessity for ascertaining the profit or loss on each separate department was explained at length in Chapter III, and it was shown that the method adopted in practice is to provide analysis columns in the various subsidiary journals, and to keep separate nominal accounts for each department.

In the case of the Purchases Book, exactly the same procedure

is followed as was described in connection with the Sales Day Book. Analysis columns are provided and the totals posted, at the end of the month or other period, to the appropriate departmental purchases accounts.

Messrs. Longley and Co., for instance, may have a large business

COLUMNAR PURCHASES BOOK

Date.	Particulars.	Purchase Ledger Folio.	Details.	Invoice Total.	Drapery.	Furnishing.	Men's Wear.
19.....			£ s. d.	£ s. d.	£ s. d.	£ s. d.	£ s. d.
Oct. 4	S. & J. Lewis, Royal Court Road, London.						
	200 Bath Towels @ 2s. each.		20 0 0				
	120 Sheets @ 16s. 6d. each.		99 0 0				
	100 prs. Witney Blankets @ 38s. 9d. a pair.		193 15 0				
			312 15 0				
	Less 33⅓% trade discount.		104 5 0				
				208 10 0	208 10 0		
„ 5	Marsden & Co., Holborn, London.						
	20 Dining Room Chairs @ 28s. each.		28 0 0				
	1 Sideboard @ £15.		15 0 0				
	1 Gate-leg Table @ £7 15s.		7 15 0				
			50 15 0				
	Less 20% trade discount.		10 3 0				
				40 12 0		40 12 0	
„ 6	H. & H. Horton, Axminster.						
	20 Carpets @ £5 17s. 6d. each.		117 10 0				
	5 Carpets @ £9 3s. 6d. each.		45 17 6				
				163 7 6		163 7 6	
„ 7	Small, Jones & Co., Eastcheap, London.						
	100 Tennis Shirts @ 8s. 6d. each.		42 10 0				
	50 prs. Flannel Trousers @ 17s. 6d. per pair.		43 15 0				
			86 5 0				
	Less 20% trade discount.		17 5 0				
			69 0 0				
	100 Ladies' Jumpers @ 16s. each		80 0 0				
	Less 20% trade discount.		16 0 0				
			64 0 0	133 0 0	64 0 0		69 0 0
			£	545 9 6	272 10 0	203 19 6	69 0 0
				This total must agree with the sum of the totals of the analysis columns.	Post this total to debit of Drapery Purchases Account.	Post this total to debit of Furnishing Purchases Account.	Post this total to debit of Men's Wear Purchases Account.

with several quite distinct departments, such as drapery, furnishing and men's wear. Separate analysis columns will then be provided in the Purchases Book, and separate Purchases Accounts will be kept in the ledger for each of the three departments.

An additional column, headed " Ledger Accounts," is frequently provided in practice for sundry items which cannot be apportioned to any particular department. Packing materials, stationery, etc., are examples of purchases which require to be included in the Purchases Book, yet which are not for the exclusive use of any particular department, and are not purchased for resale to customers. Purchases of assets may also be recorded in this column. Each item in this " Sundries " column must, of course, be posted separately to its appropriate impersonal account, instead of the total being posted in one amount.

The columnar Purchases Book as it might be kept by Messrs. Longley and Co. is given on page 72 and shows the allocation of the net invoice totals to the respective departments. This form of Purchases Book should be compared with the simpler form given on page 70.

It will be noticed that the analysis columns of the Purchases Book are headed quite differently from those of the Sales Day Book of Messrs. Lewis given in Chapter III, although the first entry in both books concerns the same transaction. This is accounted for by the fact that the departments into which a business is divided depend upon the particular nature of the business and vary according to the requirements of the proprietor. Thus it will be found in practice that the departmental divisions of a wholesale drapery business such as that of Messrs. Lewis will differ from that of a retail store such as that of Messrs. Longley and Co.

It should be borne in mind that the rule of double entry applies with equal force to the columnar Purchases Book as it does to the simple form of journal. At the close of the period the total of the individual amounts credited to the various personal accounts must equal the total amount debited to the departmental purchases accounts.

RETURNS BOOKS

The methods adopted in practice for recording the two main classes of transactions, *i.e.*, Sales and Purchases, have been explained in detail, and it therefore remains to consider the smaller class of transactions which involve the return of goods by the purchaser to the seller.

Returns Outwards Book.

When large quantities of goods are bought, generally without being seen at the time of ordering, it sometimes happens that some

articles, on arrival, prove to be inferior to the quality ordered.
They may also not be in accordance with the sample from which
they were ordered ; or again, they may be defective in some
important respect or may have been damaged in transit.   In such
cases it is usual to return the goods to the supplier (*i.e.*, the seller),
and it therefore becomes necessary to record the transaction in
the books of the purchaser.

If the ordinary form of journal were used, the entry might be
given as :—

Supplier's Personal Account   *Dr.*
To Purchases Account

as the seller becomes a debtor for goods which are returned to him,
while the Purchases Account has given value, *i.e.*, the goods
have gone out of the business, therefore this account must be
credited.

In actual practice, however, entries relating to the return of
goods *outwards*, *i.e.*, the return of goods purchased, are usually
recorded in a separate book known as the Returns Outwards, or
Purchases Returns Book, in exactly the same way as purchases
are recorded in the Purchases Book.   The Returns Outwards Book
is ruled to correspond with the Purchases Book, the simple form
having columns for the date, particulars, ledger folio, details and
total.   Entries are made in the same way, the trade discount (if
any) being shown, and the *net* amount extended to the total
column.   Furthermore, it is usual to make a brief note below each
entry, indicating the reason for the return of the goods.

The items are posted from the Returns Outwards Book to the
debit of the various personal accounts, while the total amount
returned during the month, or other period, is transferred in one
amount to the credit of Returns Outwards Account.   When the
books are closed, the balance of this latter account is transferred
to the Trading Account, and it is usually shown on the debit side
as a *deduction* from the total amount of purchases and not as a
separate item on the credit side of the Trading Account.   A
moment's thought will show that the ultimate result is identical
whether the item be deducted from a debit entry, or entered as a
separate credit entry.

For example, in the specimen ruling of a Returns Outwards
Book given on page 77, the total amount to be credited to Returns
Outwards Account is £23 18s. 8d.   Assuming this to be the total
returns for the trading period, the entry in the Trading Account
would appear thus :—

Dr. TRADING ACCOUNT Cr.

	£	s.	d.	£	s.	d.
To Purchases						
(*say*).	1,018	7	6			
Less Returns						
Outwards.	23	18	8			
				994	8	10

If, on the other hand, the purchases item of £1,018 7s. 6d. were given on the debit side and the returns outwards item of £23 18s. 8d. were given on the credit side the net result would be exactly the same, *i.e.*, a net debit balance of £994 8s. 10d.

The entry is given in this way because the actual net value of the goods purchased over the period is the total amount received *less* the amount returned. In other words, the total of the returns outwards represents goods which to all intents and purposes have never been purchased, for they were returned as soon as they were received, and so the value must be deducted from the gross amount of purchases in order to bring this to the true figure.

An alternative method that is sometimes adopted is to transfer the balance shown on Returns Outwards Account, at the end of the trading period, to Purchases Account, the balance of the latter account being transferred to and shown in the Trading Account as " To Purchases (less Returns) £——."

Credit Notes and Allowances.

When the return of goods is accepted by the seller, *i.e.* when he receives them back and agrees to deduct their value from the amount due from the purchaser, it is usual for him to send the purchaser a *credit note*. This document has the opposite effect to that of an invoice, for it is a statement that the purchaser is *credited* with the value of the goods detailed therein, whereas an invoice is a statement that the purchaser is *debited* with the value of the goods specified. Credit notes are usually printed in red so that they may be easily distinguished from invoices, which are generally printed in black.

In addition to the actual return of goods, the Returns Outwards Book is also used to record allowances which are made to the purchaser in respect of goods other than those actually returned. For example, goods are sometimes damaged during the course of transit and may be saleable only at a reduced figure. It is then usual for the purchaser to request the seller to make him an allowance equal to the loss in value attributed to the damage suffered by the goods.

If the allowance made is adequate from the point of view of the purchaser he retains the goods, thereby obtaining them at a

lower net price. Naturally the seller prefers to receive a reduced sum for the damaged goods rather than to take them back into his stock, and, in addition, to incur the expense of the return carriage upon them. Thus, in practice, it is usually found that a reasonable allowance is agreed upon between purchaser and seller.

On hearing that the allowance offered has been accepted, the seller issues a credit note. This is recorded in exactly the same way as if goods to the amount of the allowance had actually been returned. An entry is made in the Returns Outwards Book by the purchaser, and the amount allowed is posted to the debit of the seller's personal account.

Columnar Returns Outwards Book.

If it is desired to ascertain the trading results of each of the departments of a business the entries in all the subsidiary journals must be analysed. Thus, the Returns Outwards Book must be ruled on the columnar principle.

The ruling for a columnar Returns Outwards Book is similar to that already described in connection with the columnar Purchases Book. The entries are made in exactly the same way, with the exception that a note is usually made after each entry, stating the reason for the return of the goods or the making of an allowance.

At the end of the month or other period, the totals of the analysis columns are transferred to the appropriate Returns Outwards Accounts, there being a separate account for each department corresponding to the separate Purchases Accounts.

A specimen ruling of a Columnar Returns Outwards Book is given on page 77. This is assumed to be the returns book of Messrs. Longley and Co., whose Purchases Book was set out earlier in the present chapter. For purposes of illustration, it has been assumed that a return of some kind has taken place in respect of each of the four transactions entered in the Purchases Book. The reader will, however, realize that this would not necessarily occur in actual practice. The number of cases where goods have to be returned is comparatively rare, although it varies with different trades, but it would be extremely unusual for there to be returns in respect of each of four consecutive entries in the Purchases Book.

It must not be forgotten that where trade discount was allowed on the original purchase a similar allowance must also be deducted from the gross value of the goods returned. Thus, if the twenty towels returned to Messrs. Lewis were to be debited to their account at their gross price, ignoring trade discount, the effect would be that the purchaser would benefit at their expense. In other words, their personal account in Messrs. Longley and Co.'s books would be debited with twenty towels at 2s. each, *i.e.*, £2, and credited with a similar number at 2s. each (less 33⅓%) *i.e.*, £1 6s. 8d. Thus

Messrs. Lewis would suffer an unfair loss of 13s. 4d. The amount of the trade discount, therefore, should be deducted from individual items, as has been done in the entries included in the specimen Returns Outwards Book.

Returns Inwards Book.

It is as necessary to record the return of goods sold, *i.e.*, Returns Inwards, as it is of those purchased, *i.e.*, Returns Outwards. The book-keeping procedure is almost identical, for one individual transaction will represent the returns outward of the purchaser and the returns inward of the seller, the sole difference being that the transaction is regarded from different points of view.

COLUMNAR RETURNS OUTWARDS BOOK

Date.	Particulars.	Purchase Ledger Folio.	Details.	Invoice Total.	Drapery.	Furnishing.	Men's Wear.
			£ s. d.	£ s. d.	£ s. d.	£ s. d.	£ s. d.
19... Oct. 8	S. & J. Lewis, Royal Court Road, London. 20 Bath Towels @ 2s. each.		2 0 0				
	Less 33⅓% trade discount.		13 4				
	Goods defective.			1 6 8	1 6 8		
„ 9	Marsden & Co., Holborn, London. 1 Gate-leg Table @ £7 15s.		7 15 0				
	Less 20% trade discount.		1 11 0				
	Damaged in transit.			6 4 0		6 4 0	
„ 11	Small, Jones & Co., Eastcheap, London. 10 Ladies' Jumpers @ 16s. each.		8 0 0				
	Less 20% trade discount.		1 12 0				
	Goods sent in excess of order.			6 8 0	6 8 0		
„ 14	H. & H. Horton, Axminster. Allowance for damage to goods.		10 0 0	10 0 0		10 0 0	
				£ 23 18 8	7 14 8	16 4 0	

This total must agree with the sum of the totals of the analysis columns.

Post this total to the credit of Drapery Returns Outwards Account.

Post this total to the credit of Furnishing Returns Outwards Account.

When goods previously sold are returned to the seller, particulars thereof are recorded in the Returns Inwards (or Sales Returns) Book, and are posted individually to the *credit* of the purchaser's personal account. The total of the Returns Inwards Book is transferred periodically to the *debit* of Returns Inwards Account, as goods have come *in* to the business. The balance of this latter account is transferred, at the time of closing the books, to the Trading Account, where instead of being shown as a separate debit entry, it is deducted from the *credit* entry of sales. As was explained in connection with Returns Outwards, the effect of both methods is the same from the double entry point of view, but the figure given in the Trading Account more accurately represents the actual net sales. For example, a typical entry would appear as follows:

Dr.	TRADING ACCOUNT	*Cr.*

	£ s. d.	£ s. d.
By Sales (*say*)	1,209 11 1	
Less Returns		
Inwards (*say*)	42 8 6	
		1,167 2 7

The ruling of the Returns Inwards Book is practically identical with that of the Returns Outwards Book. The example of a columnar form of Returns Outwards Book already given would serve equally as an example of a Returns Inwards Book if the headings were altered to correspond with those of the Sales Day Book and the posting explanations at the foot of the analysis columns were adjusted. A specimen ruling of the Returns Inwards Book need not therefore be given.

In practice, where returns inwards and outwards are few in number, they are recorded at the end of the Sales Day Book (returns inwards), and Purchases Book (returns outwards).

EXERCISE 4

A. Give a definition of the Purchases Book.

B. Discuss the uses and advantages of the Columnar Purchases Book.

C. How are Returns Inwards and Returns Outwards recorded ? Discuss the rulings of the necessary books.

D. What is a credit note ? How does a credit note differ from an invoice ?

E. Write up the Purchases Book of M. Arthur for the following transactions :—

19.....

Jan. 3. Bought from J. Roberts, 6 dozen gents' umbrellas, @ 8s. 3d. each, less 5% trade discount.

„ 5. Bought from W. Simpson, 2½ dozen children's coats @ 10s. 11d. each net, 3¾ dozen maids' coats @ 14s. 6d. each, less 10% trade discount, and 3 ladies' costumes. @ 42s. 6d. each, less 5% trade discount.

„ 7. Bought from C. Thompson, 3 dozen pullovers @ 72s. 6d. a dozen net.

„ 9. Bought from J. Booth, 2½ dozen cardigans @ 39s. 11d. a dozen, less 2½% trade discount.

„ 10. Bought from W. Saunders, 3 dozen boys' suits @ 18s. 11d. each, less 5% trade discount, and 2 dozen gents' suits @ 73s. 9d. each net.

F. Write up the Purchases Book (with analysis columns) of W. Peet for the following transactions :—

19.....

April 1. Bought from Black Collieries, Ltd., 100 tons of house coal @ 47s. 6d. per ton.

„ 3. Bought from T. Jackson & Co., 37 tons of slack coal @ 29s. 3d. per ton, less 10% trade discount, 40 tons of coke @ 19s. 10d. per ton net, and 50 tons of anthracite @ 84s. 6d. per ton net.

„ 5. Bought from J. Parry, Ltd., 230 tons of house coal @ 46s. 4d. per ton net, 45 tons of slack coal @ 27s. 9d. per ton, less 5% trade discount, and 50 tons of anthracite @ 80s. per ton, less 2½% trade discount.

„ 7. Bought from Coalfields, Ltd., 420 tons of house coal @ 43s. 6d. per ton net.

G. Write up the Returns Outwards Book of A. Merchant from the following particulars :—

19.....

Sept. 1. Returned to B. Black, 3 dozen boxes cigars @ 11s. 3d. each, not up to sample.

„ 3. Received credit note from H. Thomas for £2 5s., allowance on damaged tobacco pouches.

„ 12 Returned to J. Dewar, 1,000 cigarettes @ 4s. per hundred, not ordered.

„ 17. Received credit note from P. Proctor, for £22 7s. 6d. in respect of cigars lost in transit.

„ 20. Returned to H. Eden, cigars value £7 10s. 9d., damaged by water.

H. Write up the Sales Day Book, Purchases Book and Returns Books of Steel and Co., Cutlers and Silversmiths, from the following particulars :—

19.....

Jan. 2. Purchased from H. Rankin, 5 dozen table knives @ 29s. per dozen, 2 dozen razors @ 7s. 6d. each, and 3 dozen pocket knives @ 38s. 3d. per dozen, all being subject to 10% trade discount.

„ 2. Sold to H. Hassal, 1 dozen pairs of scissors @ 2s. 3d. per pair, and 6 table knives @ 3s. each.

Jan. 4. Returned to H. Rankin, 2½ dozen table knives as damaged and received credit note.

,, 5. Sold to J. Lloyd, 3 dozen table forks @ 37s. 9d. per dozen and 1 canteen of cutlery @ £4 10s.

,, 7. Purchased from M. Beck, 6 silver salvers @ £3 15s. each, less 15% trade discount.

,, 8. H. Hassal returned 2 pairs of scissors damaged.

,, 10. Purchased from N. Roberts, 9 cases E.P. fish servers @ £2 5s. per case, subject to 10% trade discount, and 4 dozen sets of carvers @ 12s. 9d. per set, subject to 7½% trade discount.

,, 11. Returned 1 dozen sets of carvers to N. Roberts, as inferior to quality ordered.

,, 12. Sent J. Lloyd credit note for 15s., allowance on damaged canteen of cutlery.

,, 15. Sold B. Legge, 1 tea and coffee set @ £3 10s. 6d., less trade discount of 5%.

CHAPTER V
THE CASH BOOK

It has already been explained that, unlike all other accounts, the Cash Account is not included in the ledger but is recorded, for purposes of convenience, in a separate volume known as the Cash Book.

The Cash Book fulfils two functions ; it is a ledger (consisting of one ledger account) in which cash receipts are debited and cash payments credited ; and, unlike other ledgers, it is also used as a book of first entry. Cash receipts and payments are entered direct in the Cash Book for posting to the other ledger accounts, instead of being first passed through the Journal.

In its simplest form the ruling of a Cash Book is similar to that of any other ledger account, receipts, *i.e.*, value coming in, being entered on the debit side, while payments, *i.e.*, value going out, are entered on the credit side.

In the present chapter it is proposed to consider the more advanced forms of the Cash Book used in practice : but sight must not be lost of the fact that the Cash Book is primarily an ordinary ledger account in which dealings in the commodity " cash " are recorded.

Cash Discount.

It will be remembered that, when considering trade discount in Chapter III, reference was made to *cash discount*, and it was pointed out that these two kinds of discount are not similar and are treated differently in the books of account.

Trade discount is simply an allowance which is made in order to adjust the selling price of a commodity. The amount of the trade discount is merely noted in the book of first entry, only the net invoice price being recorded in the sales and purchases books.

Cash discount, on the other hand, is an allowance which is offered in order to induce customers to pay their accounts immediately or within a specified time. A percentage allowance by way of cash discount is sometimes offered by a retailer to his customers when goods purchased are paid for promptly, but more

81

usually it is allowed by wholesalers, manufacturers and others in respect of transactions with retailers if payment is made " within one month."

The exact interpretation of the term " within one month " varies in different trades. Thus, in certain cases it may mean that each item is due for payment within one month of the date of the invoice, while in others it is assumed to mean that all goods invoiced during any given month must be paid for by the middle, e.g., the 15th, of the following month, if advantage is to be taken of the cash discount. Accounts not paid before the expiration of the agreed period or fixed date are " net," i.e., they must be paid in full without the deduction of cash discount.

One of the main points of difference between trade and cash discount is that the former is allowed *automatically*, irrespective of the date of actual payment, whereas cash discount is allowed *conditionally*, and if the stipulated conditions as to time of payment are not fulfilled it ceases to be allowable.

For example, if Bates purchases furniture to the value of £250 from Wholesalers, Limited, on 18th August, subject to 20% trade discount and $2\frac{1}{2}$% cash discount for payment within one month of date of invoice, the trade discount is a definite allowance made unconditionally, so that the net invoice price, i.e., the net amount due, will be £250 less 20% of £250, or £200. The cash discount, however, will be allowed only if payment is made by 18th September, in which case the amount to be remitted will be £195, i.e., £200 less $2\frac{1}{2}$% of £200. Note that the cash discount is calculated on the net invoice price and not on the gross amount. Unless payment is made by the aforementioned stipulated date, the net invoice price of £200 will be payable and the account will be " net," i.e., no cash discount can be deducted.

The Treatment of Discount Allowed.

Cash discount may be regarded as a definite business transaction in which cash is paid in return for a service received, in the same way as cash is exchanged for labour when wages are paid. The service in the case of cash discount is the prompt payment of a debt. In return for the prompt payment of accounts and the advantages resulting therefrom, a trader is willing to pay a certain sum as cash discount.

The simplest entry to record the allowance of cash discount in the books of the creditor would in theory be :—

Debit Discount Account
Credit Cash Account

because Cash Account has given value, whereas Discount Account has received value, i.e., a service.

In actual practice, however, instead of cash going out of the business, the allowance of cash discount results in less cash coming in, which ultimately amounts to the same thing. Thus, when a debtor pays his account under discount there are, in effect, two distinct transactions, *viz.* :—

(1) Cash is received for the full amount of the debt owing ; and
(2) Part of this cash is refunded to the debtor in the form of discount.

The first transaction is a familiar one, requiring a debit to cash and a credit to the debtor's personal account. The entry for the second transaction is given above.

The necessary cash entries are simplified in practice, for the same effect is obtained, with less clerical effort, if cash is debited with the actual amount received instead of cash being debited with the full amount of the debt and credited with the amount of discount allowed. This may be illustrated by referring to the example quoted above, and assuming that Bates paid the amount due, less discount, on 17th September. In order to comply with the principles of double entry in the books of Wholesalers, Limited, cash is debited with £195 and Discount Account with £5, and the personal ledger account of Bates is credited with £200.

Therefore in order to record a cash receipt when discount is allowed the necessary entries in the books of the seller will be :—

> *Debit* Cash with the net amount received.
> *Debit* Discount Account with the amount of discount allowed.
> *Credit* Debtor's Account with the full amount of the debt.

or, in the above example the entries in the books of Wholesalers, Limited, will be :—

> *Debit* Cash, £195
> *Debit* Discount Account, 5
> *Credit* Bates's Account, £200

The personal account of the debtor, Bates, will appear thus :

Dr.				A. BATES				Cr.
19..... Aug. 18	To Sales.	£ 200	s. 0	d. 0	19..... Sept. 17	By Cash.	£ 195	s. 0	d. 0
					„ „	„ Discount.	5	0	0
		£ 200	0	0			£ 200	0	0

The following more practical method, however, is usually adopted by which a composite entry is made, viz. :—

Dr.   A. BATES   *Cr.*

19.....		£	s.	d.	19.....		£	s.	d.
Aug. 18	To Sales.	200	0	0	Sept. 17	By Cash and Discount.	200	0	0

In practice, items of discount allowed are not debited individually to a nominal account of that name in the ledger, but are grouped together in the same way as are purchases and sales. It has already been explained that purchases, sales and returns are recorded in separate journals for purposes of convenience in posting to the nominal accounts. Cash discounts are grouped together in a similar way and posted to the Discount Account in the ledger in total, at the end of the specified periods.

In order to ascertain these periodical totals, cash discounts allowed are not recorded in separate journals, but the Cash Book is made to serve the same purpose by the provision of an additional column on the debit side, alongside the cash column. When a transaction is entered in the Cash Book the amount of cash actually received is entered in the cash column, and at the same time the amount of the discount allowed is entered in the discount column on the same side (see example on page 88). At the end of the month or other period, the total of the discount column is posted to Discount Account in the ledger, and of course the balancing of the cash columns of the Cash Book is carried out in the usual way.

The Treatment of Discount Received.

Where discount is received, that is when considering the books of the trader who *pays* the account and *receives* the discount, the book-keeping procedure is similar, but in this case the entries are reversed. The actual amount of cash paid is credited in the cash column of the Cash Book, the amount of discount is entered in the discount column on the same side, and the full amount is debited to the creditor's personal account. Thus the entries in Bates's books to record the transactions already referred to would be :—

Debit Wholesalers, Limited, £200
    Credit Cash,   £195
    Credit Discount Account,   5

The discount would not be credited direct, as has already been explained, but would be recorded in the discount column on the credit side of the Cash Book, the totals of this column being posted periodically to the credit of Discount Account in the ledger. Thus in the above specimen entries Discount Account is *credited* because Bates has *given* out a service (the service of paying cash promptly). It will be noticed that the total of the discount column on the debit side of the Cash Book is posted, as previously explained, to the *debit* of Discount Account, and, similarly, the total of the *credit* column to the *credit* of Discount Account. This fact usually causes difficulty to the beginner, as it does not appear to be in accordance with the fundamental rule of posting items to the opposite side of other accounts, *i.e.*, debit items being posted to the credit side and *vice versa*. The difficulty arises from the mistake made by the student of regarding the discount columns of the Cash Book as being part of a ledger account, whereas actually they must be considered as *Discount Journals*, or books of first entry, which are incorporated in the Cash Book for purposes of convenience to obviate undue detail in the Discount Account in the ledger.

It follows, therefore, that the column on the credit side of the Cash Book relates to discount to be *credited*, and that on the debit side to discount to be *debited*, to the Discount Account.

The principle of double entry is adhered to, as the various items in the discount allowed column on the debit side of the Cash Book have been posted, in detail, to the credit side of the various personal accounts in the ledger at the same time as the cash items to which they refer, and the total of these items is posted to the *debit* of Discount Account. Conversely, the double entry is completed in regard to the items in the discounts received column on the credit side of the Cash Book by debiting the various personal accounts concerned and *crediting* the total to Discount Account.

The *totals* of the discount columns are posted to the corresponding sides of Discount Account and *not* the difference between the totals of the two columns. The posting is similar to that when, say, total purchases are posted from the Purchases Book to Purchases Account in the ledger ; in either case there is a posting of total debits or credits from books of first entry to the appropriate ledger accounts. In practice it is safer to insert the discount totals on the same line as that on which the cash totals appear, as there is thus less likelihood of their being overlooked in posting to the ledger.

The double entry in respect of cash discounts may now be summarized as follows :—

DISCOUNT RECEIVED : *Debit* Supplier's Account.

Credit Discount Account (in periodical total from credit column in Cash Book).

DISCOUNT ALLOWED : *Debit* Discount Account (in periodical total from debit column in Cash Book).

Credit Customer's Account.

A useful rule to bear in mind is that the entry for discount in the personal account appears on the *same* side as the cash entry in the personal account.

Many students have difficulty in understanding why a customer who " receives " discount should be credited. This appears to be an exception to the theoretical principle of " debit the receiver, credit the giver," but it should be remembered that discounts allowed by a trader are losses or expenses and must consequently be *debited* to Discount Account, whilst the customer is regarded as having *given* a service by prompt payment to the value of the discount. Conversely, discounts received by a trader are gains to the business, and must be *credited* to Discount Account, whilst the supplier is regarded as having *received* a service to the value of the discount.

The preceding remarks relate to the settlement of accounts relating to goods sold or bought on credit terms, for cash discounts on cash sales or cash purchases are *not* entered in the Cash Book as no personal account is affected. Thus the Cash Book entry is confined to the *net* amount received in the case of a cash sale and the *net* amount paid in the case of a cash purchase.

The theoretical aspect of this subject has been clearly explained in this chapter, and it is now proposed to consider, by way of illustration, a practical example showing the use of a simple form of Cash Book in which discount columns are incorporated.

EXAMPLE

On 15th September, 19...., Bates had a balance of cash in hand of £641 3s. 8d. Write up his Cash Book from the following particulars :—

19.....

Sept. 16. Paid account of Wholesalers, Limited, £200, less 2½% discount.

„ 17. Received £24, less 2½% discount, from R. King.

„ 18. Received £87 15s. from S. Parsons.

„ 19. Paid wages, £19.

„ 20. Paid Samson and Company, £151, less 2½% discount.

„ 21. Received £33, less 2½% discount, from B. E. Saul.

„ 23. Paid carriage on goods, £2 5s. 3d.

„ 24. Received £21 10s., less 2½% discount from R. Knowles.

„ 25. Received £41 9s. 8d. from N. A. Stall.

„ 26. Paid wages, £19.

Sept. 28.   Paid Lawson & Co.'s account, £103 10s., less 2½% discount.
 „   30.   Paid Sorter & Co., £17 10s., less 2½% discount.
 „   30.   Received £19, less 2½% discount, from H. Small.
                (*For worked solution, see page* 88.)

It should be noticed that the cash columns are balanced in the usual way, the amount £365 0s. 4d. representing the cash in hand at the end of the month. The total of the discount column on the debit side of the Cash Book, £2 8s. 9d., is posted to the *debit* of Discount Account and the corresponding credit total of £11 16s. 0d. to the *credit* of the same account. In practice, separate accounts are sometimes kept for Discount Allowed and Discount Received, but in theory it is sufficient to post both classes of discount to the same account. The Discount Account, after the transfers from the Cash Book have been made, would appear as follows :—

Dr.	DISCOUNT ACCOUNT						Cr.	
19.....		£	s.	d.	19.....		£	s. d.
Sept. 30	To Sundries as per Cash Book.	2	8	9	Sept. 30	By Sundries as per Cash Book.	11	16 0

The Banking System.

Hitherto it has been assumed that all transactions involving payment by one person to another have been made in actual cash, and the existence of banks, cheques, and the whole remarkably developed banking system of the present day, has been ignored. In actual fact, however, a banking account is kept by practically every business concern, and the cheque now plays a far greater part in the settlement of debts than do notes or coins. The effect which this has upon book-keeping methods must therefore be considered, but it will first be advisable for the reader to gain a general idea of the banking system as far as it affects the average business concern.

In England, banking developed originally from the activities of the money-changers who came from Lombardy, and the goldsmiths of London. At first it involved nothing more than keeping the gold and valuables of the wealthy merchants in safe custody and restoring them when required. Then came the idea of issuing a note or promise of repayment in respect of the gold received, and of lending some of the gold in the meantime to others who needed it. Thus, slowly there developed the present-day system of receiving money from those who have a surplus, and of lending it to those who require it for productive and other purposes.

Within the last century, the use of bank notes has been very

CASH BOOK

Dr.

Date	Particulars	Led. Fo.	Discount Allowed £ s. d.	Amount Received £ s. d.
19....				
Sept. 15	To Balance	b/d		641 3 8
" 17	" R. King.		12 0	23 8 0
" 18	" S. Parsons.			87 15 6
" 21	" B. E. Saul.		16 6	32 3 6
" 24	" R. Knowles.		10 9	20 19 3
" 25	" N. A. Stall.			41 9 6
" 30	" H. Small.			18 10 6
			£2 8 9 Total debited to Discount Account.	865 9 7
Sept. 30	To Balance.		b/d	365 0 4

Cr.

Date	Particulars	Led. Fo.	Discount Received £ s. d.	Amount Paid £ s. d.
19....				
Sept. 16	By Wholesalers, Ltd.		5 0 0	195 0 0
" 19	" Wages.			19 0 0
" 20	" Samson & Co.		3 15 6	147 4 6
" 23	" Carriage.			2 5 3
" 26	" Wages.			19 0 0
" 28	" Lawson & Co.		2 11 9	100 18 3
" 30	" Sorter & Co.		8 9	17 1 3
" 30	" Balance.	c/d		365 0 4
			£11 16 0 Total credited to Discount Account.	865 9 7

considerably replaced by the cheque system, which is far more convenient for all general business purposes. The principle remains the same, however ; the customer pays his money into the bank from time to time, and withdraws it as required by means of cheques, which are orders to the banker to pay money to the persons specified on such cheques.

Banking Accounts.

Bankers receive money from their customers in two different ways, *viz.* :—

        (*a*) On Current Account ; and
        (*b*) On Deposit Account.

A CURRENT ACCOUNT is a running account, that is, one which is intended to be used as frequently as is required for payments in and out, withdrawals being made by cheque. The current account is invariably used for ordinary business purposes.

The cash, notes and cheques received from debtors are paid in daily or weekly, according to the particular circumstances of the business, while payment of creditors' accounts or of the various trading expenses is made by cheques, which are eventually received by the banker and debited to the customer's account. Thus the position of a banker and his customer is that of a debtor and a creditor, the banker in this case being the debtor. It sometimes happens that a trader or manufacturer requires money to develop his business, extend his factory or engage upon some other activity involving heavy expenditure in the present which will not be repaid, in the form of profits, for some considerable time. In such cases it is usual for the trader to obtain a *loan* from his banker, giving in return substantial security to protect the latter from possible loss. The security deposited may take the form of title deeds to property, rights to the possession of goods, assignments of insurance policies or of investments, or personal guarantees by third parties who undertake to repay the amount lent in the event of the trader failing to do so.

When a loan is granted to a customer, the normal relationship of banker and customer becomes reversed, as the trader becomes the banker's debtor.

The practice of bankers in connection with advances varies in different parts of the country, the overdraft being used in some cases and the loan account in others. When the advance takes the form of an overdraft, the customer is allowed to draw cheques against his account although he has no amount to his credit, *i.e.*, to run his account into debt, up to a certain limit, say £1,000 in a particular case. Thus the actual state of the account will, of course, vary from day to day ; sometimes it may be perhaps

only £650 overdrawn, while at others it may be in debit almost up to the limit of £1,000.

The alternative method that is sometimes adopted is to transfer the full amount of the loan required, *e.g.*, £1,000, to the current account of the customer for him to draw against, so that this account will always be in credit. The amount of the loan is also debited by the banker to a Loan Account in the customer's name. The latter account will therefore always show a debit balance equal to the full amount of the loan, *e.g.*, £1,000 in this particular case, and the customer will be required to pay interest on this amount as long as the loan is in force.

In regard to current accounts generally, it is the usual practice not to allow any interest on the credit balances of current accounts, and to charge a commission, in the form of a percentage, on the total withdrawals for the period.

A DEPOSIT ACCOUNT is one which, as its name implies, is intended for the deposit of money, *i.e.*, for money which is in excess of the ordinary requirements of a person and which, as it is not likely to be needed in the immediate future, can be placed on one side in a deposit account to earn interest. Money may, of course, be paid in to this account at any time, and may be withdrawn either whenever the customer requires it, or sometimes only after a certain period of notice has been given. Cheques cannot usually be drawn against money on deposit account, and thus its utility for ordinary business purposes is considerably less than that of a current account.

The only instance in which a trader is likely to use a deposit account is when the credit balance on his current account has steadily accumulated and a portion of it is in excess of his ordinary requirements. A transfer of this surplus is then made to a deposit account, sufficient, of course, being left in the current account for all general purposes, and thus interest is earned on money which would otherwise bear no interest.

The terms " debit " and " credit " with reference to banking accounts and their operation in the preceding and following paragraphs are used from the banker's viewpoint ; in the trader's books a debit balance on his banking account indicates a balance in hand while a credit balance represents the amount overdrawn.

Cheques.

A cheque may be described as an unconditional order, addressed by a customer to his banker, instructing the banker to pay a stated sum of money, when requested, to the person named in the cheque or to the bearer of it. The actual meaning of a cheque will be better indicated if an illustration is given of a form of cheque

in common use. For example, if we assume that the transaction referred to previously in this chapter between Bates and Wholesalers, Limited was settled by a cheque in place of cash, the completed form of the cheque would usually be as follows :—

No. PR10227	No. PR10227	17th September, 19.....	
17th Sept., 19....			
	The MIDLAND BANK, LIMITED,		2d.
	Lower St., Bristol.		stamp.
Wholesalers, Limited.	PAY *Wholesalers, Limited*........................OR ORDER		
	One hundred and ninety-five pounds—	£195 : 0 : 0	
£195 : 0 : 0		*A. Bates.*	

The banker supplies his customer with printed cheque forms, bound up in books in convenient numbers, such as 24, 60, 120, 240, etc., according to the requirements of the customer, which in turn will depend upon the frequency with which cheques are drawn upon the particular account. The cheques are perforated so that they can be torn out as required, a note of the essential particulars first being made on the portion which remains in the book, known as the *counterfoil*, as shown in the illustration. Thus a record of the cheques actually issued may be kept by the customer in order to check the entries in his banking account. A cheque requires a twopenny stamp, which is usually impressed on the cheque form before it is issued by the bank ; an adhesive stamp is, however, quite legal.

The person drawing the cheque is known as the "drawer"; the person to whom it is payable is the " payee " and the banker upon whom the cheque is drawn is known as the "drawee." Thus, in the above illustration, Bates is the " drawer," Wholesalers, Limited the " payee" and the Midland Bank the " drawee."

Cheques are almost always drawn " to order " as in the example given, which indicates that the money is to be paid to the person named, *i.e*, the payee, or to his order. It is then necessary for the payee to *indorse* the cheque before he can obtain payment, *i.e.*, to sign his name on the back of the cheque. Occasionally, cheques are made payable to " bearer," in which case no indorsement is necessary and the money is paid to the person who presents the cheque.

The Conduct of a Banking Account.

The actual procedure when a banking account is kept is described in the following paragraphs.

D

Before a current account is opened a banker requires an introduction from some other person of standing known to him, who will vouch for the prospective customer's reliability. The account is then opened with the money which the new customer has available, a specimen of his signature (in order to verify the genuineness of cheques presented for payment) is obtained, and a cheque book is issued. A pass book is made out by the banker for the use of the customer. The difference between the totals of the two sides of the pass book represents the customer's balance in the bank at the moment. The pass book nowadays often takes the form of loose leaf statements prepared by accounting machines and retained in a special folder.

The heading of the pass book (or loose leaf statement) may indicate that the details represent a copy of the customer's account in the books of the bank or a copy of the bank's account in the books of the customer. In the former case the pass book is headed, say, " A Customer in account with —— Bank," and payments in are shown on the credit side and withdrawals on the debit side, while in the latter case the pass book is headed " —— Bank in account with A Customer," and payments in are debited and withdrawals credited. The former method is more usual.

The customer pays in to his account, daily or weekly as the case may be, all the cash, notes, cheques, etc., which he has received in the course of business, e.g., from sales or from his debtors, using for the purpose the special printed " paying-in slips " supplied by the bank. These slips are perforated and have counterfoils which are filled up for the amount paid in and the date in each case. One portion is retained by the banker and the counterfoil is stamped by him with a rubber stamp to acknowledge receipt of the money, and handed back to the customer. These paying-in slips are also issued in book form in a similar way to cheques, the counterfoils being retained in the book.

When the trader wishes to pay an account he owes, he makes out a cheque, payable to the creditor, for the amount of the account, and sends it to him. The creditor who receives the cheque indorses it and pays it in to the credit of his own banking account. His banker sends the cheque, via the head office and the London Clearing House, to the banker upon whom it is drawn, who examines it upon receipt and, if it is in order and does not exceed the balance to the credit of the payer's banking account (or the limit of his overdraft), pays it and debits it to the drawer's account. The Clearing House is an institution for the classification of cheques into the several banks (and their respective branches) upon which they are drawn, thereby avoiding the clerical work in forwarding cheques direct from one bank to another.

The foregoing remarks may be illustrated by considering again

the transactions of Bates with Wholesalers, Limited. In this specific instance Bates draws a cheque upon his bankers, The Midland Bank, Lower Street, Bristol branch, payable to Wholesalers, Limited, and posts it off to them, at the same time recording the transaction in his cash book. Wholesalers, Limited, indorse the cheque and pay it, along with others, into their own banking account with, say, Barclays Bank, Tottenham Court Road, London branch, who then send it, through their Head Office and the Clearing House, to the Midland Bank at Bristol. The latter bank examines the cheque and, if everything is in order, debits it to the current account of Bates, thus reducing his bank balance by £195.

When Bates leaves his pass book with his banker to be written up, which he should do at regular intervals, the debit in respect of the cheque will be entered in it along with the other items, and thus the procedure in regard to this particular transaction will be complete. Where the pass book takes the form of loose leaf statements, the debit will appear on the next statement sent by the banker to Bates.

Unpaid Cheques.

It was mentioned above that the banker examines the cheque before paying it and debiting it to the customer's account. This examination is made to ensure that the cheque is correctly drawn up and indorsed, that the amounts in words and figures agree, that the cheque is not post dated or out of date, that the drawer is not dead or has not requested the bank to stop payment of the cheque on presentation, and, most important of all, that the balance standing to the drawer's credit is sufficient to meet the cheque.

If the cheque fails to comply with any of the above conditions, it is not paid but is returned, marked with a brief note as to the reason for non-payment (e.g., R/D (Refer to drawer), words and figures differ, etc.), to the banker who first received it. This banker debits the account of the customer who paid in the cheque and returns it to him. The latter has then to communicate with the drawer, i.e., his customer, in order to have the defect rectified, or, in the case of there being insufficient funds in the account, to ask that arrangements be made to meet the cheque.

Crossed Cheques.

When a cheque is sent by post it is a usual and useful precaution to cross it, i.e., to draw across it two parallel transverse lines with or without the words " and Co." There are other forms of crossing which may be adopted and other words which are sometimes added, thereby constituting what is known as a " special crossing," as distinguished from the aforementioned " general crossing." The main form to remember, however, is the crossing with two

parallel lines, unless the name of the payee's banker is known, in which case it is sufficient to write such name across the cheque without the transverse lines.

The effect of the crossing is to diminish the possibility of fraud, as it acts as an instruction to the "drawee" banker not to pay the cheque across the counter but only to a customer's account or to another banker. The cheque then cannot be "cashed" but must be paid in to the credit of some banking account, which greatly minimizes the chance of a thief's obtaining cash for the cheque by fraud.

If the name of a banker is written across the cheque, with or without the parallel lines, the proceeds of the cheque must be paid only to the banker named in the crossing, thereby providing an additional safeguard against loss. Thus, if Bates knew that Wholesalers, Limited, banked at Barclays Bank, Tottenham Court Road, London, he might have written the name of this particular bank across the cheque, and it would then have had to be paid into an account at that bank and there only.

The Record of Bank Transactions.

The reader should by now have gained a fairly clear idea of the procedure in connection with the keeping of a banking account, and of the various matters in regard to cheques which may affect the trader from the book-keeping point of view. It remains, therefore, to explain the entries necessary in the trader's own books, where bank transactions require to be recorded.

In the first place it must be understood that money in the bank is similar to money in the till, the former, however, being retained for purposes of convenience by an outside party, on behalf of the trader. In other words, just as a Cash Account was opened to record dealings in the commodity "Cash in Hand," so a Bank Account must be opened to record dealings in the commodity "Cash in the Bank." The balance of cash at the bank is an asset in a similar way to the balance of cash in hand. If this fact is thoroughly understood no difficulty should be experienced in recording bank transactions.

It would, of course, be correct to keep a "Cash" Cash Book to record cash receipts and payments, and a "Bank" Cash Book to record payments into and withdrawals from the bank. In practice, however, it is found to be simpler and more effective to provide extra columns in the Cash Book to record all payments into or out of the bank. This has exactly the same effect as two separate cash books, but as in the case of the columnar system explained in connection with the sub-division of the Journal, the use of one book containing additional columns is much more convenient than the use of separate books.

The Three-Column Cash Book.

The three-column Cash Book has three separate money columns on each side to record entries relating to discount, cash transactions and bank transactions respectively. Entries are made and discount is dealt with in exactly the same way as in the case of the Cash Book already explained, except that there are two balances, representing the cash balance and the bank balance respectively. In this form of Cash Book the two cash columns and the two bank columns are balanced separately and independently.

The only difficulty that can arise is when cash is paid into the bank or when money is drawn from the bank for office cash. This difficulty, however, is dispelled if it is remembered that the two " cash " columns and the two " bank " columns are entirely separate and represent two quite distinct accounts, the debit and credit cash columns being the Cash Account and the debit and credit bank columns being the Bank Account. Thus, transfers between cash and bank must be recorded in exactly the same way as if they were transfers between two accounts in different parts of the ledger.

Therefore, when cash is received, it is debited in the cash column in the usual way. When a certain amount of the cash in hand is paid into the bank, the *bank* column is *debited*, because it has received value, while the *cash* column is *credited* because it has given value. If a cheque is received and paid into the bank immediately the cash account need not be both debited and credited, but an entry can be made direct to the debit of the bank column.

When a cheque is made out, the bank column alone is affected and must be credited because value has gone out. If, however, an amount is drawn from the bank by cheque as, for example, to cover wages, the *bank* column is *credited* because value has gone out and the *cash* column is *debited* because it has received value. The cash column itself will be credited with the exact amount of the wages when they are paid from the cash in hand.

When cash is paid into the bank from the balance of cash in hand or cash is withdrawn from the bank for internal use, the corresponding entries in the cash *and* bank columns are identified by the use of the symbol " c " in the ledger folio column to indicate that the corresponding debit (or credit) is to be found in the cash (or bank column) on the opposite side of the Cash Book (see illustration on page 97).

As already mentioned on page 59, in order to cancel an entry the original double entry should be reversed ; crossing out must never be resorted to. Thus if a cheque received from a customer and paid into the bank is later returned by the bank dishonoured,

the former entries are reversed—debit Customer's Account and credit bank column in the Cash Book.

It must be remembered that if the bank columns of the Cash Book show a balance in hand at the bank, this will be a debit balance since, from the point of view of the trader, the banker is indebted to him.

More cash than is on hand cannot be paid away, so that the total of the cash column on the credit side of the Cash Book cannot exceed the total of the corresponding debit column. This does not apply to the bank column and if the banking account is *overdrawn* this column will show a *credit* balance, since the bank is a creditor of the business for the amount in question.

The worked example of the simple two-column cash book given earlier in this chapter recorded Bates's cash transactions for the period 15th September to 30th September. It is now proposed to consider the effect of the opening of a banking account by Bates, and this will be illustrated by an example of a three-column cash book.

EXAMPLE

On the 1st October, Bates, who had a balance of cash in hand of £365 0s. 4d., opened a banking account with £350, and commenced to use a three-column Cash Book to record his cash and bank transactions. Write up his Cash Book from the following particulars and show the balances of cash in hand and at the bank on 18th October.

19.....

Oct.	1.	Paid Barling & Co.'s account of £85 10s. by cheque, deducting 2½% cash discount.
,,	2.	Received £19 10s. less 5% discount, in cash from A. Burns.
,,	3.	Paid wages, £19, by cash.
,,	4.	Received cash remittance of £48 17s. 3d. from H. B. Nuttall.
,,	5.	Received £23 10s. less 2½% discount, in cash from R. Sims.
,,	,,	Paid £70 into the bank.
,,	7.	Paid Holson & Co.'s account of £16 by cheque, deducting 2½% cash discount.
,,	9.	Received from R. King by cheque, £62 10s., less 2½% cash discount, and paid into bank.
,,	10.	Cashed cheque for £20, and paid wages in cash, £19.
,,	12.	Received £178 5s. less 5% discount, in cash from S. Parsons.
,,	14.	Received cash, £15 8s. 3d., from R. F. Holmes.
,,	,,	Paid £180 into the bank.
,,	15.	Paid carriage in cash, £3 7s. 2d.
,,	16.	Paid Wholesalers, Limited's account of £83 by cheque, less 2½% cash discount.
,,	17.	Cashed cheque for £20, and paid wages in cash, £19.

(*For worked solution, see page* 97.)

The Bank Cash Book.

The three-column Cash Book is still in use to a considerable extent, but the method now more generally adopted in practice is to bank all cash and cheques on the day of receipt and to draw cheques for the exact amount of any *cash* payments which have

THREE-COLUMN CASH BOOK

Dr.

Date	Name of Account	Led. Fo.	Discount £ s. d.	Cash £ s. d.	Bank £ s. d.
19.... Oct. 1	To Balance.	b/d		365 0 4	350 0 0
" 2	Office Cash.	c		18 10 6	
" 4	A. Burns.		19 6	48 17 3	
" 5	H. B. Nuttall.		11 9	22 18 3	
" 7	R. Sims.				70 18 0
" 9	Office Cash.	c		20 0 0	
" 10	R. King.		1 11 3	169 6 9	60 18 9
" 12	Bank.			15 8 3	
" 14	S. Parsons.		8 18 3		
" 14	R. F. Holmes.			20 0 0	
" 17	Office Cash.	c			
" 17	Bank.	c			180 0 0
			£12 0 9 Total debited to Discount Account.	680 1 4	660 18 9
Oct. 18	To Balances.	b/d		19 14 2	441 1 0

Cr.

Date	Name of Account	Led. Fo.	Discount £ s. d.	Cash £ s. d.	Bank £ s. d.
19.... Oct. 1	By Bank.	c		350 0 0	
" 2	Barling & Co.		2 2 9		83 7 3
" 3	Wages.			19 0 0	
" 5	Bank.			19 0 0	15 12 0
" 7	Holson & Co.		8 0		20 0 0
" 10	Office Cash.	c		19 0 0	
" 14	Wages.			180 0 0	
" 15	Bank.			3 7	
" 16	Carriage.				
" 16	Wholesalers, Ltd.		2 1 6		80 18 6
" 17	Office Cash.	c		20 0 0	20 0 0
" 18	Wages.			19 0 0	
" 18	Balances.	c/d		19 14 2	441 1 0
			£4 12 3 Total credited to Discount Account.	680 1 4	660 18 9

to be made (*e.g.*, wages) and periodical cheques for petty cash disbursements, thereby doing away with the necessity for any cash (as distinct from Petty Cash) in hand and any record of it. This method is rendered possible by the adoption of the *Petty Cash* system described in the next chapter, which provides for the payment of all small cash expenses and outgoings.

The Bank Cash Book is similar to the three-column Cash Book just described, except that the two " cash " columns are dispensed with, their place being taken by an " Amount Received " column on the debit side and a " Details " column on the credit side.

Each cash receipt is entered first in the " Amount Received " column and only the total amount actually banked at one time is extended into the " Bank " column. This has the advantage of keeping the latter free from unnecessary detail, and of facilitating the comparison of the Cash Book with the Bank Pass Book (or bank statements), as the total amounts entered in the " Bank " column of the former correspond with the daily " paying-in " totals in the latter. Furthermore, as all receipts are paid direct into the bank, the clerical labour of making contra entries to record transfers between office cash and bank is avoided.

The " Details " column on the credit side of the Cash Book is mainly used to record the analysis of cheques drawn for office purposes (*e.g.*, where a cheque for £27 10s. is drawn in respect of wages, £15 and salaries, £12 10s.), these latter figures will appear in the " Details " column, each individual item being debited to its appropriate ledger account and the total of the cheque appearing in the Bank column.

For the purpose of illustration it is assumed that Bates has made considerable progress in the two years which have elapsed since the previous example and now keeps his Cash Book on the " Bank " system, paying in all receipts to the bank daily and making all payments by cheque.

EXAMPLE

On the 21st September, 19...., A. Bates had a bank balance of £642 10s. Write up his Cash Book from the following particulars and bring down the balance as at 27th September.

19.....
Sept. 21. Received cheque £48 10s., less 2½% discount, from R. Barlow.
Received cheque £15, less 2½% discount, from N. P. Naylor.
Received cash £12 6s. 3d. from R. O. Jackson.
Paid H. Hulton & Co. £124 10s., less 2½% discount.

,,   22. Received cheque £73 10s., less 2½% discount, from A. Holmes.
Received money order, £10 7s. 6d., from H. B. Nuttall.
Paid Barling & Co.'s account £105, less 2½% discount.

,,   23. Received cheque £37 10s., less 2½% discount, from O. Footman.
Received cheque £8 7s. 5d. from P. Newson.
Cashed cheque for £60 and paid Wages £50 and Salaries £10.

Dr.   "BANK" CASH BOOK   **Cr.**

Date.	Led. Fo.	Name of Account.	Discount			Amount Received.			Daily Total paid into Bank.		
			£	s.	d.	£	s.	d.	£	s.	d.
19.....Sept. 21	b/d	To Balance.							642	10	0
		,, R. Barlow.	1	4	3	47	5	9			
		,, N. F. Naylor.		7	6	14	12	6			
		,, R. O. Jackson.				12	6	3	74	4	6
22		,, A. Holmes.	1	16	9	71	13	3			
		,, H. B. Nuttall.				10	7	6	82	0	9
23		,, O. Footman.		18	9	36	11	3			
		,, P. Newson.				8	7	5	44	18	8
25		,, D. A. Nelson.				50	0	0	50	0	0
27		,, R. Sims.		6	3	42	10	0			
		,, N. E. Maile.				7	3	9	49	13	9
			£4	13	6				£943	7	8
			Debited to Discount Account.								
Sept. 27	b/d	To Balance.							610	12	5

Date.	Led. Fo.	Name of Account.	Discount Details			Discount			Details			Cheques Drawn.		
						£	s.	d.	£	s.	d.	£	s.	d.
19.....Sept. 21		By H. Hulton & Co.				3	2	3				121	7	9
22		,, Barling & Co.				2	12	6				102	7	6
23		,, Wages.							50	0	0	60	0	0
23		,, Salaries.							10	0	0	49	0	0
27		,, Rent.										610	12	5
27	c/d	,, Balance.												
						£5	14	9				£943	7	8
						Credited to Discount Account.								

19.....
Sept. 25.   Received cheque, £50, on account, from D. A Nelson.
   „   27.   Paid Rent, £49.
             Received cheque, £42 10s., from R. Sims.
             Received cheque, £7 3s. 9d., from N. E. Maile, allowing him 6s. 3d.
             cash discount.
             (*For worked solution, see page 99.*)

Bank Reconciliation Statement.

It has already been explained that the banker supplies his
customer with a " Pass Book " in bound or loose-leaf form, which
contains a copy of the ledger account of the customer as it appears
in the banker's books.   In order to prevent any possibility of
fraud or error, the customer should have this book written up at
regular intervals or obtain periodic statements of his account and
compare the information shown in detail with his own Cash Book.

He will almost invariably find that the pass book balance does
not agree with that of the Cash Book.   The difference between
the balances shown on the two books at any given date is usually
found to be due to one or more of the following causes :—

(1) Cheques received and paid into the bank have not yet been
     credited in the pass book.

(2) Cheques drawn and paid to creditors have not yet been
     presented for payment.

(3) Bank charges for commission and cheque books, or for
     interest on an overdraft, have been debited in the pass
     book, but are not shown in the cash book.

(4) Bank interest has been credited in the pass book, but
     does not appear in the cash book.

(5) Errors have occurred in either the pass book and/or the
     cash book.

With regard to item (1) it may be argued that it is the usual
practice for the bank to credit its customer's account as soon as
cheques are paid in.   In fact, however, it will be found that it
is usually necessary to reconcile the cash book balance of one
day with the pass book balance of the *previous* day.   Obviously
if cheques are lodged with the bank and the pass book is called
for at the same time the latter will contain no record of the items
just paid in.

Item (2) is the most frequent cause of disagreement between
the pass book and the cash book, as there are almost always
some cheques outstanding which have been sent to creditors but
have not been presented for payment at any given date.   Thus,
in the illustration given in connection with the payment of £195
by Bates to Wholesalers, Limited, it was explained how time
must elapse before the cheque which Bates drew would actually

reach his own banker and be debited to his account. If, in the meantime, Bates had had his pass book written up he would have found a difference between the balance given therein and that shown in his own cash book, as an item of £195 would appear in the latter but not in the former.

Items (3) and (4) are frequently not brought to the notice of the customer until he receives his pass book, so that no entry in respect of these charges, etc., can previously have been passed through his cash book.

In order to agree the balances shown on the pass book and the cash book a *Bank Reconciliation Statement* must be drawn up. Any items under (3), (4) or (5) above must first be disposed of, errors being corrected and entries for any bank interest or charges being passed through the cash book. A statement can then be prepared by taking the balance as shown by the pass book and *adding* thereto any items paid in but not yet credited and *deducting* any cheques drawn but not yet presented for payment. The following example will illustrate the method adopted.

EXAMPLE

A. Bates's Pass Book shows a balance to his credit at 30th June, 19....., of £1,351 6s. 3d. The total debits in his Cash Book at the same date amount to £2,793 8s. 4d. and the total credits to £1,602 1s. 9d., but it is found that cheques for £109 5s. 0d. (S. J. Lewis) and £83 6s. 6d. (A. N. Jewison) have not been credited in the Pass Book, while cheques for £208 10s. 2d. (N. O. Mawley) and £141 9s. 6d. (B. B. Somes) have not been presented for payment. On the other hand, the Pass Book includes two items which do not appear in the Cash Book, viz., £10 1s. 6d. (Bank Interest credited) and £7 10s. 0d. (Bank Charges debited). Prepare a Bank Reconciliation Statement as at the 30th June.........

Before the reconciliation statement is drawn up the necessary entries must be made in the Cash Book to record the bank interest and charges.

Dr. CASH BOOK *Cr.*

Date.	Name of Account.	Bank.			Date.	Name of Account.	Bank.		
19.....		£	s.	d.	19.....		£	s.	d.
June 30	To Total Debits.	2,793	8	4	June 30	By Total Credits.	1,602	1	9
„ 30	„ Bank Interest for half year.	10	1	6	„ 30	„ Bank Charges for half year.	7	10	0
					„ 30	„ Balance c/d.	1,193	18	1
		£ 2,803	9	10			£ 2,803	9	10
June 30	To Balance b/d	1,193	18	1					

The reconciliation statement may then be prepared, in the form shown below, to agree the pass book balance with the new balance now appearing in the cash book.

RECONCILIATION STATEMENT—30TH JUNE, 19.....

	£	s.	d.	£	s.	d.
Balance as per Pass Book.				1,351	6	3
Add Cheques paid in but not credited at 30th June, 19..... :—						
S. J. Lewis.	109	5	0			
A. N. Jewison.	83	6	6			
				192	11	6
				1,543	17	9
Less Unpresented Cheques :—						
N. O. Mawley.	208	10	2			
B. B. Somes.	141	9	6			
				349	19	8
Balance as per Cash Book				£1,193	18	1

If the bank account happens to be overdrawn the procedure will be reversed ; cheques paid in but not yet credited will reduce the overdraft when they are credited and hence must be *deducted* from the pass book balance, while cheques issued by the business but not yet presented will increase the overdraft and must therefore be *added* to the balance as shown by the pass book.

Thus, in the above example, if the pass book had shown an overdraft of £1,351 6s. 3d. and the cash book, after the necessary adjustments for interest and charges, an overdrawn (*i.e.*, *credit*) balance of £1,508 14s. 5d., the reconciliation statement would appear as under :—

RECONCILIATION STATEMENT—30TH JUNE, 19......

	£	s.	d.	£	s.	d.
Balance as per Pass Book (overdrawn).				1,351	6	3
Deduct Cheques paid in but not credited at 30th June, 19...... :—						
S. J. Lewis.	109	5	0			
A. N. Jewison.	83	6	6			
				192	11	6
				1,158	14	9
Add Unpresented Cheques :—						
N. O. Mawley	208	10	2			
B. B. Somes	141	9	6			
				349	19	8
Balance as per Cash Book (Credit)				£1,508	14	5

The normal procedure when preparing a bank reconciliation

statement is to work *from* the pass book balance *to* the cash book balance. Sometimes, however, questions are set which make this procedure impossible, as the former balance is not given. Such a question should not cause undue difficulty and is easily answered by an adjusted application of the foregoing principles to the Cash Book balance.

EXAMPLE

The following facts relate to the banking transactions of A. Bates, who is a customer of the X Bank. You are required to produce a Bank Reconciliation Statement as at 31st December, 19......

	£ s. d.	£ s. d.
Cash Book balance at 31st December		230 2 6
Cheques paid in to bank and not credited until 2nd January following:—		
A. Jones	5 12 6	
C. Thomas	25 7 6	
Cheques issued on 31st December and not presented until the following 2nd January:—		
L. Brown	8 5 6	
S. Green	15 9 6	

Commission charged by bank on 31st December, but not entered in A. Bates's Cash Book, £2 2s. 6d.

RECONCILIATION STATEMENT—31st DECEMBER, 19......

	£ s. d.	£ s. d.
Balance as per Cash Book		230 2 6
Less Commission charged and not entered in Cash Book		2 2 6
		228 0 0
Less Cheques paid in but not credited in Pass Book:—		
A. Jones	5 12 6	
C. Thomas	25 7 6	
		31 0 0
		197 0 0
Add Unpresented Cheques:—		
L. Brown	8 5 6	
S. Green	15 9 6	
		23 15 0
Balance as per Pass Book		£220 15 0

If the Cash Book balance happens to be overdrawn, the above procedure will be reversed.

The reconciliation statements are usually filed in a suitable manner, or they may be noted in the cash book (in red ink) in order that a permanent record of the outstanding items may be available for future reference.

EXERCISE 5

A. What are the two functions of a Cash Book ?

B. What is Cash Discount ? How is it recorded in the books of a trader ?

C. Distinguish between a current account and a deposit account.

D. Explain the meaning and use of (1) cheques; (2) crossed cheques; (3) paying-in slips; and (4) bank pass book.

E. Explain the alternative methods of recording banking transactions in the books of account.

F. What is a Reconciliation Statement, and how is it prepared ?

G. From the following particulars write up the Cash Book (with Discount columns) of G. Ward, and bring down the balance as at 15th January.

19.....
Jan. 1. Cash in hand, £123 7s.
  „ 2. Received from R. Newton, £75, less 5% discount.
  „ 4. Paid carriage, £3 7s.
  „ 5. Paid £30 on account to R. Hall.
  „ 7. Paid B. Paul, £110 7s. 9d., less 3¾% discount.
  „ 9. Paid wages, £4 10s.
  „ 10. Cash sales, £12 7s. 11d.
  „ 11. Received from M. Roulston, £47 8s., less 2½% discount.
  „ 12. Paid to R. Hall, £45, balance of account, less discount of £7 10s.
  „ 13. Received from J. Dyer, £14 8s. 4d.
  „ „ Paid for stationery, £4 7s. 10d.
  „ 14. Cash sales, £9 10s. 4d.
  „ 15. Purchased and paid for a new trolley, £17 15s., less cash discount of 5%.
  „ „ Paid wages, £4 10s., postage stamps, 15s.

H. Rule the form of a Cash Book and enter therein the following items :—
19....., 1st January : Balance at bank, £235 6s. 2d. ; Balance of cash in hand, £86 4s. 10d. 2nd January : Paid wages in cash, £17 6s. 5d. 3rd January : Paid into bank cheque received from Smith & Sons in settlement of their account of £65 10s., they deducting 5% discount from this amount. 4th January : Paid Wm. Williams, by cheque, the amount due to him, £76 6s. 8d., less 5% discount. 5th January : P. Peters paid £100 on account. 6th January : Paid by cheque £56 rent due 25th December. 8th January : Sold an old table for 15s. in cash. Paid into bank all cash in hand with the exception of £10.
Balance the Cash Book as on 8th January.

J. From the following transactions of John Giles write up his Cash Book (three-column form) bringing down the balances as at 31st May :—
19.....
May 1. Balance at bank, £150.
  „ 2. Drew from bank for office cash, £50.
       Bought stationery for cash, £2 10s.
  „ 3. Bought office furniture for cash at sale, £32.

19.....

May 5. Obtained cheque book from bank, 16s. 8d. Paid wages, £15 by cash.

,, 13. Drew from bank for office cash, £25.

,, 14. Paid wages from cash, £15.

Sold goods for cash, £22 10s.

Received cheque from Norris & Co. in settlement of their account, £75, less 5% discount and paid same direct to bank.

,, 17. Sold goods for cash to J. Jenkins, £8 5s.

,, 20. Sold goods for cash, £18.

Paid into bank, £10.

,, 21. Paid wages from cash, £15.

,, 28. Drew cheque £25 for cash, and paid wages, £15, and self, £10.

,, 31. Paid Parker's account, £30, by cheque, less 2½% discount.

K. Record the following particulars in a suitable form of Cash Book and bring down the balance. All money received is paid into the Bank on the day when received, in one amount.

			£	s.	d.
19.....					
July	1.	Balance at Bank.	820	6	10
,,	2.	Received from Best & Co. on account.	25	0	0
,,	2.	Read Bros. paid their account, *viz.* and were allowed 2½% discount.	40	10	0
,,	5	Drew cheque for :— Wages, £106 ; salaries, £22 10s. ; National Insurance, 8s. 6d. ; petty cash, £1 1s. 6d.	130	0	0
,,	8.	Parkers, Ltd., remitted on account.	100	0	0
		H. Hill paid balance of his account, *viz.* and was allowed 2½% discount.	62	6	8
,,	9.	Paid rent, by cheque.	19	8	4
,,	12.	Paid electric light account.	8	10	5
		Received from Stevens & Co.	12		4
		Cash sale.	18	9	4
		Drew cheque for Adams & Co.	7	5	0
		Drew cheque for :— Wages, £117 ; salaries, £22 10s. ; National Insurance, 8s. 6d. ; self, £10.	149	18	6
		Paid A. Cook's account for being allowed 1¼% discount.	30	0	0

L. (a) On 30th June the Cash Book showed a balance of £1,250 as cash at bank, but the bank pass book made up to the same date showed that cheques for £130, £45 and £73 10s. 9d. had not been presented for payment; also cheques to the amount of £217 8s. 11d. paid into the account had not yet been credited to the pass book. Find, by means of a Reconciliation Statement, the balance shown in the pass book.

(b) If the above balance of £1,250 represented the total amount overdrawn as shown in the Cash Book, find the amount of the balance shown in the bank pass book at the same date.

CHAPTER VI

THE PETTY CASH BOOK

In every business, no matter how small it may be, there must arise from time to time a number of items of petty expenditure for such miscellaneous purposes as postages, telegrams, cleaning, stationery, etc.

It has been found advisable for purposes of convenience to omit these items of petty disbursements from the Cash Book, and to adopt a special method of dealing with the necessary bookkeeping records. This object is achieved by the use of a *Petty Cash Book* in which all small payments are recorded.

There are several reasons why a special method should be adopted for dealing with these small items of expense. In the first place the use of a separate Petty Cash Book enables all the smaller expense items to be grouped together, analysed (if desired) into classes, and posted in periodical totals to the respective nominal accounts in the ledger. The use of such a system therefore relieves not only the Cash Book but also the Nominal Accounts of unnecessary detail.

Furthermore, unless a petty cash system of some description is adopted the modern " Bank " Cash Book method, described in the previous chapter, would be impracticable, as the latter depends upon the assumption that all payments are made by cheque. Obviously it would not be possible to draw a cheque for each item of petty expense as it arose, for this would involve much unnecessary clerical labour and expense, and delay in obtaining the actual cash required for small disbursements.

In actual practice the above-mentioned difficulties are overcome if a clerk (the *petty cashier*) is supplied with a round sum of money, out of which to make all necessary disbursements for small expenses.

There are various methods available for dealing with petty expenditure. By the oldest method no provision was made for the analysis of the payments by means of separate columns, nor for the renewal of the amount of cash in the hands of the petty cashier at regular intervals. When the balance in his hands was almost exhausted, a further round sum was handed to him and a laborious analysis of his expenditure was necessary.

The Columnar Petty Cash Book.

The form of Petty Cash Book now used almost universally is ruled in columnar form, with analysis columns for the more usual classes of expenditure.

On the debit side there is a column to record the amount of cash received periodically from the general Cash Book. Unlike the usual form of cash book or ledger account, only one " Date " and one " Particulars " column are provided, between the debit and the credit " Total " columns ; these two single columns are utilized to record details of both petty cash receipts and payments.

On the credit side, a total column together with analysis columns are provided for the more usual classes of expenditure, in accordance with the division of the nominal accounts in the ledger, together with a column for sundry items. The headings of these columns vary according to the business. In some cases, for example, separate expense accounts would be kept for " Postages " and for " Telegrams," with the result that a separate column would be required for each class of expenditure in the Petty Cash Book. In other cases these two classes of expenditure would be combined, and thus only one petty cash analysis column and one nominal account would be necessary. A separate column, headed " Ledger Accounts," or " Sundries," is usually provided to record the small payments relating to personal accounts which occasionally require to be made in cash, and for any infrequent items of expenditure for which the analysis columns provided are unsuitable.

When a petty cash payment is made, the amount is entered in the " Total " column on the credit side and is extended into the appropriate analysis column. The totals of all the columns are carried forward from page to page until the end of the month or other agreed period, when the book is closed off. The totals of the analysis columns are then posted to the debit of the appropriate nominal accounts in the ledger, while the individual items in the " Ledger " column are posted to the debit of the various personal or other accounts affected.

In balancing the book it will be obvious that the sum of the totals of the analysis and " Ledger " columns must equal the total expenditure for the period as shown by the " Total Payments " column, and a useful method of checking the clerical accuracy of the entries is thereby provided.

The Imprest System.

The imprest system of dealing with petty cash transactions is now almost universally adopted by up-to-date firms. It is

found that this system has many advantages over the older method referred to previously in this chapter.

The imprest system is based upon two essential requirements ; namely, that further sums of money are handed to the petty cashier *at regular intervals* (monthly, or otherwise, as arranged), and that in each case *the sum* must be equivalent to *the exact amount of petty cash disbursed for the period concerned.*

In the first instance a round sum of say £20 or £30, estimated to cover the expenditure for the fixed period, is handed to the petty cashier. This specified sum is known as the "imprest" amount, and it remains at the same figure, unless at any time a general and decided increase or decrease in petty cash expenditure takes place and renders it advisable to raise or reduce the fixed "imprest" amount. At regular intervals, usually at the end of each month, the Petty Cash Book is balanced, the various columns totalled and cross-checked, and a further sum is drawn from the general Cash Book for the exact amount expended during the month, as indicated by the "Total Payments" column.

Thus, at the commencement of each succeeding period, the balance of petty cash in hand is restored to the original "imprest" amount. The usual procedure is for a cheque to be drawn for the exact amount of the petty cash expenditure for the period. This cheque is credited in the general Cash Book in the same way as any other bank payment. The amount of the cheque is then entered on the debit side of the Petty Cash Book, the cheque being cashed at the bank by the petty cashier.

The "imprest system" of keeping the petty cash has many advantages. The general Cash Book is relieved of small cash disbursements and can therefore be kept on the "Bank" system. The risk of error is reduced, and there is much less opportunity for fraud, provided that proper supervision is exercised over the petty cashier. An excellent check is kept upon the amount of petty cash expenditure by a comparison of the monthly or periodical payments to the petty cashier, and extravagance or an unusual volume of expenditure is revealed by the exhaustion of the balance before the end of the fixed period.

The amount of petty cash in hand for inclusion in the Balance Sheet is usually the fixed "imprest" amount, as the Petty Cash Book is invariably closed off at the end of the trading year or other period.

Furthermore, as the balance of cash in hand should never exceed a certain fixed figure (the "imprest" amount or "float") the clerk in charge of the petty cash is prevented from making a series of defalcations and covering them each time by a corresponding fictitious increase in the balance in hand.

Before explaining the effect of the system as far as double

entry book-keeping is concerned, a practical example will be given, together with a specimen ruling of a columnar Petty Cash Book kept on the "imprest system."

EXAMPLE

On 1st June, 19...., the balance of A. Bates's petty cash in hand was £12, this being the imprest amount allotted to the petty cashier. Record the following transactions for the month of June in his Petty Cash Book, which is kept on the imprest system, close off the book at the 30th June, and bring down the balance restoring the petty cash balance to the agreed "imprest" amount of £12.

19.....

June	4.	Paid carriage to Leek & Co., £1 8s. 6d.
"	7.	Purchased postage stamps, £3 0s. 0d.
"	11.	Purchased carbon copy paper, 15s. 6d.
"	18.	Paid B. A. Mortlake's account in cash, 13s. 3d.
"	20.	Paid H. N. Tate for travelling expenses to London, £3 8s. 6d.
"	22.	Paid office cleaning, 5s.
"	25.	Paid telegram to Launts, 1s. 6d.
"	28.	Purchased ink, pens, etc., 8s. 3d.

(*For worked solution, see page* 110.)

In the above example, the petty cash disbursements for the month amount to £10 0s. 6d., and a cheque for this amount has been drawn from the general cash book and is entered on the debit side of the Petty Cash Book. When the cheque is changed at the bank, the petty cashier will thus have a balance of petty cash in hand equal to the fixed "imprest" amount of £12, with which he will commence the succeeding period.

The totals of the analysis columns are posted to the debit of the appropriate nominal accounts in the ledger, and the item of 13s. 3d. in the "Ledger" column is posted to the debit of Mortlake's personal account.

Thus the principle of double entry is complied with, as is shown by the following summary :—

		£	s.	d.	£	s.	d.
Petty Cash Book.	Dr.	10	0	6			
To Cash Book.					10	0	6
Sundries.	Dr.						
To Petty Cash Book.					10	0	6
Sundry Expenses Account.			5	0			
Postages and Telegrams Account.		3	1	6			
Travelling Expenses Account.		3	8	6			
Carriage Account.		1	8	6			
Stationery Account.		1	3	9			
B. A. Mortlake's Account.			13	3			
		£20	1	0	£20	1	0

In this connection it must be remembered that the Petty Cash Book, like the general cash book, is an essential part of the double entry book-keeping system and represents the ledger account which records dealings in petty cash. Thus it is not

PETTY CASH BOOK

Dr. Amount Received £ s. d.	C.B. Fol.	Date	Details	Voucher No.	Payments Total £ s. d.	Sundry Expenses £ s. d.	Postages & Telegrams £ s. d.	Travelling Expenses £ s. d.	Carriage £ s. d.	Stationery £ s. d.	Led. Fol.	Cr. Ledger Accounts £ s. d.
12 0 0	86	19.... June 1	To Balance *brought down.*									
		,, 4	By Carriage—Leek & Co.	1	1 8 6				1 8 6			
		,, 7	,, Postage Stamps.	2	3 0 0		3 0 0					
		,, 11	,, Carbon Paper.	3	15 6					15 6	171	
		,, 18	,, B. A. Mortlake.	4	13 3							13 3
		,, 20	,, Tate's Expenses to London.	5	3 8 6			3 8 6				
		,, 22	,, Office Cleaning.	6	5 0	5 0						
		,, 25	,, Telegram to Launts.	7	1 6		1 6					
		,, 28	,, Ink, Pens, etc.	8	8 3					8 3		
10 0 6	94	,, 30	,, To Cash.		10 0 6	5 0	3 1 6	3 8 6	1 8 6	1 3 9		13 3
		,, 30	By Balance *carried down.*		12 0 0							
£22 0 6					£22 0 6							
12 0 0		June 30	To Balance *brought down.*									

Totals are debited to the nominal accounts concerned.

Items are debited individually to the accounts concerned.

only a book of original entry, but also a part of the ledger, and as such the balance in hand requires to be included in the Trial Balance and shown on the Balance Sheet with the balances of the other ledger accounts. This balance represents the commencing amount for the next period.

It should be observed that the term "imprest" is not confined to petty cash as it can be applied to any case where the original fixed amount is restored by making up the amount expended or used, *e.g.*, it may be applied to a stock of goods.

"Memorandum" Petty Cash Book.

An alternative system, which is also in fairly common use, regards the Petty Cash Book as a *memorandum* record only. The method adopted is to open a Petty Cash Account in the Ledger and post thereto from the Cash Book the amount of the Petty Cash imprest, £5, £10, as the case may be. A record of petty cash receipts and expenditure is kept on the analysis principle, as already explained, and periodically the Memorandum Petty Cash Book is "balanced," the analysed totals of expenditure being entered on the credit side of the Petty Cash Account and posted therefrom to the appropriate personal and impersonal accounts. The renewal of the imprest is then posted from the

Dr. PETTY CASH ACCOUNT *Cr.*

19.....			£	s.	d.	19.....			£	s.	d.
June 1	To Balance	b/d	12	0	0	June 30	By Sundry Expenses			5	0
„ 30	„ Cash		10	0	6		„ Postages and Telegrams		3	1	6
							„ Travelling Expenses		3	8	6
							„ Carriage		1	8	6
							„ Stationery		1	3	9
							„ Sundry Ledger Accounts R. A. Mortlake			13	3
									10	0	6
							„ Balance	c/d	12	0	0
			£22	0	6				£22	0	6
June 30	To Balance	b/d	12	0	0						

Cash Book to the Petty Cash Account, which will then show as a balance the original imprest amount.

The Petty Cash Account (corresponding to the Petty Cash Book on page 110) would appear as on the previous page.

The Voucher System.

It will be noticed that a column headed " Voucher Number " is shown in the specimen ruling of a Petty Cash Book given in this chapter. This particular column is necessary where the " voucher " system is adopted in connection with the petty cash disbursements.

In many firms it is found that the petty cashier is not sufficiently experienced to undertake the responsibility for authorizing petty cash payments, and it is for this reason that the " voucher " system is adopted.

When the necessity for any small business disbursements arises, the clerk concerned must apply to some responsible official for a " chit," or " voucher," authorizing the requisite expenditure. This is presented to the petty cashier, who retains the voucher and issues the necessary cash in exchange. The vouchers are numbered in chronological order, and the corresponding numbers are recorded in the column provided in the Petty Cash Book.

At the end of the month or other agreed period it is usual for the chief cashier, or some other responsible official, to check the Petty Cash Book before issuing a cheque for the amount of the petty cash disbursed during the period concerned. When the Petty Cash Book is being checked in this way, the responsible official should also ascertain that there is a duly signed and receipted voucher for every disbursement.

If this, or some similar system is not adopted, the clerk in charge of the petty cash, often quite a junior clerk, has complete freedom to issue cash at anyone's request and thus there is no check upon extravagant or unauthorized expenditure, particularly as receipts are not available for certain small expenses, e.g., bus fares. An additional advantage of this " voucher " system, when utilized in conjunction with the " imprest " system, is that at any given date the petty cashier should be in possession of unexpended cash and petty cash vouchers issued during the current period equivalent to the fixed " imprest " amount.

When the number of petty cash transactions is sufficiently large voucher forms are printed, and it is then only necessary to fill in the details and obtain the signature of a competent official. Otherwise the same effect is achieved, where the petty cash transactions are less frequent, if a note is made on a slip of paper,

using the same wording as that given for the voucher form, and the note is signed by the authorizing official.

The following is a specimen of a voucher form in general use :—

Petty Cash Voucher.

No. 8   28th June, 19.....
ACCOUNT TO BE DEBITED   Stationery
———pounds *eight* shillings and *three* pence
for *ink*.

Authorized by
£—: 8 : 3   *B. LAWRENCE.*
Received by : *R. TRAP.*

Postages Book.

Just as the petty cash book is used to relieve the cash book of numerous small items of expenditure, so a Postages Book is employed in many offices in which to record details of expenditure on postages. The stamps are purchased in the first instance out of petty cash, the petty cashier recording the payment in the usual way and the postages clerk entering the receipt of the stamps in his Postages Book. Expenditure on postages will then be detailed in this book. Whilst the imprest system could be adopted for such expenditure, this is not usual owing to the fact that the volume of expenditure varies widely over different periods. The person authorizing the purchase of stamps should, however, before doing so, examine the Postages Book as a check against petty defalcations. The Postages Book is not usually regarded as part of the double entry system.

EXERCISE 6

A.   How are small items of expense usually recorded in the books of accounts ?

B.   What are the advantages of a columnar Petty Cash Book ?

C.   What is meant by the Imprest system of dealing with petty cash ? In what ways does this system provide a check on the petty cashier ?

D.   What is the "Voucher" system as applied to petty cash transactions, and what are the advantages resulting from the adoption of this system ?

E.   Explain the manner in which the Petty Cash Book is part of the double entry system of book-keeping.

F.   From the following particulars compile a suitable Petty Cash Book (on the Imprest system) for James Thompson.
19.....
Jan. 1. Petty cash in hand, £10.
  ,,   2. Paid office cleaning, 10s. 6d.
  ,,   4. Paid J. Jones's account for goods supplied, £3 7s. 3d.

Jan. 5   Bought for cash, stationery, 17s. 9d.

,, 7.   Paid carriage on parcel, 1s. 3d.

,, 8.   Bought postage stamps, 5s.

,, ,,   Paid for foolscap paper, 6s. 6d.

,, 10.   Paid travelling expenses of P. Jenkins to Rugby, £1 17s. 9d.

,, 12.   Paid for telegram to J. Jackson, 3s. 3d.

,, ,,   Bought postage stamps, 7s. 6d.

,, 13.   Paid carriage on samples, 4s. 10d.

,, 14.   Paid cartage on goods, 17s. 10d.

,, 15.   Received cash from Cashier to adjust account to date.

G. Show the ruling of a Petty Cash Book on the Imprest system, with six analysis columns (including one for ledger accounts), enter the following transactions therein, and bring down the balance as at 31st August.

19.....

Aug. 1.   Received cash (imprest amount), £10.

,, 2.   Paid carriage on parcel, 2s. 9d.

,, 3.   Bought postage stamps, £1.

,, 6.   Settled Baxter & Co.'s account, 7s. 4d.

,, 8.   Bought envelopes, 6s. 4d.

,, 10.   Paid travelling expenses of C. Cox, 10s. 6d.

,, 16.   Paid for blotting paper, 4s. 3d.

,, 18.   Paid fares of J. Jones, 1s. 6d.

,, 22.   Bought matches and duster, 2s. 6d.

,, 27.   Bought postage stamps, 10s.

,, 31.   Received cash from Cashier to adjust account to date.

H. From the following transactions of G. Emerson write up his Petty Cash Book, containing analysis columns for the following classes of expenditure:—Stationery, Postages and Telegrams, Carriage, Travelling Expenses, Sundries, Cleaning and Ledger Accounts. Bring down the balance as at 28th February, and show how the necessary double entry is effected.

19.....

Feb. 1.   Received cheque from Cashier, £30 (" Imprest " amount).

,, 2.   Paid for postage stamps, £1.

,, 4.   Paid carriage on empties, 7s. 4d.

,, 5.   Bought ink, pens, etc., 1s. 4d.

,, 7.   Paid T. Brown's expenses to Manchester, £1 7s. 10d.

,, 11.   Paid for postage stamps, £1.

,, 12.   Bought typewriting paper, 6s. 9d.

,, 13.   Bought new typewriter, £7 7s. 6d.

,, 15.   Paid sundry 'bus fares, 2s. 4d.

,, 17.   Paid carriage on samples, 3s. 6d.

,, 19.   Paid Howe & Co.'s account, £2 2s.

,, 20.   Paid for office cleaning, 5s.

,, 21.   Paid for postage stamps, £1.

,, ,,   Paid for sundry telegrams, 4s. 9d.

,, 22.   Paid W. Green's expenses to London, £1 4s. 10d.

,, ,,   Bought railway guide, 1s.

,, 24.   Paid for envelopes, 12s. 6d.

,, 25.   Paid Jones & Co.'s account, £2 14s.

,, 26.   Paid for ink, waste-paper basket, etc., 2s. 9d.

,, 27.   Paid for telegram to Paris, 7s.

,, 28.   Paid for postage stamps, £1.

,, ,,   Received cash from Cashier to adjust petty cash balance

CHAPTER VII

BILLS OF EXCHANGE AND BILL BOOKS

Nature of Bills of Exchange.

The important part played by the cheque in modern commercial transactions has been explained in an earlier chapter. It is now necessary to consider the nature and uses of the *Bill of Exchange*, which actually existed long before the introduction of the cheque and which may be regarded as the parent of the cheque itself.

A bill of exchange is legally defined as " an unconditional order in writing, addressed by one person to another, signed by the person giving it, requiring the person to whom it is addressed to pay on demand or at a fixed or determinable future time a sum certain in money to, or to the order of, a specified person, or to bearer."

The creditor who draws and signs the bill and to whom the money is owing is called the *drawer*. The debtor who is ordered to pay the amount of the bill and by whom the money is owing, *i.e.*, the person drawn upon, is termed the *drawee*. The person named on the bill as the one to whom the money is to be paid is known as the *payee*. Thus the *drawer* and the *payee* may be one and the same person.

The drawee cannot be legally liable to pay the bill until he has indicated his acceptance of the terms. This is effected by the drawee " accepting " the bill, *i.e.*, writing across its face the word " accepted " accompanied by his signature and the date. When this has been done the drawee is then known as the *acceptor* and as such is legally liable to all parties to the bill.

A bill may be payable " to order " or " to bearer." If payable to order, it must be indorsed, *i.e.*, signed on the back, by the person named in it as payee, who then becomes an indorser. He may himself present the bill for payment or he may transfer it, after indorsement, to another person or *holder*, who may then present it for payment.

If a bill is payable to bearer no indorsement is necessary before either transfer or payment, and payment must be made to any person presenting the bill to the acceptor.

A bill which is not drawn " on demand " or " at sight " must be payable on some fixed future date or at some future time which can be definitely ascertained. Usually bills are drawn at so many days

or months " after date," or " after sight." In the first case the due date of payment is calculated from the date of the bill, whereas in the latter the period is calculated from the date of acceptance.

It is customary in this country to allow three *days of grace*, which are added to the period in order to ascertain the actual date upon which payment is due. These days of grace are *not* allowed in the case of bills drawn " on demand " or " at sight."

Thus, a bill dated 3rd March, drawn at three months after date, is due for payment on 6th June, *i.e.*, three calendar months from 3rd March gives 3rd June, to which the three days of grace must be added. On the other hand, if the same bill had been drawn " three months after sight " and was sighted (and accepted) on the 6th March, the due date would be 9th June.

The following illustrates the usual form of a bill :—

INLAND BILL OF EXCHANGE

No. 92
£600 : 10 : 6   LONDON, 9th July, 19.....

(7s.)   Three months after date pay to our Order the sum of Six hundred pounds ten shillings and sixpence for value received.

To MR. ARNOLD BATES,   per pro. WHOLESALERS, LIMITED.
    9, MORTON STREET,   R. PORTER,
       BRISTOL.   Director.

It will be observed that the above bill complies with all the requirements of the legal definition. Thus it is an unconditional order in writing addressed by one person (Wholesalers, Limited) to another (Mr. Arnold Bates), signed by the person giving it (Wholesalers, Limited) requiring the person to whom it is addressed (Mr. Arnold Bates) to pay at a fixed future time (three months after date) a sum certain in money (£600 10s. 6d.) to the order of a specified person (Wholesalers, Limited).

In this case Wholesalers, Limited are both the drawers and the payees of the bill ; Bates will become the acceptor when he writes across the face of the bill his assent, whilst the actual due date will be three months from 9th July plus three days of grace, *i.e.*, 12th October.

Promissory Notes.

A Promissory Note is defined by the Bills of Exchange Act, 1882, as " an unconditional promise in writing made by one person to another signed by the maker, engaging to pay, on demand or at a fixed or determinable future time, a sum certain in money, to, or to the order of, a specified person or to bearer."

Promissory notes are seldom used except in money-lending businesses, and whether payable on demand or not, they must bear *ad valorem* stamps at the same rates as for bills of exchange payable after date (see below). Promissory notes payable on demand are sometimes given as an acknowledgement of a debt, on the understanding that this payment shall not be enforced without due notice.

Stamping of Bills.

Bills for any amount payable on demand, at sight, or within three days' date, require a twopenny stamp, which may be impressed or adhesive. All other bills require *ad valorem* impressed stamps, *i.e.*, stamps of varying amounts based upon the amount of the bill. The scale of *ad valorem* stamp duties payable on bills of exchange is as follows :—

Where the amount does not exceed £10				.	.	.	.	2d.
Where it exceeds		£10 but does not exceed	£25	.	.	.	.	3d.
„	„	£25 „	„	£50	.	.	.	6d.
„	„	£50 „	„	£75	.	.	.	9d.
„	„	£75 „	„	£100	.	.	.	1s.
„	„	£100 for each £100 or any part thereof		.		.		1s.

Thus the specimen bill given on the previous page requires a 7s. impressed stamp, as the monetary value is in excess of £600 but does not exceed £700.

The Uses of Bills of Exchange.

Manufacturers, wholesalers and merchants almost invariably allow their customers, the retailers, a period of credit so that the latter may be able to sell at least a portion of the goods purchased before they are required to pay for them. For example, goods may be sold on terms by which payment need not be made until " three months from date of delivery."

The sale of goods on credit terms, in this way, however, results in a large part of the manufacturer's capital becoming locked up in book debts, as his own productive expenses have to be paid before the goods are in a condition to be sold. Furthermore, as he does not receive payment until several months after the goods have been sold, the difficulty of the manufacturers in this connection can readily be appreciated.

This difficulty is overcome by the use of bills of exchange, which provide a means (as explained overleaf) whereby the producer can receive immediate payment for goods sold without in any way curtailing the credit allowed to the purchaser. The bill

of exchange serves a further useful purpose in that it acts as legal evidence of the debt, enabling payment to be enforced in case of need without involved or costly litigation.

When the goods are sold, the creditor draws a bill upon the debtor for the amount of the debt, payable at the end of the agreed period of credit. Immediately the bill is accepted, it confirms the transaction and its terms as between the two parties, and gives the creditor a certain amount of security, by way of the debtor's written undertaking to meet the debt incurred at the agreed future date.

Discounting a Bill.

The above section, however, does not explain the manner in which the creditor is enabled to obtain immediate payment of the debt which is not actually due until a future date. The explanation is to be found in the intervention of the banker, for it is by discounting the bill with his banker that the creditor is able to receive present cash in exchange for a future debt.

It was explained in Chapter V that the chief function of the banker is to receive money from customers who have more than they require and to lend it out again to those who need it for productive and other purposes. One of the chief methods by which a banker lends out money is by discounting bills of exchange.

To discount a bill is to pay out the face value of the bill, less a deduction representing interest on the amount for the period the bill has to run, in exchange for the right to receive payment of the bill from the acceptor on its due date.

In the example previously given, Wholesalers, Limited have drawn a bill on Bates for the value of goods supplied, and upon acceptance of the bill by Bates they will have legal evidence of the debt. Bates will not, however, be under the necessity of providing cash to the extent of £600 10s. 6d. until the bill falls due on 12th October, when it will be presented to him, or to his bankers if he so arranges, for payment. If Wholesalers, Limited wish to receive the use of the money immediately they may, provided that their financial position is known to be good, indorse the bill and hand it to their banker for discounting. Their account will then be credited with the full value of the bill and debited with the deduction, for interest, which is known as " banker's discount " ; and the transaction will thus be closed as far as they are concerned. The banker has in this way purchased the bill and taken over the responsibility for obtaining the proceeds in due course, therefore Wholesalers, Limited are no longer concerned with it provided payment is duly made at the date of maturity of the bill.

They will become interested again, however, if Bates fails to pay the bill at maturity, *i.e.*, if the bill is *dishonoured*, for the banker has then a right of recovery against them and is entitled to debit their account with the full amount of the dishonoured bill. The bill is then handed back to them and it is for them to communicate with the debtor, Bates, and to make some satisfactory arrangements regarding settlement, or, alternatively, to take legal action against him.

Sufficient has now been said to give a clear indication of the important part which the bill of exchange plays in modern commercial transactions and of the general procedure which is adopted in connection therewith. It may be added that the greatest use of the bill of exchange is in settling foreign trade transactions, but foreign bills and the method of dealing with them are outside the scope of the present work.

The bill of exchange having been explained in detail, it is advisable to indicate the close relationship between a bill of exchange and a cheque. A cheque is actually a particular form of bill of exchange, *i.e.*, it is a bill of exchange drawn upon a banker and payable on demand.

In the case of a cheque the customer is the creditor or drawer, the banker is the drawee, and the person to whom the cheque is payable is the payee, but there is no acceptor, as a cheque is always payable *on demand*.

Although a cheque is, from the legal point of view, merely a particular form of bill of exchange, the two are regarded as entirely distinct in commercial usage and must not be confused by the reader.

The Books in which Bill Entries are Made.

In a small business, or in one where transactions in bills of exchange are few in number, no special bill books are kept and the necessary book-keeping entries, when the occasion does arise, are made in the Journal and Ledger.

Where dealings in bills are at all numerous, however, the original entries are made in two specially ruled books, known as the BILLS RECEIVABLE BOOK and the BILLS PAYABLE BOOK respectively. This procedure is in accordance with the same principle of sub-division of the Journal and classification of entries into convenient groups as was found in the case of the Purchases, Sales and Returns Books. Similarly, the number of nominal ledger entries is reduced, as only the monthly or periodical totals are posted from the Bills Books to the respective bill accounts in the ledger, and thus the necessity for detailed daily entries direct from the journal is avoided.

Bills which a trader *receives from his debtors* are known as

Bills Receivable, while those he *gives to his creditors* are termed *Bills Payable*.

The Bills Receivable Book.

The Bills Receivable Book is one in which are recorded full details of bills received from debtors. It should be noted that these are not necessarily bills drawn upon the debtor by the trader himself (although in actual practice they usually are), for a debtor may send in settlement of his debt a bill which he himself has received from someone else, *e.g.*, from one of his own customers.

A specimen ruling of a Bill Receivable Book is given on page 121, and the following explanatory notes should assist the reader in memorizing the actual ruling by indicating the uses of the various columns :—

(*a*) NUMBER OF BILL. Each bill, as it is received, is given a serial number, which serves to identify it in case of further entries or of correspondence in regard to it.

(*b*) DATE RECEIVED. This records the date upon which the bill is received and is, therefore, the date to be entered in the personal ledger accounts.

(*c*) FROM WHOM RECEIVED. This column records the name of the debtor whose account is to be credited in respect of the bill, *i.e.*, the person who has given the bill in satisfaction of his debt. Although this is usually the same as the name given in the column " Acceptor," it is not always the case, as was explained above.

(*d*) DRAWER. This is usually the trader himself, but it may not always be so. The drawer, it must be remembered, is an important party to a bill.

(*e*) ACCEPTOR. See note to (*c*) above. As explained previously, the acceptor is the person primarily liable to pay the bill at its date of maturity.

(*f*) WHERE PAYABLE. If no indication of the actual place of payment is given when the bill is accepted, it is payable at the acceptor's address as given on the bill, or if no address is given, at his place of business. Frequently, however, the place of payment is indicated in the acceptance, and in most cases it is payable at the acceptor's bank.

(*g*), (*h*) and (*i*) DATE OF BILL, ETC. These columns are necessary in order to give all the information in connection with the date upon which the bill is due for payment.

BILLS RECEIVABLE BOOK

(a) No. of Bill	(b) Date Received	(c) From Whom Received	(d) Drawer	(e) Acceptor	(f) Where Payable	(g) Date of Bill	(h) Term	(i) Due Date including Days of Grace	(j) Sales Ledg. Folio	(k) Amount of Bill	(l) Disposal
	19....					19....		19....		£ s. d.	
1	July 11	A. Bates	Selves	A. Bates	Midland Bk. Bristol	July 9	3 months	Oct. 12	172	600 10 6	Discounted 12th July.
2	,, 12	R.T.Loftus	,,	R.T.Loftus	Barclays Bk. Loughborough.	,, 10	2 ,,	Sept. 13	183	200 0 0	Paid 13th September.
3	,, 14	H. Soames	,,	H. Soames	Midland Bk. Brighton.	,, 11	3 ,,	Oct. 14	74	500 10 0	Dishonoured 14th October.
4	,, 17	N. T. Lent & Co.	H. Martyn.	B. Rook.	7, East St. Burton.	June 19	6 ,,	Dec. 22	103	250 0 0	Discounted 20th July.
		Total (posted to the debit of Bills Receivable Account).								£ 1,551 0 6	

The above may be assumed to represent the Bills Receivable Book of Wholesalers, Limited, the first entry representing the bill received from A. Bates referred to previously in this chapter.

(*j*) LEDGER FOLIO. This column is provided to record the folio in the ledger of the personal account of the debtor from whom the bill is received. The debtor's account must be credited with the amount of the bill.

(*k*) AMOUNT OF BILL. The full face value of the bill is entered in this column, the value being credited to the debtor's personal account, and the periodical total being debited to Bills Receivable Account.

(*l*) DISPOSAL. This column is used to record how the bill is finally disposed of, *i.e.*, whether paid at maturity, dishonoured on presentation, discounted with the bank or transferred over to a creditor in payment of a debt owing to him by the trader.

Bills Payable Book.

The Bills Payable Book records details of bills given to creditors, *i.e.*, bills accepted by the trader which he must eventually meet by means of a cash payment or a transfer of bank credit.

A specimen ruling is given on page 123, and the following explanatory notes indicate the usefulness of the various columns.

(*a*) NUMBER OF BILL. Bills payable are numbered in the same way as bills receivable.

(*b*) DATE ACCEPTED. This column records the date upon which the trader accepts the bill. It is particularly important in the case of bills payable " after sight," as it then fixes the due date.

(*c*) DRAWER. The drawer of the bill is the creditor and this column therefore indicates the name of the personal account in the ledger which requires to be debited in respect of the bill.

(*d*) TO WHOM PAYABLE. This is usually, but not always, the same as the drawer and serves to identify the bill more completely.

(*e*) WHERE PAYABLE. The details entered in this column are particularly important, for they enable the necessary arrangements to be made for the bill to be met at maturity. Bills are usually payable, in practice, at the acceptor's bank.

(*f*), (*g*) and (*h*) DATE OF BILL, ETC. The due date of a bill payable is very important, for if arrangements are not made for the bill to be met, there is a considerable risk of dishonour, with its serious effect upon the trader's credit.

(*i*), (*j*) and (*k*) LEDGER FOLIO, AMOUNT, ETC. Nothing further need be added to the remarks given in respect of the corresponding columns in the Bills Receivable Book.

BILLS PAYABLE BOOK

(a) No. of Bill.	(b) Date Accepted.	(c) Drawer.	(d) To Whom Payable.	(e) Where Payable.	(f) Date of Bill.	(g) Term.	(h) Due Date.	(i) Bought Ledger Folio.	(j) Amount.	(k) How dealt with.
	19......				19......		19......		£ s. d.	
1	July 9	Wholesalers, Ltd.	Wholesalers, Ltd.	Midland Bank, Lower Street, Bristol.	July 9	3 months date.	Oct. 12	101	600 10 6	Paid at Maturity.
2	,, 13	B. A. Sills.	B. A. Sills.	,,	,, 123	,,	,, 15	192	300 0 0	,,
3	,, 15	N. Knowles & Co.	N. Knowles & Co.	,,	,, 133	,,	,, 16	177	349 9 6	,,
4	,, 16	T. Smith, Ltd.	Midland Bank.	,,	,, 152	,,	Sept. 18	98	400 0 0	,,
			Total (posted to the credit of Bills Payable Account).						£ 1,650 0 0	

The above may be assumed to represent the Bills Payable Book of A. Bates, the first entry representing the bill given to Wholesalers, Ltd., referred to previously in this chapter.

E

The amount of each individual bill is posted to the debit
of the respective personal ledger account of the creditor
to whom the bill is given, and the periodical total is
credited to Bills Payable Account.

It will be noticed that no column is provided for the name of
the acceptor, this being unnecessary because the trader himself
is the acceptor in each case.

Recording Bill Transactions.

On receipt of a bill receivable from a debtor the bill must be
numbered with its correct serial number and the necessary details
entered in the Bills Receivable Book. If the bill is not to be
discounted but to be retained until maturity it is placed in a *Bill
Folio* and a note of the due date made in the diary. A bill folio
is merely a folder in which bills are placed for safe custody and
convenience until they are due for payment, the memorandum
entries in the diary facilitating the collection of the amounts of
the bills on their due dates.

The entry in the Bills Receivable Book is posted to the credit
of the debtor's personal account in the ledger, because he has
given value, while Bills Receivable Account is debited, because it
has received value. The latter entries are not made individually,
but in one periodical total when the book is closed off, usually at
the end of each month.

Thus, the entries on receipt of a bill receivable are :—

Debit Bills Receivable Account
Credit Customer's Personal Account.

In the specimen ruling of the Bills Receivable Book of Wholesalers, Limited, already given, the personal ledger accounts of
Bates, Loftus, Soames and Lent and Co. will be credited with the
respective amounts of the bills given by them as shown in the book.
The total amount of the money column, *i.e.*, £1,551 0s. 6d., will
be periodically posted to the debit of Bills Receivable Account
in the ledger.

Conversely, when a bill payable is given to a creditor, his
personal account in the ledger is debited from the Bills Payable
Book, and the total of the money column is periodically posted
to the credit of Bills Payable Account. Therefore the entries on
giving a bill payable are :—

Debit Supplier's Personal Account
Credit Bills Payable Account.

Thus in the specimen ruling of the Bills Payable Book of
A. Bates, already given, the creditors' personal accounts will be
debited with the amounts of the bills given to them, and Bills

Payable Account will be credited with the total of £1,650 at the end of the month or other agreed period.

In regard to payment, the trader who possesses a bill receivable may either (a) discount it with his banker (see page 118) or (b) hold it until maturity and then present it through his banker for payment. In the latter case, the entries required at maturity will be :—

Debit Bank (in the Cash Book)
Credit Bills Receivable Account.

In the case of a bill payable the usual procedure is to arrange with the bank to pay the bill on presentation and the entries on the due date of payment are :—

Debit Bills Payable Account
Credit Bank (in the Cash Book).

Discounting Bills—Treatment in Books.

It has already been explained that traders frequently discount bills receivable with their bankers, *i.e.*, sell the bills to the banker for less than their face value, the banker in return taking over the responsibility of obtaining payment at maturity.

The difference between the sum paid to the customer and the face value of the bill, known as *Bankers' Discount*, represents the amount of interest on the bill for the period between the date of discount (not the date of the bill) and the date of maturity of the bill. This discount is calculated at the discount rate ruling at the moment, *i.e.*, the rate per cent. charged by the bank for discounting bills of exchange.

The amount of the discount may be calculated by the following formula :—

$$\text{Discount} = \frac{\text{Amount of Bill} \times \text{Rate} \times \text{Time in years}}{100}.$$

Thus for example, if a trader wished to discount a bill receivable for £1,000 which was due for payment in three months from the date of discounting, the discount rate being 5%, the amount of the discount would be ascertained as follows :—

$$\frac{1000}{1} \times \frac{5}{100} \times \frac{1}{4} = \text{£12 10s. 0d.}$$

The banker would therefore pay his customer £1,000 less £12 10s. for the bill, and the trader would lose £12 10s. for the privilege of having his money three months earlier than would otherwise be the case.

When the discount period is not an even fraction of a year, the number of days from the day of discount to the last day of grace must be calculated and given in the numerator of the formula

and 365 must be included as a factor in the denominator. In calculating the number of days in this way either the date of discounting or the date of maturity must be omitted. Thus, if a bill maturing on 13th June is discounted on 3rd May, the number of days for which " discount " is calculated will be 41 (May 28 days, June 13 days) and not 42.

The discount in the case of an uneven period is therefore as follows :—

$$\text{Discount} = \frac{\text{Amount of Bill} \times \text{Rate of Interest} \times \text{No. of Days}}{100 \qquad 365}.$$

When a bill receivable is discounted the book-keeping entries in the trader's books are quite straightforward. The cash book " Bank " column is debited with the face value of the bill, because it receives this amount from the banker, and Bills Receivable Account is credited as it has given out value to the same extent. Bank Charges Account (or Interest Account) is debited with the amount of the discount which is an expense, and the cash book (" Bank " column) is credited because the banker takes this amount out of the customer's account. Thus the necessary entries in the case of the above transaction would appear as follows :—

```
                                        £   s. d.      £   s. d.
Bank Account (in the Cash Book). Dr. 1,000  0  0
   To Bills Receivable Account.                     1,000  0  0
Bank Charges Account (or Interest
   Account).                    Dr.    12 10  0
   To Bank Account (in the Cash Book).                 12 10  0
```

It is the custom of bankers to record the two entries in the customer's account separately and not merely to credit him with the net amount allowed for the bill, and a similar procedure is adopted in practice in the accounts of a trader. This method will be found to facilitate the reconciliation of the individual entries in the cash book and the bank pass book, and will furthermore be found convenient for posting purposes.

It should be noted that bank discount is quite distinct from the cash discount allowed to debtors on payment of their accounts. Banker's discount may be regarded as a payment of interest for the use of the bank's money, whereas cash discount is an allowance for prompt payment to the trader of his own money. Banker's discount is therefore given as an ordinary credit in the Cash Book (" Bank " column) and posted thence to the debit of Bank Charges Account. It would not be correct to enter discount of this nature in the discount column on the debit side of the Cash Book, for it would then eventually be transferred to the Discount Account, which records *cash* discounts alone.

EXAMPLE

On 1st June, 19....., Wholesalers, Limited sold goods to A. Bates for £450 and drew a bill upon him for this amount, payable at three months' date. The bill was duly accepted by Bates, and was discounted by Wholesalers, Limited with their bankers on 23rd June at $4\frac{1}{2}\%$ discount. Find the amount of the discount charged by the bank and enter the transactions in the ledger of Wholesalers, Limited.

The amount of discount is calculated as follows :—

$$£\frac{450}{1} \times \frac{4\frac{1}{2}}{100} \times \frac{73}{365} = £4 \text{ 1s. 0d.}$$

The discount period is 73 days, arrived at by counting the number of days from 23rd June to the last day of grace, *i.e.*, 4th September.

In this case there are three distinct transactions to be recorded, *viz.*:

(1) The sale of goods to Bates ;
(2) The receipt from Bates of a bill receivable ; and
(3) The discount of the bill with the bank.

Dr.	SALES ACCOUNT			Cr.
			19..... June 1 By A. Bates.	£ s. d. 450 0 0

Dr.	A. BATES				Cr.
19..... June 1 To Sales Account.	£ s. d. 450 0 0	19..... June 1 By Bills Receivable.			£ s. d. 450 0 0

Dr.	BILLS RECEIVABLE ACCOUNT				Cr.
19..... June 1 To A. Bates.	£ s. d. 450 0 0	19..... June 23 By Bank.			£ s. d. 450 0 0

Dr.	CASH BOOK				Cr.
19.... June 23 To Bills Receivable.	£ s. d. 450 0 0	19.... June 23 By Bank Charges.			£ s. d. 4 1 0

Dr.	BANK CHARGES ACCOUNT		Cr.
19..... June 23 To Bank.	£ s. d. 4 1 0		

In practice, the sale would be recorded in the Sales Day Book and would be credited to Sales Account in the grand total at the end of the month or other agreed period. Similarly the bill of exchange would be recorded in the Bills Receivable Book and Bills Receivable Account would only be debited in total at the end of the period. The individual entries are given in the above example in order to illustrate the complete double entry.

Dishonour of a Bill Receivable.

When for any reason payment of a bill is refused by the acceptor or drawee at its maturity the bill is said to be dishonoured. When this occurs it is usual for the bill to be "noted," *i.e.*, it is handed to a notary public who re-presents the bill to the acceptor for payment. If the bill is not met he attaches a note to it to the effect that payment has been refused and states the reason given for non-payment. This procedure enables independent evidence of the dishonour of the bill to be obtained.

The notary makes a small charge which is usually stated on the slip attached to the bill. This expense is passed on to the drawer, who naturally charges it to the acceptor, *i.e.*, his debtor, as it arose through his action in refusing payment of the bill.

The dishonour of a bill receivable is recorded in the creditor's books by a reversal of the previous entries, in order to restore the debtor's account to the position it was in before the bill was received from him in the first instance.

Thus in the previous example, the account of A. Bates showed a debit entry of £450 before the bill was drawn upon him. This was cancelled by a credit entry for the same amount in respect of the bill given by him. In the event of this bill being dishonoured his account must be debited with the amount of the bill so as to restore it to the original position (*i.e.*, of being £450 in debit).

The corresponding credit entry would be made in the "Bank" column of the Cash Book, since the bill was discounted, and the bank, upon dishonour of the bill, would exercise their right of recovery against their customer and would charge his account with the amount of the bill.

Thus the entries in the accounts already given would be :—

		£ s. d.	£ s. d.
A. Bates.	*Dr.*	450 0 0	
To Bank Account (in the Cash Book).			450 0 0

If, for example, the expenses charged by the notary public amounted to 3s. 6d., further entries would be necessary, as follows :

		£ s. d.	£ s. d.
A. Bates.	*Dr.*	3 6	
To Bank Account (in the Cash Book).			3 6

If the trader holds the bill until maturity and then presents

it through his banker for payment, we have already seen (see page 125) that Bank Account will then be debited and Bills Receivable Account will be credited. If the bill is then dishonoured by the acceptor, the debtor's personal account will require to be debited with the amount of the bill and with any expenses, Bank Account being credited to the same extent.

If the bill were retained by the trader himself until maturity and presented personally and not through a bank, for payment, then the Bank Account (or the " Bank " column in the Cash Book) will not be concerned in the transactions. The Bills Receivable Account will have been debited when the bill was received and no *contra* entry will yet have been made. If payment is refused this account will be credited with the amount of the bill and the debtor's account will be debited. Noting charges will then be debited to the debtor's account and credited to cash, or petty cash, as the case may be.

EXAMPLE

On 15th July, 19....., Wholesalers, Limited sold goods to Smith and Son for £750 and drew a bill upon them for this amount, payable three months after sight. The bill was accepted by Smith and Son on 18th July. On the due date of the bill, Wholesalers, Limited handed the bill to their bankers for collection, but on the following day they received a communication from the bank stating that the bill had been dishonoured, and that their account had accordingly been charged with its value and also with 3s. noting charges. Show the entries recording the transactions in the ledger of Wholesalers, Limited.

In this case it will be noted that there are four distinct transactions to be recorded :—

(1) The sale of goods to Smith and Son ;
(2) The receipt of a bill receivable from Smith and Son ;
(3) The payment of the bill into the bank on maturity ; and
(4) The dishonour of the bill.

Dr.   SALES ACCOUNT   *Cr.*

			19.....		£	s.	d.
			July 15	By Smith & Son.	750	0	0

Dr.   SMITH AND SON   *Cr.*

19....		£	s.	d.	19.....		£	s.	d.
July 15	To Sales.	750	0	0	July 18	By Bills Receivable.	750	0	0
Oct. 22	To Bank (Bill dishonoured).	750	0	0					
„ „	„ do. (Noting charges).		3	0					

Dr. BILLS RECEIVABLE Cr.

19..... July 18	To Smith & Son.	£ s. d. 750 0 0	19.... Oct. 21	By Bank.	£ s. d. 750 0 0

Dr. BANK ACCOUNT (Cash Book) Cr.

19..... Oct. 21	To Bills Receivable.	£ s. d. 750 0 0	19.... Oct. 22 ,, ,,	By Smith & Son (Bill dis- honoured). ,, do. (Noting charges).	£ s. d. 750 0 0 3 0

If the bill has been negotiated by the trader to one of his own creditors, when the bill is dishonoured the account of the customer from whom the bill was received will be debited and the creditor's personal account credited, thus restoring both personal accounts to the position prior to the negotiation of the bill.

If the bill is not paid owing to temporary lack of funds on the part of the debtor, the creditor may agree to accept a new bill for the full amount plus expenses and interest for the extended period. The debtor will then be debited with interest, etc., Interest Account being credited, while the new bill receivable will be entered in the books in the usual manner.

EXAMPLE

Upon dishonour of the above-mentioned bill for £750, Smith and Son offered to accept a new bill, payable three months after maturity of the first bill, for the same amount plus all expenses and interest at 5 per cent. per annum. Their offer was accepted and the new bill was presented through the bank at maturity and was duly honoured. Show the necessary entries in the books of Whole-salers, Limited.

Dr. SMITH AND SON Cr.

19.... Oct. 22 ,, ,, ,, ,, ,, ,,	To Bank (Bill dishonoured). ,, do. (Noting charges). ,, Interest. ,, Stamp.	£ s. d. 750 0 0 3 0 9 7 6 8 0 £ 759 18 6	19..... Oct. 22	By Bills Receivable.	£ s. d. 759 18 6 £ 759 18 6

Dr.   BILLS RECEIVABLE   Cr.

19..... Oct. 22	To Smith & Son.	£ s. d. 759 18 6	19..... Jan. 24	By Bank.	£ s. d. 759 18 6

Dr.   INTEREST ACCOUNT   Cr.

			19..... Oct. 22	By Smith & Son.	£ s. d. 9 7 6

Dr.   SUNDRY EXPENSES ACCOUNT.   Cr.

			19..... Oct. 22	By Smith & Son (Bill Stamp).	£ s. d. 8 0

Dr.   BANK ACCOUNT (Cash Book)   Cr.

19..... Jan. 24	To Bills Receivable.	£ s. d. 759 18 6	19..... Oct. 22	By Smith & Son (Bill dishonoured).	£ s. d. 750 0 0
			,, ,,	,, do. (Noting charges).	3 0

" Retired " Bills of Exchange.

When a bill is paid by the acceptor before its due date it is said to be " retired." An allowance is made for payment before the due date, and the bill is said to be " retired under rebate," the acceptor paying the amount of the bill less an agreed allowance for rebate calculated from the date of payment to the due date. This rebate is treated in the holder's books in a similar manner to banker's discount.

EXAMPLE

A. Bates draws a bill of £100 on R. Charles on 1st January, 19...., payable three months after date. Charles finding himself in funds on 28th February decides to retire the bill. Indicate the amount which Charles must pay to Bates to discharge the bill assuming interest at 5 per cent. per annum.

The rebate will be calculated as follows :—

28th February to 4th April (due date) = 35 days.

$$\therefore \; £\frac{100}{1} \times \frac{5}{100} \times \frac{35}{365} = 9s. \; 7d.$$

∴ The amount required is £100 less 9s. 7d. = £99 10s. 5d.

The entries in Bates's books will be as follows :—

> Debit Bank Account, £99 10s. 5d.
> Credit Bills Receivable Account, £99 10s. 5d.
> Debit Banker's Discount (or Rebate on Bills) Account, 9s. 7d.
> Credit Bills Receivable Account, 9s. 7d.

If the bill had been discounted by A. Bates, prior to retirement, the entries consequent upon the retirement of the bill will not affect Bates's books as Bates is no longer the holder of the bill.

The entries in Charles's books will be as follows :—

> Debit Bills Payable Account, £99 10s. 5d.
> Credit Bank Account, £99 10s. 5d.
> Debit Bills Payable Account, 9s. 7d.
> Credit Rebate on Bills Account, 9s. 7d.

Dishonour of a Bill Payable.

Exactly the same rules apply in the case of the dishonour of a bill payable. When the bill was accepted the creditor's account was debited and Bills Payable Account credited. If the bill was met at maturity Bills Payable Account would have been debited and Bank Account would have been credited in due course.

If, however, the trader is unable to find sufficient funds to meet the bill, the position must be restored to that which existed before the bill was accepted in the first instance. That is, the creditor's account must be credited so that the amount will still be shown as owing to him, for the dishonour of the bill may be said to have cancelled the conditional settlement of the account made when the bill was given. The Bills Payable Account must be debited in the same way, in order to cancel the amount at present given therein as representing a bill payable outstanding.

If the creditor states that there are noting charges to be paid in connection with the dishonour, the trader will debit a Noting Charges Account, and credit the creditor's personal account with the amount of these charges. These entries will be made through the journal, a note being made in the last column of the Bills Payable Book to the effect that the bill was dishonoured.

EXAMPLE

On 10th September, 19....., Wholesalers, Limited purchased goods valued £1,000 from Johnson, Vickers and Co., and gave in settlement a two months' bill for this amount. At the date of maturity of the bill they were in temporary financial difficulties, and the bill was dishonoured. Johnson, Vickers and Co. have the bill noted, the charges incurred amounting to 3s. 6d.

Wholesalers, Limited then offered to accept a new bill for £1,000 14s. 6d. (including 11s. stamp on the new bill) payable in a further three months' time, together with interest on the amount of the original bill at 5 per cent. per annum, which was agreed to. The bill was dated 16th November and was duly met at maturity. Show the entries recording the transactions in the ledger of Wholesalers, Limited.

Dr.   PURCHASES ACCOUNT   Cr.

19.....		£	s.	d.					
Sept. 10	To Johnson, Vickers & Co.	1,000	0	0					

Dr.   JOHNSON, VICKERS & CO.   Cr.

19.....		£	s.	d.	19.....		£	s.	d.
Sept. 10	To Bills Payable.	1,000	0	0	Sept. 10	By Purchases.	1,000	0	0
Nov. 16	,, Bills Payable.	1,013	4	6	Nov. 13	,, Bills Payable (dishonoured).	1,000	0	0
					,,	,, Noting Charges Account.		3	6
					,,	,, Stamp on Bills Account.		11	0
					,,	,, Interest Account.		12	10	0
		£1,013	4	6			£1,013	4	6

Dr.   BILLS PAYABLE ACCOUNT   Cr.

19.....		£	s.	d.	19.....		£	s.	d.
Nov. 13	To Johnson, Vickers & Co. (dishonoured Bill).	1,000	0	0	Sept. 10	By Johnson, Vickers & Co.	1,000	0	0
19.....									
Feb. 19	,, Bank.	1,013	4	6	Nov. 16	,, Johnson, Vickers & Co.	1,013	4	6

Dr.   BANK ACCOUNT (Cash Book)   Cr.

				19..... Feb. 19	By Bills Pay- able.		£ s. d. 1,013 4 6

Dr.   NOTING CHARGES ACCOUNT   Cr.

19..... Nov. 13	To Johnson, Vickers & Co.	£ s. d. 3 6			

Dr.   STAMP ON BILLS ACCOUNT   Cr.

19..... Nov. 13	To Johnson, Vickers & Co.	£ s. d. 11 0			

Dr.   INTEREST ACCOUNT   Cr.

19..... Nov. 13	To Johnson, Vickers & Co.	£ s. d. 12 10 0			

It should be observed that where an arrangement such as this is made in practice, the new bill is generally drawn for an amount to cover the value of the old bill, together with noting and stamping expenses, and interest for the extra period of credit allowed. Interest has been calculated in the above example for one quarter of a year, but in actual practice interest would be charged for the *exact* number of days, including days of grace, that the new bill has to run.

EXERCISE 7

A. What is a bill of exchange?

B. What are the uses of a bill of exchange?

C. What do you understand by the following terms:
Acceptor; drawer; drawee; payee; dishonour; days of grace; retirement under rebate?

D. Explain the distinction between bills receivable and bills payable.

E. How does a bill of exchange (*a*) resemble, and (*b*) differ from a cheque ?

F. What is meant by " discounting " a bill of exchange ?   How is this form of discount calculated ?

G. Morton Bros. owed Dean & Co. £325.   By arrangement Dean & Co. drew on 1st September, 19...., a bill at three months' sight on Morton Bros., which was duly accepted on 3rd September, payable at the National Bank, Birmingham.   Show the form of bill, indicating stamp and due date.

H. Rule a form of Bills Receivable Book for the use of Thomas & Co., and enter therein the following bills received, indicating the due dates of the bills.
19.....
Mar. 23.   Received from Johnson & Co., bill of exchange, value £750, drawn by Thomas & Co., in their own favour, and accepted by Johnson & Co. on 20th March, at 3 months' date.   Payable at Lloyds Bank, Leeds.
„ 27.   Received from J. Beatty, bill of exchange drawn by Beatty on Jones Bros. for £175 12s. 6d. in favour of Thomas & Co. due for payment on 14th April.   Payable at The British Bank, Hereford.
„ 29.   Received from T. Dixon, bill of exchange, value £53 9s., drawn by Thomas & Co. in their own favour, and accepted by Dixon on 25th March, at three months' sight.   Payable at Bank of Scotland, Edinburgh.

J. Rule a form of Bills Payable Book for the use of J. Arthur, and enter therein details of the following bills accepted by him :—
19.....
June 4.   Gave Harris & Co. bill of exchange value £350, payable to their order three months after date.
„ 6.   Accepted bill drawn by Jack, Ltd., in favour of T. Forth, value £37 18s., and payable at six months after sight.
„ 7.   Gave Lewis & Son bill of exchange value £475 15s., payable to their order, two months after date.
All the above bills are payable at the Midland Bank, Dunstable.

K. On 1st June, 19...., Hugh Dickson sold goods amounting to £300 to F. Forrester.   On receipt of the goods Forrester sent Dickson a cheque for £100 on account, and a duly-accepted bill dated 1st June at two months for the balance.   Dickson discounted this bill on 5th June at 5%.   Show how these transactions would appear in Dickson's books.

L. On 17th July, 19...., W. Frost sold goods to Church & Co. for £870, and drew a bill upon them for this amount, payable four months after sight.   The bill was accepted by Church & Co. on 21st July, and on 11th August was discounted at 4½% by Frost with his bankers.   On maturity of the

bill Church & Co. were only able to find £300 in cash, which they paid to Frost. The bill was dishonoured and the bank recovered the amount of the bill, together with notarial charges amounting to 4s. 3d., from Frost. Church & co. then agreed to accept a new bill for the balance outstanding, together with notarial charges on the dishonoured bill and stamp duty on the new bill. This bill was accepted on 24th November, and was payable in two months. Show the entries recording the transactions in Frost's ledger at 30th November.

M. On 4th December, 19...., W. Bell accepts a bill for £250 drawn on him by S. Wise at four months after acceptance in respect of goods supplied. At the date of maturity of the bill he is unable to meet it and the bill is dishonoured, notarial charges amounting to 3s. 9d. being incurred. On 7th April he accepts a new bill payable in three months' time for £250 3s. 9d., together with interest at 6% per annum on £250, and this bill was duly met at maturity. Show the entries recording the transactions in Bell's ledger, ignoring the stamp on the new bill.

CHAPTER VIII

THE LEDGER ; THE TRIAL BALANCE

In its simplest form the ledger is a collection of all the accounts which record a trader's dealings in commodities, in services or in debts. In more precise language, the ledger may be defined as the book of account which contains, in classified form, the final and permanent records of a trader's transactions.

It has already been stated as a fundamental rule that no entry must be made in the ledger unless it has first been passed through a book of prime entry. The seeming exception to this rule is that cash transactions are entered direct in the cash book, which is explained by the fact that the cash book may be considered to fulfil the dual function of both a book of prime entry and a ledger account.

Sub-division of the Ledger.

All accounts have hitherto been regarded as being kept in one volume, with the exception of the cash account and the petty cash account already referred to, but in practice this state of affairs would be possible only in the smallest business. Just as it became necessary to sub-divide the journal in order to enable more than one clerk to be engaged upon the work at once, and in order to keep the various books from becoming unwieldy, so it becomes necessary to divide the ledger into various sections, each of which may be bound into one or more separate volumes.

Furthermore, the same method of sub-division is adopted for the ledger as in the case of the journal. It will be remembered that the great majority of the transactions passed through the journal were found to fall into a few main classes, and it was, therefore, an easy and obvious step, as the business grew in size, to allocate a separate book or section of the journal to each main class of entry.

In an exactly similar manner the ledger is divided into separate volumes, in accordance with the main classes into which accounts fall, each volume being given a distinctive name which clearly indicates the kind of account to be found in it.

It was shown in Chapter I that ledger accounts are of three kinds :—

(a) PERSONAL ACCOUNTS, recording dealings with persons ;

137

(b) REAL ACCOUNTS, recording dealings in material things, *e.g.*, property or goods ; and

(c) NOMINAL ACCOUNTS, recording the intangible items of gain and loss, income and expenses.

It will be remembered that the majority of the transactions which book-keeping has to record involve either the purchase or the sale of goods, and consequently the most important sub-divisions of the journal are the Purchases and the Sales Day Books. Obviously, therefore, it will not be sufficient to combine all personal transactions involving both purchases and sales into one ledger, and thus separate ledgers are kept for purchases accounts and for sales accounts respectively.

THE PURCHASES LEDGER contains the accounts of persons from whom goods are purchased, *i.e.*, those who are normally the creditors of the business. THE SALES LEDGER contains the accounts of persons to whom goods are sold, *i.e.*, those who are generally debtors to the business.

Real and nominal accounts are kept in the GENERAL LEDGER, although this is sometimes divided into (a) the NOMINAL LEDGER, containing accounts of gain, loss, income and expenses, and (b) the PRIVATE LEDGER, containing the accounts relating to property, capital, profit and loss, etc.

An alternative division of the General Ledger is into (a) the IMPERSONAL LEDGER, containing real and nominal accounts in ordinary use, and (b) the PRIVATE LEDGER, containing accounts of a more private nature which disclose the financial standing of the business, such as the Capital Account, the Profit and Loss Account, etc.

The most important sections into which the ledger is divided may therefore be tabulated as follows :—

> (a) PURCHASES LEDGER (or CREDITORS' LEDGER).
> (b) SALES LEDGER (or DEBTORS' LEDGER).
> (c) GENERAL LEDGER—
>
> > (i) Impersonal Ledger or Nominal Ledger; and
> > (ii) Private Ledger.

Further Sub-division.

Theoretically, the above sub-division of the ledger may be considered as that to be found in general use in an ordinary trader's business. In actual practice, however, it is frequently necessary to make further extensive sub-divisions in order to cope with the volume of business and to enable a large book-keeping staff to be continuously employed.

Large firms may have 10,000 or more active accounts in their books, and in such cases very careful and systematic organization is essential if hopeless confusion is to be avoided.

The sections into which the ledgers are divided depend, of course, entirely upon the nature and circumstances of the individual firm, but naturally the chief need for division arises in the Sales Ledger, and, in a lesser degree, in the Purchases Ledger. The Impersonal and Private Ledgers seldom contain a number of accounts, or have to record a number of transactions, sufficiently large to justify their being split up into further sections.

Alphabetical Division.

A convenient and frequently adopted sub-division of a personal ledger is on an alphabetical basis. In the ordinary way, accounts are entered in a ledger in alphabetical order, and, in the sub-division just referred to, advantage is taken of this fact.

The alphabet is divided into a number of sections, varying with the total number of accounts to be dealt with, and a separate section of the ledger is allotted to each. Thus, the division might be A-C ; D-H ; I-R ; and S-Z.

The Sales Ledger labelled " A-C " would then contain the accounts of all customers whose surnames began with A, B or C. The account of any person whose name commenced with D, E, F, G or H would be found in " D-H " ledger, and so forth.

Geographical Division.

Another method is to divide the country into areas and to allot a separate ledger to each area. Each ledger will then contain the accounts of all persons whose address is in a certain specified area, the actual arrangement of the accounts in each ledger being, of course, alphabetical.

The advantage of this method is that customers' accounts can be grouped together in areas, to coincide with the sections into which the country is divided for sales purposes. If the areas chosen are those of the travellers or agents, there is a considerable saving of time when statistics or information are required in regard to the accounts or the sales for which each traveller is responsible.

Again, it is a common practice for a firm to " try out " a new sales scheme in a chosen area, and to tabulate carefully all statistics which can be obtained as to the results achieved. This enables the probable success or failure of the scheme to be ascertained by means of the results from one area only, and, if the verdict is unsatisfactory, prevents the heavy loss which might possibly have occurred if the scheme had been applied to the whole country in the first instance. In such cases, a geographical division of the ledgers will obviously facilitate the experiment and effect considerable clerical economy.

A typical area classification is as follows :—

(1) London and Home Counties.
(2) Southern Area.
(3) Western Area.
(4) Midlands.
(5) Northern Area.

Inter-relationship of Ledgers and Subsidiary Books.

The chart set out on page 141 gives a graphic representation of the inter-relationship between the ledger and the books of first entry and will repay careful study, because it will enable the reader to gain a clear understanding of the manner in which the various books and ledgers are linked up.

Reading horizontally across the chart, the double entry aspect is clearly indicated. For example, entries on the debit side of the Cash Book result in entries on the credit side of any of the four ledgers. Similarly, entries in the Purchases Book result in debit entries in the Nominal Ledger and in credit entries in the Purchases Ledger and so on.

Reading vertically down the columns, the various *classes of entry* found in each ledger can be seen. Thus, the Sales Ledger is credited with cash received from debtors, with goods returned by debtors and with bills receivable given by debtors, while it is debited with goods sold to debtors and with repayments to debtors.

The Journal has been omitted from the chart, not because it is unimportant, for the contrary is the case, but because it records miscellaneous transactions which may affect either side of any of the individual ledgers.

The Treatment of Ledger Balances.

In view of the thorough explanation of the essential principles of double entry given in the earlier chapters, there should be no necessity to state again the rules for debiting and crediting the various classes of ledger accounts.

It will, however, be useful to set out briefly the nature of the entries and the meaning of a debit or a credit balance in each case.

(a) PERSONAL ACCOUNTS.

(i) SALES LEDGER ACCOUNTS.

A Sales Ledger Account is *debited* with goods sold, bills receivable dishonoured, interest charged on overdue accounts, and with cash repayments made for allowances, rebates, etc. (in cases where the debtor to whom the allowance is due had previously settled his account in full), and is *credited* with cash remitted by debtors, goods returned, bills receivable given by debtors and discounts and allowances made to debtors.

CHART OF DOUBLE ENTRY.

Book of First Entry.	Personal Ledgers.				Nominal Ledger (or Impersonal Ledger).		Private Ledger.	
	Purchases Ledger.		Sales Ledger.					
	Dr.	Cr.	Dr.	Cr.	Dr.	Cr.	Dr.	Cr.
Cash Book—Dr. Side		Repayments by Creditors.		Receipts from Debtors.		Income.		Capital Introduced. Proceeds of sale of assets, etc.
Cash Book—Cr. Side	Payments to Creditors.		Repayments to Debtors (Allowances, etc.).		Expenses.		Withdrawal of Capital. Purchase of assets.	
Purchases Book		Purchases from Creditors.			Purchases (in total).			
Purchases Returns Book	Purchases Returned to Creditors.					Purchases Returns (in total).		
Sales Book			Sales to Debtors.			Sales (in total).		
Sales Returns Book				Sales Returned by Debtors.	Sales Returns (in total).			
Bills Receivable Book				Bills Receivable from Debtors.	Bills Receivable (in total).			
Bills Payable Book	Bills Payable to Creditors.					Bills Payable (in total).		

The fundamental rule is thus clearly fulfilled, for the debit entries obviously represent incomings, while the credit entries in each case represent outgoings as far as the personal account of the debtor is concerned.

(ii) PURCHASES LEDGER ACCOUNTS.

A Purchases Ledger Account is *debited* with cash paid, goods returned, bills payable given to creditors and discounts and allowances received from creditors, and is *credited* with goods purchased, bills payable dishonoured, interest charged on overdue accounts, and cash allowances received in cases where the trader had previously settled his creditor's account in full.

Here again the fulfilment of the fundamental rule can be clearly seen.

In both cases, the *balance* of a Personal Account represents a debt. In a Sales Ledger Account the debt is owing by the customer to the business, and is thus a *debit* balance. In a Purchases Ledger Account the debt is owing by the business, and so the account is that of a *creditor* and the balance is a *credit* one.

Where a person both buys goods from and sells goods to the trader, he may have two accounts in the trader's books, one in the Sales Ledger and one in the Purchases Ledger. It is customary in such a case to transfer the smaller balance to the other account periodically, thus leaving only one balance outstanding. Such an entry is termed a *contra entry*. It should be noted that a transfer of this nature will almost invariably be a debit in the Purchases Ledger and a credit in the Sales Ledger. To ensure the completion of the double entry such contra entries are usually recorded in the Principal Journal.

(b) REAL ACCOUNTS.

A Real Account is *debited* with the outlay on the acquisition or extension of an asset, and is *credited* with the proceeds of the sale of the whole or a portion of such assets. It is also *credited* with depreciation, or with any amount which is written off the book value of the asset.

Cash Account is *debited* with cash received and *credited* with cash paid, while Bank Account is *debited* with money paid into the bank and *credited* with money withdrawn from the bank.

A Real Account always has a *debit* balance, because it represents property which belongs to the business, *i.e.*, it represents a benefit received by the business. When cash at bank is overdrawn, this rule is not violated, for cash itself cannot be " overdrawn." What has happened, in effect, is that a real account has temporarily become a personal account representing a debt owing by the business to the banker.

(c) NOMINAL ACCOUNTS.

Nominal Accounts are *debited* with losses and expenses, *i.e.*, incomings of services, and *credited* with income and gains, *i.e.*, outgoings of services.

An expense, or loss, account shows a debit balance, because it represents a service received, while an income or gain account has a credit balance for the contrary reason.

(d) CAPITAL ACCOUNT.

The Capital Account should be considered as a special type of ledger account contained in the Private Ledger. It generally shows a credit balance, which represents the amount owing *to the owner* by the business ; in the rare cases where it shows a debit balance, the balance represents the deficiency which the trader owes *to his business*.

Thus the main classes of ledger balances may be tabulated as follows :—

LEDGER BALANCES.

Debit Balances	Credit Balances.
Personal Accounts of Debtors (Sales).	Personal Accounts of Trade Creditors (Purchases).
Real Accounts (Assets).	Personal Accounts of Creditors (Liabilities, *e.g.*, Bank Overdraft).
Nominal Accounts (Losses and Expenses).	Nominal Accounts (Gains and Income).
Capital Account (if insolvent).	Capital Account (if solvent).

If this chapter, including the chart, has been thoroughly studied up to the present point, the reader should possess a sound knowledge of the system of double entry book-keeping as a whole. An endeavour should now be made to visualize the complete system, noting in particular the inter-relationship of the subsidiary books with the various sub-divisions of the ledger.

THE TRIAL BALANCE

The foregoing statement of the chief classes of account which have debit and credit balances respectively provides a suitable opportunity for an explanation of the trial balance.

A Trial Balance may be defined as a statement of all the debit and credit balances of the ledger accounts at any given date, arranged systematically in order to check the arithmetical accuracy of the ledger postings. Thus the trial balance should be taken out immediately after the completion of the postings and *not* immediately prior to drawing up the Balance Sheet, as the main

object of the Trial Balance is to ascertain that the books are arithmetically correct before proceeding with the preparation of the final accounts.

A Trial Balance has also a secondary purpose in providing a concise statement of all the items which require to be included in the Trading Account, Profit and Loss Account, and Balance Sheet. Thus, in the statement of balances given above, the debit balances which represent assets (including in this term the debts owing by the debtors in the Sales Ledger) will appear on the right-hand side of the Balance Sheet, while those which represent losses and expenses will appear on the debit side of the Trading or Profit and Loss Accounts. Similarly, the credit balances which represent liabilities (including the amounts due to creditors) will appear on the left-hand side of the Balance Sheet, and those which represent income or gains on the credit side of the Trading or Profit and Loss Accounts.

It is extremely important to note that the trial balance is merely a statement prepared in order to check the arithmetical accuracy of the book-keeping entries and to facilitate the preparation of the final accounts. It is not a ledger account to which postings can be made, nor is it part of the journal.

Errors the Trial Balance Discloses.

It was explained in Chapter I that the result of the double entry principles, if correctly applied, is that the sum of all the debit balances of the ledger accounts must equal the sum of all the credit balances at any given date. If the two totals fail to agree, it is a certain indication that an error of some nature has occurred in the book-keeping records.

Thus, if an entry for £22 0s. 10d. in the Sales Day Book is posted therefrom to the customer's account in the Sales Ledger as £22 10s., the two sides of the trial balance will fail to agree in that the total of the debit balances will exceed that of the credit balances by 9s. 2d., unless there is some other compensating error, and the arithmetical *in*accuracy of the postings will be proved.

If the item in the Sales Day Book is entirely missed when the day's entries in that book are being posted to the Sales Ledger, the trial balance will indicate a discrepancy of the full amount of £22 0s. 10d., as the total of the credit balances will exceed that of the debit balance by that amount.

To take yet another instance, if the item is posted to the debtor's account in the ledger and the correct amount is entered, there can still arise an error if the amount is posted to the *credit* instead of to the *debit* side of the account. In this case the error will be indicated by an excess of the credit balances over the debit balances of £44 1s. 8d. (*i.e.*, twice the amount of the entry).

A trial balance, therefore, is an extremely useful means of testing or proving the arithmetical accuracy of the postings to the ledger. The preparation of a trial balance is always the first step taken in preparing the final accounts at the end of the trading period.

A trial balance should also be prepared at intervals as a means of checking the accuracy of the clerical work over shorter periods, for in this way any errors are "localized" and considerably less time requires to be spent in searching for them than is the case if a check is made every six or twelve months only.

In working exercises involving the writing up of book-keeping entries, a rough trial balance should always be taken out, even if none is required by the question, in order to check the ledger entries.

Errors not disclosed by the Trial Balance.

The Trial Balance, it has been shown, may be taken as satisfactory evidence that there is a corresponding credit entry for every debit entry in the books, and *vice versa*. It is important to note, however, that a trial balance the two sides of which agree is not proof of the absolute accuracy of the whole of the entries in the books.

The errors which a trial balance does not disclose, and which may therefore exist in spite of the agreement of the two sides of the trial balance, may be divided into the following classes :—

    (1) Errors of omission ;
    (2) Errors of commission ;
    (3) Errors of principle ;
    (4) Compensating errors ; and
    (5) Errors of original entry.

ERRORS OF OMISSION. When the entries for a transaction are entirely omitted from the books of account, an error of omission has been made, and the agreement of the two sides of the trial balance will not be affected. For example, if goods value £31 9s. 6d. are sold to T. A. Thomas, but the transaction is entirely overlooked and no entry is made in the Sales Day Book, the amount will not be posted to the debit of the personal account of Thomas nor will it be posted, with the other items for the period, to the credit of Sales Account in the nominal ledger, and the omission of both the debit and the credit entries for the same transaction will not affect the agreement of the trial balance.

ERRORS OF COMMISSION. An error of commission is one whereby an entry in respect of a transaction is made in a wrong account of the same class. For example, if the above transaction had been correctly entered in the Sales Day Book but was posted in error to the personal account of T. T. Thomas instead of T. A.

Thomas, the trial balance would not disclose the error, although the balances of the accounts of both debtors would be incorrect.

ERRORS OF PRINCIPLE. An error of principle is one whereby an entry in respect of a transaction is made in the wrong class of account, e.g., in an expense account instead of an asset account or *vice versa*. If, for example, £30 were paid for repairs to plant and machinery, the correct entry would be to debit an expense account such as "Repairs Account." If, however, the payment were regarded as an addition to the asset and debited to Plant and Machinery Account, the error would be one of principle and would affect the position of the business as disclosed by the books, yet once more the trial balance totals would not be affected.

COMPENSATING ERRORS. When two or more errors are made of the same amount but with an opposite effect, they counteract each other, and are known as compensating errors. Thus, when explaining the errors which the trial balance discloses, it was imagined that a Sales Day Book entry of £22 0s. 10d. was posted to the personal account of the customer as £22 10s., thereby causing a difference of 9s. 2d. between the two sides of the trial balance. But if, say, the Sales Day Book is overcast by 9s. 2d. the excess credit in the Sales Account will offset the excess debit in the personal account and the trial balance totals will agree, although two of the individual balances will be wrong.

ERRORS OF ORIGINAL ENTRY. Occasionally it happens that a transaction is wrongly recorded in a subsidiary book. Thus if a purchase of goods value £67 is entered in the Purchases Book as £76 the wrong amount will be credited to the supplier's account and the purchases account will eventually be debited with £9 too much. Such a mistake would not be apparent from an examination of the trial balance. Similarly, if a transaction is entered twice in the subsidiary book no difference in the Trial Balance will be revealed if the complete double entry was duplicated.

Generally, however, it may be assumed that the agreement of the trial balance is a fairly conclusive proof of the arithmetical accuracy of the books for all ordinary purposes, particularly if an efficient system of internal check is maintained, *i.e.*, if the entries in the books are checked against one another and examined systematically and regularly.

Location of Errors disclosed by Trial Balance.

When the totals of the trial balance fail to agree it is obvious that the first step must be to locate the error which is causing the discrepancy. This is by no means an easy task, particularly when the volume of transactions is large, and it is therefore always advisable to work upon a systematic basis instead of performing a haphazard check.

The possible causes of a difference in the trial balance may be divided into the following broad groups :—

1. Errors in posting ;
2. Errors in addition ;
3. Errors in balancing ; or
4. Errors in extraction.

ERRORS IN POSTING were illustrated at length earlier in the present chapter when the errors disclosed by the trial balance were explained.

ERRORS IN ADDITION may occur (a) in the trial balance itself ; (b) in the subsidiary books, e.g., in the total of the Sales Day Book ; or (c) in the ledger accounts.

ERRORS IN BALANCING usually result from faulty arithmetic in calculating the balances of the ledger accounts, or in bringing down these balances.

ERRORS IN EXTRACTION refer to the inaccurate insertion of balances in the trial balance itself, e.g., reading off hurriedly the balance of Discount Account as £32 9s. 6d. instead of £32 19s. 6d. Sometimes a balance is omitted entirely.

The first step in the location of an error is to check carefully the additions of the Trial Balance and the extraction of the balances. It is a very annoying experience to discover after hours of search that the books themselves were correct all the time, and that the error lay in the incorrect preparation of the trial balance itself.

Having proved the trial balance to be correct, the next step is to ascertain the actual amount of the difference, as this is often an indication of the source of the error. An even amount, e.g., £10, £1, will probably be found to be due to an error in addition, although of course this is by no means necessarily so, and it is usually advisable in this case to check the additions of the subsidiary books and ledger accounts.

If the difference is not a round sum, e.g., is £9 3s. 6d., the additions should not be checked except as a last resort, for the error is most likely to be in the postings or possibly in the balancing of the ledger accounts. The books should, therefore, be searched, and any entries of this amount should be carefully examined to ensure that the double entry has been correctly completed in each case.

Similar action should then be taken in regard to amounts of exactly half the difference, where the latter is an even sum, in view of the possibility of an item having been debited or credited twice to the same side, e.g., an error of £9 3s. 6d. may be caused by an item of £4 11s. 9d. being debited to two accounts instead of being debited to one and credited to another.

It is also advisable to pay particular attention to such errors as £43 9s. posted as £4 3s. 9d., causing a difference of £39 5s. 3d.,

or £1 0s. 6d. posted as £1 6s., etc.   A careful examination of the amount of the difference may suggest the possible source of the error.   A difference of 5s. 6d., for instance, would indicate the advisability of scrutinizing any items of £1 0s. 6d. or £1 6s., in case the debit entry has been made for one amount and the credit entry for the other.

If figures have been transposed when posting or carrying forward, an error which is always a multiple of 9 will be caused. For example, £19 posted as £91 would result in an error of £72, a multiple of 9.   It does not, of course, necessarily follow that an error which is a multiple of 9 has been caused by transposed figures.

There are other methods of tracing errors, without necessarily having to check laboriously every entry for the whole of the period, and these methods may be acquired quickly as the result of experience.   The trial balance should be compared with the previous one to trace any balance completely omitted (e.g., Petty Cash, which is easily overlooked), and the subsidiary books should be examined in order to discover any unposted item, indicated by the absence of the folio number.

An error in book-keeping can always be traced if sufficient time and labour are expended upon the task, but the exercise of care, intelligence, and the skill born of experience can always reduce to a very considerable extent the time required to locate the error.

EXERCISE 8

A.   What is the use of the ledger ?   Explain clearly the reasons for the subdivision of the ledger and outline a system of sub-division with which you are acquainted, explaining its specific advantages.

B.   Show clearly the inter-relationship of the ledger and the various subsidiary books.

C.   Explain precisely the significance of a debit or credit balance in the different types of ledger accounts.

D.   Discuss carefully the nature and purpose of the Trial Balance.

E.   What types of error does the Trial Balance fail to disclose ?   Explain fully the method of location of those errors which are disclosed.

F.   George Dickson is in business as a cutler and silversmith.   On 1st January, 19..., his financial position was as follows : Creditor :—Totnes & Co., Ltd., £304 8s. ; Debtors :—G. Dartmouth, £72 8s. ; P. Plymouth, £32 17s. ; Stock in hand, £342 19s. ; Cash in hand, £10 8s. ; Cash at Bank, £119 4s. ; Fixtures and Fittings, £126 12s.

Open the accounts necessary to record the above particulars in the ledger, and post thereto, through the proper subsidiary books, the following transactions :—

19....

Jan. 4. Purchased on credit from H. Gilbert, 10 dozen table knives at 29s. per dozen, 24 razors at 5s. 6d. each, and one tea and coffee set at £10 18s., the whole invoice being subject to 10% trade discount.

„ 7. Sold for cash, 1 dozen pairs of scissors at 1s. 6d. per pair, and 24 table forks at 32s. per dozen.

„ 8. Paid in cash, wages £7 10s., trade expenses £3 2s.

„ 9. Returned to H. Gilbert, 3 dozen table knives and 4 razors as damaged, and received credit note.

„ 10. Drew and cashed cheque, £25, for cash payments.

„ 12. Sold on credit to P. Plymouth, 4 cases E.P. fish servers at £2 10s. per case, 2 silver salvers at £5 5s. each and 2 dozen razors at 7s. each, packing charges £1 2s., the whole invoice subject to 10% trade discount.

„ 14. Received cheque from P. Plymouth for amount due from him and allowed him £5 cash discount. Paid cheque into Bank.

„ 15. Paid in cash, wages £8 2s., and trade expenses, £2 1s. 6d.

„ 17. G. Dartmouth paid £50 on account by cheque. Paid cheque into Bank.

„ 19. Purchased new typewriter, £16 16s., by cheque.

„ 22. Paid in cash, wages £7 19s.

Balance the ledger, bring down the balances, and extract a Trial Balance as on 22nd January, 19....

G. E. Burnett commenced business on 1st January, 19...., as a dry goods merchant. On that date he paid £1,000 into the Midland Bank. His stock in hand consisted of ten rolls of tweed, which cost £28 per roll, purchased in December on credit from G. Notcut & Sons, but not yet paid for. Burnett's transactions for the month of January, 19...., were as follows :—

19...

Jan. 1. Drew and cashed cheque for £10 for Petty Cash.

„ 2. Purchased out of Petty Cash, stamps 10s., and stationery £1 10s.

„ 3. Purchased on credit, from Chatenay & Co., velvet £92, less 10% trade discount.

„ 4. Sold on credit, to George Dickson, 3 rolls tweed, at £34 per roll.

„ 5. Paid wages from Petty Cash, £7 10s.

„ 6. Sold for cash, 5 yards of tweed at 20s. per yard, and paid the money into Petty Cash.

„ 7. Received cheque (which was paid into Bank) from George Dickson for the amount of his account, less 5% cash discount.

„ 8. Paid G. Notcut & Sons their account by cheque, less 5% cash discount.

„ 10. Returned to Chatenay & Co., velvet value £12, damaged.

„ 11. Drew and cashed cheque for £10 for Petty Cash.

„ 12. Paid wages from Petty Cash, £8 15s.

Jan. 13.   Paid carriage from Petty Cash, £1 2s. 6d.

„   14.   Purchased on credit, from D. Barton, tweed, £64 8s. 6d.

„   15.   Sold on credit, to R. Alexander & Co., tweed, £28 9s.

Open the ledger accounts and post the above transactions thereto, through the proper subsidiary books. Balance the ledger, bring down the balances, and extract a Trial Balance as on 15th January, 19.....

H. John Giles commenced business as a merchant on 1st July, 19...., with a capital of £750 in cash, which he at once placed in the Bank. His transactions during the first month were as follows :—

19...

July 2.   Bank charged to his account for cheque book, 16s. 8d.

Drew for office cash, £30.

Bought office furniture and paid for same by cheque, £42 10s.

„   3.   Bought stationery for cash, £8 10s.

„   4.   Bought on credit from Davis & Jones, goods, £370 5s., less trade discount 5%.

„   5.   Drew for office cash, £30.

„   6.   Bought for cash, goods, £4.

„   7.   Paid salaries by cash, £18.

„   9.   Sold to Elkan Bros. on credit, goods, £122 net.

„   10.   Received in Treasury notes and silver, £23 3s. for cash sale.

„   12.   Paid Davis & Jones on account, by cheque, £200.

„   13.   Paid salaries by cash, £18.

„   17.   Sold to Field & Co., on credit, goods, £168 10s.

„   19.   Sold to Elkan Bros., on credit, goods, £93 15s. net.

„   20.   Paid salaries by cash, £18.

„   23.   Received cheque from Elkan Bros. for balance of account, less 5% cash discount, and paid same direct to Bank.

„   26.   Returned to Davis & Jones, damaged goods, £5 14s. 9d. net.

„   27.   Cash sale, £27 10s. in Treasury notes.

Paid salaries by cash, £18.

Paid to Bank, £15.

Bought from Hope & Co., on credit, goods £82 net.

„   29.   Paid Davis & Jones, by cheque, the balance due to them, deducting 2½% cash discount on the net goods supplied, according to their terms "Cash within a month."

„   30.   Field & Co. returned goods, wrong colour, £22 10s., with cheque for balance of account. Paid cheque into Bank.

„   31.   Bought for cash, stationery, £2 10s.

John Giles drew by cheque for personal use, £20.

Bought goods on credit from Hope & Co., £120 net.

Make the required entries in the subsidiary books (3-column cash book : Discount, Cash and Bank), post to ledger, balance the accounts and prepare a Trial Balance.

J. Explain what effect the following mistakes would have on the accounts of a business :—

(a) A payment to a creditor of £200 entered in the Cash Book correctly and posted as £220.

(b) A payment for expenses of £60 entered in the Cash Book correctly and posted as £160.

(c) A credit sale of goods of £200 debited to the account of the wrong customer.

(d) A cash sale of £29 10s. credited to Cash Sales Account as £9 10s.

K. In taking out the balances of a set of books it is found that errors have been made as follows :—

(a) £10 paid for carriage on goods inwards has been debited to Purchases Account.

(b) An invoice for goods purchased has been rendered £10 short, and posted as rendered. The goods have been taken at their correct value in stocktaking.

How would these errors be rectified ?

THE LEDGER; THE TRIAL BALANCE 151

K. In taking out the balances of a set of books it is found that errors have been made as follows:—

(a) £10 paid for carriage on goods inwards has been debited to Purchase Account.

(b) An invoice for goods purchased has been rendered £10 short, and posted as rendered. The goods have been taken at their correct value in stocktaking.

How would these errors be rectified?

CHAPTER IX

ADJUSTMENTS AND DEPRECIATION

Before we proceed to a study of the adjustments that require to be made in certain of the nominal and real accounts after the Trial Balance has been agreed, it will be as well if we consider the nature and use of suspense accounts and the adjustments that have occasionally to be made in the personal accounts to write off bad debts.

Suspense Accounts.

A Suspense Account may be defined as an account in which items in abeyance are temporarily recorded, *i.e.*, any items which, owing to insufficient data, cannot at the time of entry be posted to their correct accounts.

If, for example, a trader on 8th April receives a postal order value 10s. 6d. without any indication of the identity of the sender, he will be unable to make the correct entries in his books. He therefore credits this amount temporarily to a suspense account, pending the discovery of the name of the customer from whom the remittance was received. The theoretical journal entry in this case would be :—

			£ s. d.	£ s. d.
19.....				
April 8.	Cash Account (Cash Book)	*Dr.*	10 6	
	To Suspense Account			10 6
	Being remittance received from unknown source.			

If it was discovered on 18th April that the postal order was sent by J. Jackson, who had written to say that he had received no receipt in respect of the sum paid, the necessary adjusting entry would be made as follows :—

			£ s. d.	£ s. d.
19.....				
April 18.	Suspense Account	*Dr.*	10 6	
	To J. Jackson			10 6
	Being adjustment of temporary entry made on 8th April.			

UNLOCATED ERRORS.—In theory, a difference in a Trial Balance should be located before preparing the Trading and Profit and Loss Accounts and Balance Sheet, but in practice it is sometimes inconvenient to hold up the preparation of the final accounts pending the discovery of the error. The Trial Balance is therefore made to " balance " by the insertion of an item " Suspense Account (Difference in Books) ". For instance, where the debit side of a Trial Balance exceeds the credit side by £50, the Trial Balance (in skeleton form) would appear thus :—

TRIAL BALANCE : 31ST MARCH, 19.....

	Dr.	Cr.
	£	£
Sundry debit balances	10,570	
Sundry credit balances		10,520
Suspense Account (Difference in Books) .		50
	£10,570	£10,570

A Suspense Account will be opened in the General Ledger which must be credited with the difference of £50, but no double entry is made, as the credit entry is equal and opposite to the net difference caused by one or more errors either in writing up the books or in extracting the Trial Balance. When these errors are discovered, corrective entries must be made *both* in the account in which the error occurred *and* in the Suspense Account. Great care is needed in making these corrective entries. In respect of each item an entry must be made in the account concerned in order to correct it and then the double entry is completed by making an entry on the opposite side of the Suspense Account. In some cases a double entry is not necessary, *e.g.*, where the error is not due to an incorrect posting or addition, but where the book entries are correct and the error has arisen through copying a figure wrongly in the extraction of balances (see (3) below). When all the errors are discovered the Suspense Account balance will be eliminated.

If, on re-checking the books, the difference of £50 revealed by the above Trial Balance is found to be due to the following errors :—

(1) Sales Day Book overcast by £10;
(2) Purchase of goods from Appleton Bros., correctly entered in the Purchases Day Book as £130, but posted to their account in error as £100;
(3) Balance on Blenkinsopp and Son's account of £35 in the Sales Ledger extracted in error as £55;
(4) Discount allowed to Cantrell and Co., £5 debited to their account,

the necessary corrections should be journalized in the following manner :—

		Dr.	Cr.
		£	£
(1)	Sales Account. Dr. To Suspense Account. *Being correction of overcast of £10 in Sales* *Day Book. Folio —.*	10	10
(2)	Suspense Account. Dr. To Appleton Bros. *Being correction of error in crediting* *account of Appleton Bros. with £100 in place* *of £130 as per Purchases Day Book. Folio —.*	30	30
(3)	Suspense Account. Dr. *To Blenkinsopp & Sons.* *Being correction of error in extracting debit* *balance on account of Blenkinsopp & Sons* *as £55 in place of £35.* (*Note.*—As a double entry is not required, the unposted credit item may be recorded in red ink.)	20	20
(4)	Suspense Account. Dr. To Cantrell & Co. *Being correction of error in debiting account* *of Cantrell & Co. with £5 discount allowed.*	10	10

The explanation of the above entries is as follows :—

(1) The double entry is completed by debiting Sales Account with £10, thus offsetting the previous over-credit of £10 to that account.

(2) The double entry is completed by crediting Appleton Bros.' account in the Purchases Ledger with £30, thus correcting the item under-credited.

(3) Blenkinsopp and Sons' account in the Sales Ledger is already correct ; the error was made in taking out the Trial Balance, and the entry of £20 in the Suspense Account merely rectifies this.

(4) Discount of £5 has been debited to Cantrell & Co.'s account instead of being credited. The double entry of the item in the Suspense Account is a credit of £10 to Cantrell & Co.'s account, made up of (i) a credit of £5 to eliminate the incorrect debit entry and (ii) a credit of £5 to record the discount allowed to them.

The Suspense Account would appear as follows :—

SUSPENSE ACCOUNT

Dr.   Cr.

			£				£
To Appleton Bros.	(2)		30	By Difference in Books.			50
„ Blenkinsopp & Sons.	(3)		20	„ Sales A/c.	(1)		10
„ Cantrell & Co.	(4)		10				
			£60				£60

These rules only apply to those errors which affect the agreement of the Trial Balance. Errors of Commission and Errors of Principle (see page 145) are dealt with by means of a transfer between the accounts concerned and *not* through the Suspense Account, since there is no balancing entry to be eliminated in respect of these errors. If, for example, machinery purchased for £200 had been debited to Repairs Account, instead of to Machinery Account, the journal entry required to make the correction would be :—

	Dr.	Cr.
	£	£
Machinery Account. *Dr.*	200	
To Repairs Account.		200
Being correction of error made in posting purchase		
of machinery (C.B. fol. ......).		

When the Trading and Profit and Loss Accounts and Balance Sheet are prepared *before* the errors are discovered, the difference, which may be either a debit item or a credit item, is usually shown in the Balance Sheet as " Suspense Account (Difference in Books)." Some authorities, however, while agreeing that a credit balance should be shown on the liabilities side, advocate the writing off of any debit balance to the Profit and Loss Account. It must be emphasized, however, that every attempt should be made to locate a difference in a Trial Balance, as the opening of a Suspense Account is merely a temporary expedient, pending location of the actual error or errors.

Adjustments in Personal Accounts—Bad Debts.

In every business, however efficiently it may be conducted, it happens from time to time that the whole or a part of an amount due from a customer who has been granted credit proves to be

F

irrecoverable. This may possibly arise where repeated applications for payment have met with no response, or have finally been returned by the Post Office marked " Gone away," or where the debtor has become bankrupt or has made some composition or arrangement with his creditors.

Whatever the cause of the bad debt, the fact of its existence remains and requires to be dealt with in the books of account. Once an account is known to be irrecoverable, no time should be lost in writing off the balance, for while the balance of the account remains in the sales ledger it is regarded as a part of the realizable assets of the business, whereas it is in fact a loss. If bad debts are ignored the financial position of the trader, as shown by the books of account, cannot be said to be true and correct, as provision has not been made for a definite known loss.

The usual procedure is to close the personal account of the debtor by writing off the irrecoverable balance by a transfer to a Bad Debts Account, in which all bad debts are collected and transferred in total to the debit of Profit and Loss Account at the end of the trading period. An example of a journal entry of this nature is as follows :—

			£ s. d.	£ s. d.
19.....				
Dec. 31.	Bad Debts Account	Dr.	4 17 6	
	To H. Abel			4 17 6
	Being bad debt written off owing to			
	bankruptcy of customer.			

It occasionally happens that some portion, or even the whole, of an amount previously written off as irrecoverable is eventually paid by the debtor or by his trustee in bankruptcy. This may be the result of a payment by the trustee in bankruptcy of a debtor whose assets were not at first expected to realize anything. To take another example, it may be caused by a customer who moved away without leaving an address, subsequently communicating again with the trader and paying his old account with a view to obtaining a further supply of goods.

In such a case, there are two methods of making the necessary entries in the books. The most direct method is merely to enter the amount received on the debit side of the Cash Book and to credit Bad Debts Account, thereby reducing the total amount to be written off to Profit and Loss Account for the period.

From a theoretical point of view the alternative method is more correct, for it regards the writing off of the bad debt as being cancelled and the personal account as being re-opened to the extent of the amount paid. The whole balance of the account, or the proportion of it paid as the case may be, is written back from Bad Debts Account to the personal account of the debtor

(debit Customer's Account credit Bad Debts Account) and the cash received is posted in the ordinary way to the Customer's Account from the Cash Book. A further advantage of this method is that the debtor's account gives a complete record of what actually takes place in regard to the balance, whereas the first method does not give any entry in the personal account to record the subsequent payment.

The following example will clearly illustrate the method of treatment of bad debts in the books of account.

EXAMPLE

On 1st January, 19....., H. Small owes A. Bates the sum of £9 15s. 0d. in respect of goods supplied, and another debtor, T. N. Fish, owes £27 3s. 6d. Both accounts have been outstanding for some time, and requests for payment have met with no response. On 3rd March a letter to Small is returned by the postal authorities marked " Gone away," and it is decided to write off the balance of his account as a bad debt. On 10th June Fish becomes bankrupt and a first and final payment of 13s. 4d. in the £ is made by his trustee.

On 20th November, a letter is received from Small stating that he has removed to new premises, and enclosing a cheque in settlement of his account. Enter these transactions in the Journal, Cash Book and Ledger, and close the books on 31st December.

JOURNAL

19.....			£	s.	d.	£	s.	d.
Mar. 3	Bad Debts Account. *Dr.*		9	15	0			
	To H. Small.					9	15	0
	Being bad debt written off as customer cannot be traced.							
June 10	Bad Debts Account. *Dr.*		9	1	2			
	To T. N. Fish.					9	1	2
	Being bad debt written off, 6s. 8d. in the £ on £27 3s. 6d., Fish being adjudicated bankrupt, a first and final dividend of 13s. 4d. in the £ being received.							
Nov. 20	H. Small. *Dr.*		9	15	0			
	To Bad Debts Account.					9	15	0
	Being bad debt recovered.							
Dec. 31	Profit and Loss Account. *Dr.*		9	1	2			
	To Bad Debts Account.					9	1	2
	Being transfer of bad debts for the year ended 31st December, 19.....							

Dr.   CASH BOOK   *Cr.*

19.....			£ s. d.	19.....			£ s. d
June 10	To T. N. Fish (per trustee).		18 2 4	Dec. 31.	By Balance.	c/d	27 17 4
Nov. 20	,, H. Small.		9 15 0				
			£27 17 4				£27 17 4
Dec. 31	To Balance.	b/d	27 17 4				

Dr.   H. SMALL   *Cr.*

19.....			£ s. d.	19.....		£ s. d.
Jan. 1	To Balance.	b/d	9 15 0	Mar. 3.	By Bad Debts.	9 15 0
Nov. 20	To Bad Debts.		9 15 0	Nov. 20.	By Cash.	9 15 0

Dr.   T. N. FISH   *Cr.*

19.....			£ s. d.	19.....		£ s. d.
Jan. 1	To Balance.	b/d	27 3 6	June 10.	By Cash.	18 2 4
				,, ,,	,, Bad Debts.	9 1 2
			£27 3 6			£27 3 6

Dr.   BAD DEBTS ACCOUNT   *Cr.*

19.....		£ s. d.	19.....		£ s. d.
Mar. 3	To H. Small.	9 15 0	Nov. 20.	By H. Small.	9 15 0
June 10	,, T. N. Fish.	9 1 2	Dec. 31.	,, Profit and Loss Account.	9 1 2
		£18 16 2			£18 16 2

It will be noticed that the second of the two methods of dealing with the recovery of a bad debt has been adopted in the above example. If the first method is utilized the journal entry on 20th November would be omitted and the amount of £9 15s.

received from H. Small posted from the Cash Book direct to the credit of Bad Debts Account, the final transfer to Profit and Loss Account being the same as in the above example.

Provisions and Reserves.

In the past the terms "provisions" and "reserves" were regarded as synonymous, but it is now generally accepted that a clear distinction should be drawn between the term "provision" as represented by any amount written off or retained by way of providing for depreciation, renewals or diminution in value of assets, e.g., provisions for depreciation, or retained by way of providing for any known liability of which the amount cannot be determined with substantial accuracy, e.g., provisions for bad debts and discounts, and the term "reserve" as represented by amounts set aside out of undivided profits and other surpluses in order to strengthen the financial position of the business, but not designed to meet any liability or contingency known to exist at the date of the Balance Sheet.

Reserves, in the accepted sense of the term, are seldom met with in the accounts of a sole trader and are therefore outside the scope of the present work.

The adjustments in nominal accounts dealt with in the following paragraphs are in the nature of provisions, as they provide for a known expense which will fall due in the future, but they are more correctly regarded as merely adjustments of the accounts with a view to showing the actual income or expenditure appropriate to the current accounting period. On the other hand, when provision is made for losses which *may* arise in connection with the balances of debtors' accounts at the date of the Balance Sheet, the liability is only contingent, *i.e.*, the loss is *possible* but not *certain* and may, in fact, not arise at all.

Adjustments in Nominal Accounts.

The first step in the preparation of the final accounts at the end of the trading period is to close off the ledger accounts, bring down their balances, and prove the accuracy of the books by taking out a Trial Balance. When this has been done, and any errors brought to light by the Trial Balance have been rectified, it is almost invariably necessary to make some adjustments in the nominal accounts before the compilation of the Trading and Profit and Loss Accounts is commenced, in order that the latter accounts may disclose the true trading result.

The true profit for a trading period is that which is arrived at after the deduction of all expenses incurred during the period, whether they have actually been paid or not, and of all losses which relate to the period, whether they have actually arisen or

have only been estimated as being likely to arise. On the other hand, expenses paid but relating to a subsequent period, or payments for expenses relating to some prior period, must *not* be deducted.

Similarly, any income or gains must relate solely to the period in question, and not in whole or in part to an earlier or later period, and income in respect of the period which is due but has not been received should theoretically be included, although in practice it is sometimes considered prudent to ignore such unrealised income.

EXAMPLE

On 1st October, A. Bates paid his rates, £210, for the six months up to the 31st March following. At the 31st December, the consumption of electricity for the three months October to December, amounted to £15 7s. 6d., but no account had been received from the suppliers. The rent of £5 for part of his warehouse which he had sub-let was due at the 31st December for the past 6 months, but had not been received at 31st December. His profit for the year, before providing for the above, amounted to £1,830. State to what extent the profit for the year to 31st December would be affected by the foregoing items.

(*a*) RATES. A sum representing the rates for the three months January to March, in the *next* trading period, has been paid. Therefore an amount of £105 has been paid in advance and should not be charged to the current period, otherwise an excessive sum would be charged to Profit and Loss Account, thereby resulting in an under-statement of profit.

(*b*) LIGHTING. The item of £15 7s. 6d. relates to the current period, but as no account has been received, Profit and Loss Account will not have been debited with this amount. Therefore, the profits appear larger than they should, for *all* expenses relating to the period have not been deducted.

(*c*) RENT RECEIVABLE. The rent of £5 due to Bates is an item of income relating to the current period, and should therefore be taken into account before computing the net profit, in spite of the fact that it has not actually been received.

Thus the figure of £1,830 requires to be increased by £105 in respect of item (*a*), decreased by £15 7s. 6d. in respect of item (*b*), and increased by £5 in respect of item (*c*); therefore the true profit for the year ended 31st December amounts to £1,924 12s. 6d.

This example makes it evident that if only items actually received or paid are taken into account when preparing the Trading and Profit and Loss Accounts and no adjustments are made, a totally incorrect result will be obtained, and the *true* profit for the period may differ by a considerable amount from that shown in the books.

The items for which adjustments in nominal accounts are necessary may be classified as follows :—

    (1) Expenses paid during the period which relate to a subsequent period, *e.g.*, rates and insurance paid in advance ;

    (2) Expenses relating to the current period which have not been paid, *e.g.*, gas and electricity accounts ;

    (3) Income received during the period, which is actually applicable to a later period, *e.g.*, rents received in advance ; and

(4) Income which applies to the current period but has not yet been received, *e.g.*, interest and dividends accrued but not yet received.

It is also necessary to make provision at the end of the trading period for possible losses relating to the current period which may or may not arise. The adjustment in this case is, however, more in the nature of a provision against a possible outgoing, rather than an adjustment in respect of a known expense, and will be considered later in this present chapter.

Method of Making Adjustments.

There are two methods of recording the necessary adjustments in nominal accounts at the end of a trading period.

From the theoretical point of view the most complete method is probably to open special suspense accounts, headed according to the nature of the items, as, for instance, " Rates paid in Advance Account," " Outstanding Expenses Account," etc.

The actual procedure is to transfer to these suspense accounts amounts representing the adjustments under items (1) to (4) above, which correspond respectively to :—

(1) Responsibility for *payments made in advance ;*

(2) Amounts sufficient to pay *expenses due but not paid ;*

(3) The amount of any *income* which has been *received in advance* ; and

(4) Responsibility for *income due but not received.*

Thus, Rates Account, in the example on page 160, has been debited with £105 too much for the current period. Therefore an adjusting entry is made crediting Rates Account with £105 and debiting " Rates paid in Advance Account " with the same amount. The balance of Rates Account will then represent the actual amount of rates chargeable against the income of the current period, and this will be transferred in due course to Profit and Loss Account.

The Lighting Account has not been debited with an item £15 7s. 6d., which nevertheless relates to the current period and should be included as an expense. Thus it is necessary to debit Lighting Account with £15 7s. 6d., as if the expense had been paid, and credit Outstanding Expenses Account with the same amount. The balance of Lighting Account will then represent the actual and full amount of the charge in respect of lighting for the current trading period.

Rent Receivable Account has not been credited with an item of £5 which represents income applicable to the period and which ought, therefore, to be taken into account. The adjustment in this case is effected by crediting Rent Receivable Account with £5 and debiting Rent Receivable Outstanding Account with the

same amount ; the balance of the former will then represent the full amount of rent income for the whole trading period.

The journal entries in respect of the above adjustments would appear as follows :—

JOURNAL

19..... Dec. 31		£ s. d.	£ s. d.
Dec. 31	Rates Paid in Advance Account. *Dr.* To Rates Account. *Being portion of rates paid in advance for three months to 31st March, 19—.*	105 0 0	105 0 0
,, 31	Lighting Account. *Dr.* To Outstanding Expenses Account. *Being expense due but unpaid in respect of electricity for three months to date.*	15 7 6	15 7 6
,, 31	Rent Receivable Outstanding Account. *Dr.* To Rent Receivable Account. *Being income due but unpaid for rent receivable for six months to date.*	5 0 0	5 0 0

The Profit and Loss Account will now be correctly adjusted and its net balance will show the true profit or loss for the period.

The balances of the suspense accounts will be shown in the Balance Sheet, debit balances appearing as assets and credit balances as liabilities. This treatment may be explained by a further consideration of the above adjusting entries. The debit balance on Rates Paid in Advance Account represents an outlay paid before the expiration of the period to which it refers. Naturally this is an asset, for if the business were to be sold at the date of the Balance Sheet the seller would expect to receive an extra allowance as he had paid something that, strictly speaking, refers to the period subsequent to the date of the sale of the business. Similarly, Rent Receivable Outstanding Account is an asset, since it may be regarded as representing a debt due to the business.

Conversely, the balance of Outstanding Expenses Account represents a liability in the shape of an amount owing for a benefit received that has not yet been paid for.

At the commencement of the next trading period, the journal entries are reversed, the balances of the Suspense Accounts being transferred back to the respective income or expense accounts.

When cash is received or paid in respect of the adjustments, the posting of the cash items to the nominal accounts will result in the automatic adjustment of the latter accounts. Thus, the Lighting Account will be credited with £15 7s. 6d., transferred back from the suspense account ; when the bill is paid, cash will be credited and Lighting Account debited with the same amount,

and the nominal account will therefore be "cleared" of items relating to the previous period. The Rates Account will be debited with £105 from the suspense account. As this represents an expense correctly applicable to the new period, the matter is in order, for the position is then the same as if the £105 had not been paid at all until 1st January in the new period, when it would have been debited to Rates Account. Rent Receivable Account will be debited from the suspense account with £5, which will be "cancelled" when the cash is actually received in the new period and credited to the same account.

There is an alternative method of dealing with the re-adjustment of expenses due but not paid and income due but not received. By this method the balances of the Suspense Accounts are not transferred back to the respective nominal accounts, the cash receipts or payments being credited or debited respectively to the former accounts instead of to the latter. Thus the suspense accounts will be automatically closed when the amounts are settled by payment. For example, when the item of £15 7s. 6d. in respect of lighting is actually paid, cash would be credited and Outstanding Expenses Account debited, and the Lighting Account for the new period would not be affected. The reader is advised, however, to adopt the first method, as apportionments of payments and receipts between the two periods may arise in the case of the second method. For example, if A. Bates paid his electricity account half-yearly for the period October–March, the payment in March would represent £15 7s. 6d. for the three months to 31st December, which must be debited to Outstanding Expenses Account, and an amount in respect of the three months January–March, which would be debited to Lighting Account.

The Practical Method of Recording Adjustments.

Although the foregoing method of recording adjustments in nominal accounts is perhaps more correct from a strictly theoretical point of view, the method usually adopted in practice and the one which is recommended to the reader is explained in the following paragraphs.

The principle is the same in both cases, but the necessity for opening suspense accounts and making transfer entries through the journal is obviated in this alternative method. The nominal account for the current period is adjusted in exactly the same way as was shown by the journal entries given on page 162, but the contra entries are made lower down in the same account instead of in a suspense account, i.e., the adjusting entry is simply carried down like a balance on the account in which it is made.

The nominal account is thus, in effect, divided into two parts, one relating to the current period and one to the succeeding period.

Instead of a transfer being made from the " old period " nominal account to a suspense account, and next day back again to the " new period " nominal account, the transfer is made direct from the " old period " to the " new period " account. Thus, in the case of an outstanding expense, the adjusting entry is made on the debit side of the nominal account, and brought down on the credit side after the account has been ruled off. The converse applies to income due but not received on the date of the Balance Sheet.

It can easily be seen that the effect is exactly the same, but when preparing the Balance Sheet the student is warned of the danger of overlooking the balance brought down in the nominal account, which corresponds to the balance of the suspense account.

The ledger accounts for the example already used (see page 160) would appear as shown below, but for the sake of completeness it has been imagined that previous payments during the year were £315 for rates and £40 6s. 9d. for lighting, and receipts £5 for rent of warehouse.

Dr.   RATES ACCOUNT   *Cr.*

19.....			£	s.	d.	19.....			£	s.	d.
Jan.–						Dec. 31.	By Provision—	c/d			
Sept.	To Cash.		315	0	0		Rates paid for three months in advance				
Oct. 1	„ Cash.		210	0	0				105	0	0
							„ Profit and Loss Account		420	0	0
			£525	0	0						
Dec. 31	To Provision	b/d	105	0	0				£525	0	0

Dr.   LIGHTING ACCOUNT   *Cr.*

19.....			£	s.	d.	19.....			£	s.	d.
Jan.–						Dec. 31.	By Profit and Loss Account				
Sept.	To Cash.		40	6	9				55	14	3
Dec. 31	„ Provision— Expense accrued for three months to date	c/d	15	7	6						
			£55	14	3				£55	14	3
						Dec. 31.	By Provision.	b/d	15	7	6

Dr.   RENT RECEIVABLE ACCOUNT   Cr.

19.... Dec. 31	To Profit and Loss Account.		£ s. d. 10 0 0	19..... June 30. Dec. 31.	By Cash. „ Provi- sion— Rent accrued for six months to date	c/d	£ s. d. 5 0 0 5 0 0
			£10 0 0				£10 0 0
Dec. 31	To Provi- sion.	b/d	5 0 0				

These adjusting entries should strictly be passed through the journal, but in practice they are usually made direct in the ledger accounts concerned. For examination purposes you should be able to give the necessary entries in either journal or ledger form, according to the requirements of the question.

By this method the nominal accounts automatically re-adjust themselves in the new period. The cash payment for £15 7s. 6d. will be debited to Lighting Account and so balance the entry for " Provision " ; the cash for rent, when it is received, will be credited to Rent Receivable Account and thus " cancel " the debit balance at present shown in this account ; while Rates Account shows an opening debit balance for the new period, which represents the correct charge for this period.

The Balance Sheet would show the items as follows :—

BALANCE SHEET

As at 31st December, 19.....

Liabilities	£ s. d.	Assets	£ s. d.
Sundry Creditors :		Sundry Debtors :	
Expenses Outstanding.	15 7 6	Rent due.	5 0 0
		Rates paid in advance.	105 0 0

Under this second method of dealing with adjustments, the double entry in respect of the four classes of adjustments set out on page 161 may now be summarized as follows :—

(1) Expenses paid during the period which relate to a sub-
    sequent period : Credit Nominal Account and bring
    down as a debit balance, which appears as an asset
    (Expenses Paid in Advance) in the Balance Sheet.

(2) Expenses relating to the current period which have not been paid : Debit Nominal Account and bring down as a credit balance, which appears as a liability (Expenses Outstanding) in the Balance Sheet.

(3) Income received during the period which is applicable to a later period : Debit Nominal Account and bring down as a credit balance, which appears as a liability (Income Received in Advance) in the Balance Sheet.

(4) Income which applies to the current period but has not yet been received : Credit Nominal Account and bring down as a debit balance, which appears as an asset (Income Due but not Received) in the Balance Sheet.

It is frequently necessary to provide for several days' wages which have accrued due up to the date of the Balance Sheet but which will not actually be paid until the following pay day ; for advertising charges which have been paid in advance in order to secure "space" in certain media ; or for insurance premiums which partly relate to the next trading period. In each case the principle is similar and exactly the same procedure is followed as that set out above.

The reader should now experience no difficulty in dealing with the necessary adjustments to any particular nominal account at the end of the trading period.

Provisions for Discounts and Bad Debts.

In the same way as known losses and expenses applicable to the current period were provided for by adjustments before the preparation of the Trading and Profit and Loss Accounts was commenced, so provision must be made for possible loss in regard to debts due which arose during the current period, and for discounts receivable and payable. The underlying principle is to show in the Balance Sheet, as nearly as possible, the net amounts that will eventually be received from debtors and paid to creditors.

A provision of this nature is essential, as if a debt created during the current period should prove, during the succeeding period, to be irrecoverable, the loss should be borne by the current Profit and Loss Account, otherwise the debtors will be overstated in the Balance Sheet.

Similarly, debts, whether owing to or by the trader, which are shown as such in the books at the date of the Balance Sheet, will usually be settled during the ensuing period, and in most cases discount upon them will be given, or received, in return for prompt payment. The amount of this discount, in one case a loss, in

the other a gain, belongs to the *current* period and should be included accordingly.

The actual loss which will be sustained through bad debts relating to the current period cannot be ascertained exactly at the end of the trading period, nor can the actual amounts which will be received or given as discount. To overcome this difficulty the amount of loss or gain, as the case may be, is estimated by fixing it as being a certain percentage of the total debtors or total creditors, the actual percentage figure being fixed in accordance with past knowledge and experience.

Thus, if it is thought that 5 per cent. of the total debtors appearing in the books may possibly prove irrecoverable, a Provision for Bad Debts is created by crediting an account bearing that title with an amount equal to 5 per cent. of the total debtors, Profit and Loss Account being debited with the same figure. Similarly, a Provision for Discounts is created by debiting Profit and Loss Account with the estimated percentage of the total debtors which will represent the discount to be allowed, and crediting Profit and Loss Account with the estimated percentage of the total creditors for the discount receivable, the contra entries being made in the respective special Provisions for Discounts Accounts.

It should be mentioned that, in practice, it is first advisable to review the debtors' accounts very carefully and to write off as bad debts any which appear to be irrecoverable. The Provision for Bad Debts is then calculated on the remaining balance of total debtors. It is preferable, if there is any doubt about a debt, to allow for the loss by means of a provision rather than by actually writing the debt off, as this will then avoid subsequent adjustments if the debt is wholly or partly paid.

The procedure, as has been stated, is to debit Profit and Loss Account and credit a Provision for Bad Debts Account with the amount of the provision created. The latter, having a credit balance, should in theory appear on the Balance Sheet as a liability, but instead it is shown in practice as a deduction from the asset Sundry Debtors.

The Provision for Discounts on Debtors is created in a similar way, and also appears as a deduction from total debtors in the Balance Sheet. When provisions are made both for bad debts and for discounts, the former percentage should first be calculated and deducted from the total debtors, and the discount percentage should then be calculated on the *net* balance. This procedure is necessary because obviously there cannot be any need to make a provision for discount in respect of the debts which are regarded as being probably irrecoverable, discount being allowed only in cases of prompt payment.

The Provision for Discounts on Creditors is shown by a debit

balance in the account of that name, and appears on the Balance
Sheet as a deduction from the liability Sundry Creditors. It
should be noted that, in practice, it is usual to make provisions
for both discounts receivable and payable, and not merely for one
type of discount, although it is considered in some businesses that
it is imprudent to provide for discounts receivable on the grounds
that possible losses should be provided for but that possible gains
should not be anticipated.

Similarly to adjustments in nominal accounts, provisions for
bad debts and discounts should be recorded in the journal for
memorandum purposes, a detailed narration accompanying each
entry.

EXAMPLE

At 31st December, 19...., Bates's Discounts Account showed discounts allowed
to debtors and discounts received from creditors amounting to £410 and £221
respectively, while the amount of bad debts written off during the year was £198.
The total amount owing by Sundry Debtors at that date, after the bad debts
had been written off, was £10,400, whilst £7,600 was owing to Sundry Creditors.
Bates decided to make a provision for bad and doubtful debts of 5 per cent. on the
total debtors, and provisions of $2\frac{1}{2}$ per cent. for cash discounts on debtors and creditors. Write up the Bad Debts and Discounts Accounts and transfer the balances
to Profit and Loss Account; also show how the items " Sundry Debtors " and
" Sundry Creditors " would appear in the Balance Sheet on 31st December.

Dr.	BAD DEBTS ACCOUNT			*Cr.*
19.....		£	19.....	£
	To Sundries.	198	Dec. 31 By Profit and Loss Account.	198

Dr.	DISCOUNTS ACCOUNT			*Cr.*
19.....	To Discounts Allowed.	£ 410	19.....	By Discounts Received.	£ 221
Dec. 31	,, Profit and Loss Account.	221	Dec. 31	,, Profit and Loss Account.	410
		£631			£631

Dr.	PROVISION FOR BAD DEBTS			*Cr.*
			19.....	£
			Dec. 31 By Profit and Loss Account.	520

Dr.   PROVISION FOR DISCOUNTS ON DEBTORS   Cr.

			19..... Dec. 31	By Profit and Loss Account.	£ 247

Dr.   PROVISION FOR DISCOUNTS ON CREDITORS   Cr.

Dec. 31	To Profit and Loss Account.	£ 190			

Dr.   PROFIT AND LOSS ACCOUNT   Cr.

FOR THE YEAR ENDED 31st DECEMBER, 19....

19..... Dec. 31	To Bad Debts. „ Provision for Bad Debts. „ Discounts Allowed. „ Provision for Discounts Allowed.	£ 198 520 410 247	£ 718 657	19..... Dec.31	By Discounts Re- ceived. „ Provision for Discounts Received.	£ 221 190	£ 411

BALANCE SHEET

AS AT 31ST DECEMBER, 19.....

Liabilities.			Assets.		
Sundry Creditors. Less Provision for Discounts.	£ 7,600 190	£ 7,410	Sundry Debtors. Less Provision for Bad £ Debts. 520 Less Provision for Dis- counts. 247	£ 10,400 767	£ 9,633

The Provision for Bad Debts is arrived at by allowing 5% on the total debtors *i.e.*, £10,400, making £520. This is deducted from the total debtors, leaving a balance of £9,880 upon which the 2½% Provision for Discounts on debtors is calculated.

As an alternative to opening accounts in respect of the provisions for bad debts and discounts, the necessary adjustments could be made in the Bad Debts and Discount Accounts themselves and the provisions carried down as debit or credit balances to the following period. By this method the transfer to Profit and Loss Account would include both bad debts written off and the provision created against possible bad debts, or the discount actually received plus the provision created for discount receivable. The Bad Debts and Discount Accounts given above would then appear as follows :—

Dr.			BAD DEBTS ACCOUNT			Cr.
19.....			£	19.....		£
	To Sundries.		198	Dec. 31	By Profit and Loss	718
Dec. 31	„ Provision.	c/d	520		Account.	
			£718			£718
				Dec. 31	By Provision. b/d	520

Dr.			DISCOUNTS ALLOWED ACCOUNT			Cr.
19.....			£	19.....		£
	To Discounts			Dec. 31	By Profit and Loss	
	Allowed.		410		Account.	657
Dec. 31	„ Provision.	c/d	247			
			£657			£657
				Dec. 31	By Provision. b/d	247

Dr.			DISCOUNTS RECEIVED ACCOUNT			Cr.
19.....			£	19.....		£
Dec. 31	To Profit and Loss				By Discounts	
	Account.		411		Received.	221
				Dec. 31	„ Provision. c/d	190
			£411			£411
Dec. 31	To Provision.	b/d	190			

It should be noted that separate accounts may be kept for "Discounts Received" and "Discounts Allowed," or that, on the other hand, one account only may be kept and only the balance transferred to Profit and Loss Account, instead of the two amounts, as shown in the example above. It is preferable, however, to

distinguish between the two types of cash discounts in the final accounts.

Where the Provision for Bad Debts at the close of a financial period differs from that created at the end of the previous period, only the difference between the provisions will be transferred to Profit and Loss Account, being debited or credited thereto, according to whether the new provision is greater or smaller, respectively, than the old provision. The *new* provision will be deducted from Sundry Debtors in the Balance Sheet.

EXAMPLE

On 31st December, 1950, Sundry Debtors amounted to £10,400 and a Provision for Bad Debts of 5% thereon was created. On 31st December, 1951, it was necessary to increase the provision to 5% of £12,200, the amount of Sundry Debtors on that date. The Provision for Bad Debts Account would appear as follows :—

Dr.	PROVISION FOR BAD DEBTS ACCOUNT						*Cr.*
1951			£	1951			£
Dec. 31	To Balance, 5% on £12,200.	c/d	610	Jan. 1	By Balance, 5% on £10,400.	b/d	520
				Dec. 31	„ Profit and Loss Account.		90
			£610				£610
				1952			
				Jan. 1	By Balance.	b/d	610

In the Balance Sheet on 31st December, 1951, the Provision for Bad Debts, £610, will be deducted from Sundry Debtors, £12,200.

DEPRECIATION

Depreciation may be defined as the gradual decrease in value of an asset due to wear and tear or effluxion of time.

It is difficult to think of any asset which is permanent and which does not become of less value each year, eventually requiring replacement. Buildings, factories, houses, all become less and less valuable with the passage of time as the result of use and of the destructive effects of the elements—wind, rain, frost, etc. Machinery wears away through constant employment and rusts away if it is kept unemployed and is neglected ; in addition to this, it tends to become obsolete or out of date in time, as new and improved machines are invented. Motor vehicles suffer severely from wear and tear.

If the books of account are to give an accurate representation of the true state of affairs and the true profit or loss for each year, some method must be found for recording therein the effects of this decrease in the value of the assets of the business.

It will be remembered that real accounts are opened in the ledger to record the assets owned by a trader. These accounts are debited at the outset with the cost price of the assets purchased and so presumably the amounts debited represent the actual values of the assets acquired at the time of purchase. If the balances on these asset accounts are to continue to represent the true value they should, strictly speaking, decrease each day at the same rate as the assets they represent fall in value.

Obviously it would be impossible in practice to record depreciation in the books each day or even each week, and in any event little benefit would be derived by doing so, for a really accurate statement of the position of the business is required only at the end of the trading period. The books will be sufficiently accurate for the purpose of any approximate statements which may be needed at intermediate stages, and if necessary the amount of depreciation to date can be readily calculated.

Depreciation, due to wear and tear or effluxion of time, is recorded in the books at the end of each trading period, and is, of course, an adjustment which requires to be dealt with before the Trading and Profit and Loss Accounts are prepared.

Depreciation and Fluctuation Contrasted.

Before describing the methods adopted to provide for depreciation in the books of account it will be as well to distinguish between *depreciation* and *fluctuation*.

Fluctuation refers to a variation in the market price of an asset. The prices of many articles, machines, etc., vary very considerably from time to time owing to market conditions, production in excess of supply, reduction in the costs of manufacture, etc. For instance, the price of an expensive machine may fall £100 within one week of the date of purchase. This is a case of fluctuation, and differs from depreciation in that it does not require to be recorded in the books of account as it does not affect the business in any way, since the asset is not held for immediate sale.

Depreciation is the decrease in the value of an asset *to the owner* of such asset, and is a definite loss to a business which ought to be taken into account in arriving at the profits of the concern for the period in which the loss is incurred. A machine which has been used for a year is one year less valuable to its owner and it is one year nearer to the time when it will have to be scrapped as useless. Thus, a loss (by way of depreciation) has occurred which requires to be written off the value of the asset, as represented by the balance of the asset account in the ledger.

On the other hand, in a case of fluctuation, the delivery van

the trader bought a week ago will in his opinion be of good service for a certain number of years. Each year its value to the trader will be less because its remaining period of usefulness will be correspondingly less. The value of the van to the business, however, will not be less merely because the market price has fallen £20 a week after the date of the purchase. A fall in price of this nature will not make the van any less useful, nor will it reduce its length of life. As far as the trader is concerned, variations in price are of no importance at the present time, and will not affect the amount of depreciation to be written off the value of the asset each year, apart from the fact that an amended scrap value may be obtained at the expiration of the life of the asset.

Obsolescence.

Fluctuation must again be distinguished from *obsolescence*. Obsolescence arises when an asset becomes obsolete, or out of date, because of the production of a similar article of a new and improved type which is able to perform the same work more efficiently, rapidly, or economically.

Thus, for example, a new type of box-making machine may be invented, which will turn out a far larger number of boxes in considerably less time and with less waste of material than was possible with the old model. The advantages are so considerable that it will pay the manufacturer to scrap his existing machine, although it may still be in sound working order, and to replace it by the new and improved model.

A trader is not compelled to replace an asset in this way, however, but if he does not make the change he may easily lose more eventually owing to the heavier running costs and smaller output of the old machine as compared with those of the improved machine than he would if he replaced his machine at once.

Obsolescence, therefore, differs from fluctuation, for there is in the former case a loss in the value of the asset to the trader, so that it is a form of depreciation which must be allowed for in the books. Furthermore, it differs from depreciation due to wear and tear or effluxion of time in that it is sudden and not gradual, and occurs at a certain point of time, when the improved type is first placed upon the market, and not over a period.

It follows, therefore, that the necessary adjustment in the books should be made as soon as the new type of machine is purchased instead of at the end of the trading period. Although obsolescence is, strictly speaking, a " capital " loss, it is usual to write off the book value of the scrapped machinery to Profit and Loss Account, either in one amount or sometimes in several amounts spread over the following two or three years. If the latter course is adopted, the loss on the realisation of the asset is transferred

to an Obsolescence Account, and the balance of this account not yet written off will appear on the assets side of the Balance Sheet, under some such title as " Obsolete Machinery—Balance not yet written off."

The Fixed Instalment System of Depreciation.

There are several methods of providing for depreciation in the trader's books, but the two simplest and the most generally used are those known as the " Fixed Instalment System " (or " Straight Line Method ") and the " Reducing Instalment System " (or " Reducing Balance Method ") respectively.

The Fixed Instalment System is one whereby a fixed amount is written off the book value of the asset each year so as to reduce it to its scrap value or entirely eliminate it, as the case may be, by the expiration of the period when the asset will cease to be useful.

This method involves a knowledge of :—

(1) The cost of the asset ;
(2) The estimated period during which the asset will give useful service ; and
(3) The estimated scrap value (if any) of the asset.

Thus the annual charge for depreciation is ascertained by deducting (3) from (1) and dividing the result by the number of years given in (2). For example, if a machine is bought for £1,000, and it is estimated that at the end of nine years it will cease to give useful service but that at the expiration of that period it will have a scrap value of £100, the annual charge for depreciation will amount to £100. The amount of £100 is ascertained by deducting the scrap value (£100) from the original book value (£1,000) and dividing the result by the number of years (9) it is estimated that the asset will be useful. It can easily be proved by simple calculation that if £100 is written off the value of the asset each year for nine years, the value at the end of that period will be given as £100, which is equal to the estimated scrap value of the asset.

Where an asset is not considered to have any scrap value the same rule holds good, the book value of the asset being divided by the number of years, and the resulting annual instalment charge will therefore reduce the book value of the asset to nil by the expiration of its estimated " life."

The amount of each annual instalment is debited to Profit and Loss Account and credited to the asset account, thus reducing the balance of the latter by the amount of the depreciation.

This method is very convenient for assets such as leases, which have a definite period of life, but it is not so useful for such assets

as plant and machinery which are constantly being changed by the disposal of worn-out items and the acquisition of new ones, for under this method every addition to an asset requires a separate computation of the depreciation applicable thereto. Certain authorities contend, however, that the Fixed Instalment System is the most suitable for general application to the majority of assets, as it spreads the provision for depreciation equally over the period of anticipated use of the assets.

EXAMPLE

On 1st January, 1947, a trader purchased a five years' lease of his shop premises for £1,050. On 31st March, 1951, he vacated the premises and sold the balance of the lease for £60. Assuming that depreciation is provided for by the Fixed Instalment System, and that the trading period is 1st January to 31st December, set out the journal entry, writing off the first year's depreciation, and show the Lease Account in the ledger for the five years.

JOURNAL

1947.			£ s. d.	£ s. d.
Dec. 31	Profit and Loss Account. Dr. To Lease Account. *Being depreciation for the year 1947* *written off, i.e., one-fifth of £1,050.*		210 0 0	210 0 0

Dr. **LEASE ACCOUNT** Cr.

1947.			£	1947.				£
Jan. 1	To Cash.		1,050	Dec. 31	By Profit and Loss Account.			210
				" "	" Balance.		c/d	840
			£1,050					£1,050
1947.				1948.				
Dec. 31	To Balance.	b/d	840	Dec. 31	By Profit and Loss Account.			210
				" "	" Balance.		c/d	630
			£840					£840
1948.				1949.				
Dec. 31	To Balance.	b/d	630	Dec. 31	By Profit and Loss Account.			210
				" "	" Balance.		c/d	420
			£630					£630
1949.				1950.				
Dec. 31	To Balance.	b/d	420	Dec. 31	By Profit and Loss Account.			210
				" "	" Balance.		c/d	210
			£420					£420
1950.				1951.				
Dec. 31	To Balance.	b/d	210	Mar. 31	By Cash			60
				" "	" Profit and Loss Account— Loss on Sale.			150
			£210					£210

The realisation of the lease before the end of the five years' term results in a loss on sale of £150, which is written off to Profit and Loss Account.

Reducing Instalment System.

This is similar in nature to the Fixed Instalment System, as a fixed *percentage* is adopted, but instead of the amount of the instalment being the same each year, the actual amount written off decreases year by year.

This is accounted for by the fact that under this system the fixed percentage is written off the *diminishing value* each year, and not off the *original cost* as in the case of the fixed instalment method.

It is, therefore, still necessary to know the cost (or present book value) of the asset, the estimated scrap value (if any), and the number of years the asset is expected to prove of utility to the business. A percentage figure is then calculated which will reduce the value of the asset to its approximate scrap value at the expiration of its life. The formula used in arriving at this percentage is by no means as simple as that used in the previous method, but the required percentage can be ascertained by reference to specially compiled depreciation tables.

The amount of depreciation written off decreases year by year, but as in the types of assets which are usually written down under this method, repairs tend to increase in later years, the total charge for depreciation *and* repairs tends to be more or less constant. But it should be remembered that depreciation and repairs are quite distinct factors in that the provision for repairs does not obviate depreciation, and that the yearly equality of the combined provision for depreciation and repairs may not materialize in actual practice.

The annual charge for depreciation is dealt with in the same way as in the system already described, Profit and Loss Account being debited and the asset account credited.

The Reducing Instalment System of providing for depreciation is that most frequently adopted in practice, particularly for plant and machinery, motor vehicles, etc., as a separate calculation need not be made in respect of each addition to the asset, although, as mentioned on page 175, certain authorities favour the Fixed Instalment System for plant and machinery and similar assets. The percentage rates vary considerably, from about 5 to 10 per cent. in the case of general plant and machinery to 20 to 25 per cent. for motor vehicles, but the actual rates used depend upon the nature of the business, the condition of the asset and its estimated life. When this method of depreciation is used the book value of the asset cannot be entirely eliminated.

It should be noted that the percentage is calculated on the balance of the asset account *at the beginning* of the current period, *not* at its close. This is because otherwise the full twelve months' charge for depreciation would be deducted from additions made during the period, which would obviously be incorrect. On the other hand, when the balance *at the beginning* of the period is taken it follows that additions to the asset during the year are not depreciated for the portion of the year from the date of their purchase to that of the Balance Sheet.

If the additions are considerable or occur early in the financial year, it is usual in practice to calculate an amount of depreciation upon their value based upon the length of the period from the date of their purchase to the end of the trading period. Thus, in the

EXAMPLE

Plant and Machinery to the value of £2,000 was purchased on 1st January, 1947. Further machinery to the value of £1,000 was purchased on 30th September, 1948. Depreciation is to be provided for by writing off 10 per cent. of the diminishing value each year, *i.e.*, under the Reducing Instalment System.

Show the journal entry to record the writing off of depreciation for the first year, and write up the Plant and Machinery Account for the five years ending 31st December, 1951.

Dr.   PLANT AND MACHINERY ACCOUNT   *Cr.*

1947.			£	s.	d.	1947.			£	s.	d.
Jan. 1	To Cash.		2,000	0	0	Dec. 31	By Profit and Loss Account.		200	0	0
						" "	" Balance.	*c/d*	1,800	0	0
		£	2,000	0	0			£	2,000	0	0
1947.						1948.					
Dec. 31	To Balance.	*b/d*	1,800	0	0	Dec. 31	By Profit and Loss Account.		180	0	0
1948.											
Sept. 30	" Cash.		1,000	0	0	" "	" Balance.	*c/d*	2,620	0	0
		£	2,800	0	0			£	2,800	0	0
1948.						1949.					
Dec. 31	To Balance.	*b/d*	2,620	0	0	Dec. 31	By Profit and Loss Account.		262	0	0
						" "	" Balance.	*c/d*	2,358	0	0
		£	2,620	0	0			£	2,620	0	0
1949.						1950.					
Dec. 31	To Balance.	*b/d*	2,358	0	0	Dec. 31	By Profit and Loss Account.		235	16	0
						" "	" Balance.	*c/d*	2,122	4	0
		£	2,358	0	0			£	2,358	0	0
1950.						1951.					
Dec. 31	To Balance.	*b/d*	2,122	4	0	Dec. 31	By Profit and Loss Account.		212	4	5
						" "	" Balance.	*c/d*	1,909	19	7
		£	2,122	4	0			£	2,122	4	0
1951.											
Dec. 31	To Balance.	*b/d*	1,909	19	7						

JOURNAL

1947.		£ s. d.	£ s. d.
Dec. 31	Profit and Loss Account. *Dr.*	200 0 0	
	To Plant and Machinery Account.		200 0 0
	Being depreciation for the year to date written off, viz., 10% on £2,000.		

example given on page 178, no depreciation has been allowed on the additional plant, value £1,000, purchased on 30th September, 1948. In practice £25 (*i.e.*, 10 per cent. on £1,000 for three months) might have been added to the amount charged for depreciation at the end of that particular year.

As between the two methods of providing for depreciation, it will be noted that a higher percentage must be used under the Reducing Instalment System in order to write down an asset to a required figure in a given number of years. Thus, in the above example, the book value of the original asset at the end of the third year is £1,458 (*i.e.* £2,000 less £200, £180 and £162), whereas if depreciation had been computed at the same rate under the Fixed Instalment System, the book value would have been reduced to £1,400 in the same length of time.

It is sometimes recommended that the items of depreciation credited to the various asset accounts should first be debited to a Depreciation Account, the balance of which is transferred to Profit and Loss Account in one amount. The items are generally so few in number, however, that the opening of a special account is hardly necessary, and the procedure is not recommended to the reader. In the Balance Sheet the usual practice is to show the asset, off which depreciation has been written, as follows :—

	£	£
Plant and Machinery.	2,000	
Less Depreciation at 10% . . .	200	
		1,800

The " Fixed " and the " Reducing " Instalment Systems of providing for depreciation are not by any means the only methods in use, but they are by far the most frequently adopted. Other systems are the " Sinking Fund," the " Endowment Insurance Policy," the " Re-Valuation," the " Annuity " and the " Depreciation Reserve " methods, a detailed description of which will be found in more advanced text-books.

EXERCISE 9

A. After the Trial Balance has been agreed, what matters require attention before the preparation of the Trading and Profit and Loss Accounts ?

B. Outline the method of making adjustments in personal and nominal accounts. Give an example of an adjustment in each kind of account.

C. (i) Define depreciation, and state why it is necessary to provide for depreciation.

(ii) Give a short description of the two chief methods of providing for depreciation.

D. State briefly why Provisions are necessary. Illustrate your answer by examples of the different types of provisions, showing the method of recording them in the accounts.

E. The ·Trial Balance of the books of a Retail Merchant, extracted as on 31st December, 19...., disclosed the fact that the total debits exceeded the total credits by £18 9s. 6d. This amount was treated as a Suspense Account in the Balance Sheet pending discovery of the error.

During the following month the following errors were discovered in the accounts of the preceding year :—H. Jones was debited instead of credited with 19s. 6d. for an allowance made to him. The sales for the month of December were under-added by £36. A claim of £10 for damaged goods had been allowed to R. Smith, and credited to his account, no other entry having been made. The amount due to George Dickson & Co., £140 4s. 8d., had been extracted as £144 8s. 0d. Discount received from W. Robinson (£5 6s. 2d.) had been entered in the Cash Book and posted to Discounts Account, but had not been posted to any personal account.

Show the entries that would be necessary to correct the above errors, assuming that the necessary adjustments were made on 31st January, 19.....

F. A wholesale merchant buys 20 motor lorries at a total cost of £15,000. He estimates the working life of the lorries at six years, and that their scrap value at the expiration of that period will amount to £1,500.

(i) Write up the Lorry Account for the whole period, depreciation being calculated at 15% under the Fixed Instalment System.

(ii) Write up the Lorry Account for the whole period, depreciation being calculated at 33⅓% under the Reducing Instalment System. State what adjustment is necessary in this case during the last year to reduce the asset account to its scrap value of £1,500 at the end of six years.

G. On 1st January, 19...., a firm's books showed a Provision for Discounts on Debtors of £85 17s. 6d. During the year the discounts allowed amounted to £79 10s. 6d. At the end of the year the debtors amounted to £2,425, and a new provision of 2½% is to be made. Make the necessary journal entry, and show the Discounts Account in the ledger.

H. The stock of a trader on 31st December, 19...., was valued at £1,050. Before preparing the Balance Sheet the following adjustments were made :—
Provision for Bad Debts, £15 ; Depreciation of Machinery, 7½% on £4,500 ; £17 10s. for Wages due ; £19 10s. for Rent paid in advance ; Provision

for Discounts, 5% on remaining debtors' balances (£1,750) and 2½%
on creditors' balances (£840). It was also decided, in view of the pros-
pects of a declining market, to create a provision of 10% on value of
stock. Show all ledger accounts affected by these adjustments, and
state to what extent the net profit will be affected.

J. The following Trial Balance was extracted from the books of L. Pirrie as on
31st December, 19.... :—

TRIAL BALANCE

	£	s.	d.	£	s.	d.
Capital Account				9,000	0	0
Drawings Account . . .	700	0	0			
Purchases	5,221	0	0			
Purchases Returns . . .				424	0	0
Sales				14,984	0	0
Sales Returns	182	0	0			
Stock, at 1st January, 19.... .	1,146	0	0			
Salaries	628	0	0			
Manufacturing Wages . .	3,856	0	0			
Leasehold Factory . . .	2,500	0	0			
Rent, Rates and Insurance .	694	0	0			
Carriage Inwards . . .	231	0	0			
Carriage Outwards . . .	324	0	0			
Office Expenses . . .	228	0	0			
Factory Expenses . . .	724	0	0			
Plant and Machinery . .	2,400	0	0			
Provision for Bad Debts, at 1st January				324	0	0
Factory Fuel	759	0	0			
Discount Account (Balance) .				18	0	0
Bills Receivable . . .	160	0	0			
Sundry Debtors . . .	3,897	0	0			
Sundry Creditors . . .				1,698	0	0
Cash at Bank . . .	1,240	0	0			
Cash in hand . . .	221	0	0			
Office Furniture . . .	350	0	0			
Travellers' Salaries and Commission	987	0	0			
	£26,448	0	0	£26,448	0	0

Before preparing the accounts the following adjustments are necessary :—
1. Depreciation is to be written off as follows :—Plant and Machinery,
10% ; Office Furniture, 5%.
2. The Provision for Bad Debts is to be made up to £400.
3. The value of the stock, as on 31st December, 19...., was £1,429.
4. Three days' wages (amounting to £57) had accrued due, but had not
been paid on 31st December, 19.....
5. Unexpired insurances, amounting to £68, are to be carried forward to
next year.
Make the necessary adjustments and show in full the ledger accounts as
adjusted. Prepare Trading and Profit and Loss Accounts for the year
ended 31st December, 19...., and Balance Sheet as at that date.

CHAPTER X

THE TRADING ACCOUNT, PROFIT AND LOSS ACCOUNT, AND BALANCE SHEET

After the ledger accounts have been closed off, the Trial Balance taken out and agreed, and all the necessary adjustments and provisions have been made, the work of compiling the Trading and Profit and Loss Accounts may be proceeded with.

The main object of these accounts is to ascertain the financial result of a trader's business operations during the period covered by the particular accounts.

Apart from the stock *at the end* of the period and the adjustments and provisions described in the previous chapter, the whole of the information required for the preparation of the Trading and Profit and Loss Accounts and of the Balance Sheet is to be found in the Trial Balance. In fact, as will be seen later, every ledger balance shown in the Trial Balance must appear once, and once only, in either the Trading and Profit and Loss Accounts *or* in the Balance Sheet. On the other hand, any adjustments, etc., made subsequent to the extraction and agreement of the Trial Balance will appear in the Trading and Profit and Loss Accounts *and* in the Balance Sheet.

The debit balances appearing in the Trial Balance represent either expenses, losses or assets, and will appear either on the debit side of the Trading and Profit and Loss Accounts or on the assets side of the Balance Sheet respectively. If the balance represents some value remaining to the business it can be regarded as an asset to be shown in the Balance Sheet. If not, then it is an expense or loss to be written off to the Trading and Profit and Loss Accounts.

On the other hand, credit balances will represent income and gains or liabilities, the former being credited to the Trading and Profit and Loss Accounts, the latter appearing on the liabilities side of the Balance Sheet. If a credit balance represents an obligation of the business (including the liability to the proprietors, which will include undistributed profits) its destination will be the Balance Sheet, whereas other credit balances must be credited to the Trading and Profit and Loss Accounts.

It is convenient at this stage to explain briefly the differences between capital and revenue receipts and expenditure.

182

Capital Receipts are those items which directly increase the cash balance and are debited in the Cash Book and credited to the particular asset account and not to the Profit and Loss Account, *e.g.*, the sale of fixed assets, the sum realized being debited to cash and credited to the asset account. A further example of a capital receipt is additional capital invested by the proprietor in the business, which would be debited to cash and credited to the capital account.

Revenue Receipts include all items of profit or gain, *e.g.*, gross profit on trading ; discounts, rents and commission received, interest, etc. All revenue receipts should be credited to either the Trading Account or the Profit and Loss Account.

Capital Expenditure consists of money expended in purchasing, constructing, equipping or permanently improving any kind of property which helps in the production of revenue. One asset (cash) is replaced by another, and Profit and Loss Account is not affected thereby. The purchase of land, buildings and machinery are examples of capital expenditure.

Revenue Expenditure consists of all money spent in maintaining the value of existing assets, such as repairs and replacements, all costs and expenses incurred in the production of saleable articles, such as raw materials and wages ; and also all expenses incidental to the working of the business, such as salaries, rent, etc. All items of revenue expenditure are shown in the Trading Account or Profit and Loss Account.

The Trading Account.

A Trading Account may be defined as one which is compiled with a view to ascertaining the result of a trader's transactions for the period under review, *i.e.*, whether he has made a gross profit or a gross loss on the goods which he buys and sells.

Gross profit may be defined as the excess of the selling price of an article (or series of articles) over the prime cost of production or purchase, *i.e.*, materials, wages and other direct expenses forming part of the cost of the goods sold. *Gross loss*, on the other hand, is the amount by which the prime cost of producing or purchasing one or more articles exceeds the price realized, and indicates that the goods are being sold below cost price.

The Trading Account is debited with all expenses or costs which vary directly with turnover. Factory wages, for example, vary according to the quantity of the goods manufactured ; the greater the output the higher the wages and *vice versa*. Rent, on the other hand, remains more or less stationary, and will not vary whether turnover increases or decreases.

The chief items usually shown in the Trading Account are, on the debit side :—

(1) The stock at the commencement of the period ;
(2) The total net purchases during the period, *i.e.*, the total gross purchases less the total returns outwards ;
(3) Productive wages (if any) ; and
(4) Any other expenses of production which vary directly with the turnover, *e.g.*, carriage inwards, manufacturing wages, manufacturing expenses, etc.

On the credit side are shown :—

(1) The total net sales (or turnover) for the period, *i.e.*, the total gross sales less the total returns inwards ; and
(2) The stock at the end of the period.

The transfers are made from the various nominal accounts by means of journal entries, as shown on page 46. The closing stock represents the value of all goods on hand unsold at the end of the period, and is ascertained by means of a carefully arranged stock-taking. The amount of the stock thus ascertained is debited to Stock Account and credited to Trading Account. As the entry of closing stock is made subsequent to the preparation of the Trial Balance, the debit balance on this account will require to be shown in the Balance Sheet, as shown on page 49.

A gross profit is represented by a *credit* balance and a gross loss by a *debit* balance on the Trading Account. The latter is naturally uncommon ; for a trader very rarely sells his goods, for any considerable period of time, at less than cost price. Where a loss is sustained, it is usually a *net* loss, which means that the goods were not sold at a price sufficiently high to cover *all* the expenses of production, distribution, etc.

A *pro forma* Trading Account is as follows :—

TRADING ACCOUNT

Dr.   FOR THE YEAR ENDED 31ST DECEMBER, 19.....   *Cr.*

	£ s. d.		£ s. d.
To Stock at 1st January, 19....		By Sales. £	
„ Purchases. £		*Less* Returns In-	
Less Returns Out-		wards.	
wards.		———	
„ Wages.		„ Stock at 31st Decem-	
„ Carriage Inwards.		ber, 19.....	
„ Balance, being Gross Profit			
transferred to Profit			
and Loss Account.			
	£		£

The Profit and Loss Account.

A Profit and Loss Account may be defined as one compiled with a view to ascertaining the *net profit*, or *net loss*, from the trading operations of the period covered by the account.

The term *net profit* indicates the excess of the total amount realized by the sale of goods, plus any incidental gains, over the total cost of manufacturing, purchasing, selling, maintenance and administration expenses for the period under review. In other words, the net profit represents the excess of the gross profit, plus any gains, over the various expenses and losses. A *net loss*, on the other hand, is the reverse of this, and arises when the total expenses or costs exceed the total gains or income. Thus a net loss may be said to be the excess of the expenses over the gross profit plus gains, or the excess of the gross loss plus the expenses over the gains.

The gross profit is transferred from the Trading Account to the credit, and a gross loss to the debit, of the Profit and Loss Account. The balances of all nominal accounts which have not already been closed by transfer to the Trading Account are then transferred, by means of journal entries, to the Profit and Loss Account.

Once it has been decided which items should be debited to the Trading Account, there is naturally no difficulty in dealing with the remaining items, as the balance of every nominal account must be transferred either to the Trading Account or to the Profit and Loss Account.

Thus the chief items shown in the Profit and Loss Account are, on the debit side :—

(1) The gross loss (if any).
(2) Establishment charges, *e.g.*, rent, rates, etc.
(3) Distribution expenses, *e.g.*, carriage outwards.
(4) Selling expenses, *e.g.*, travellers' salaries.
(5) Financial charges, *e.g.*, loan interest.

On the credit side are shown :—

(1) Gross profit (if any).
(2) Sundry gains and income, *e.g.*, discounts and interest received.

When all items have been dealt with, the Profit and Loss Account is closed off and the balance ascertained. If there is a *credit* balance a net profit has been made during the period, while a *debit* balance indicates that a net loss has been incurred. The balance is then transferred by means of a journal entry to the trader's Capital Account.

As the balance of the Capital Account is normally a credit, the transfer of a credit balance from the Profit and Loss Account, *i.e.*, a net profit, will increase the amount of the trader's capital, while the transfer of a debit balance from the Profit and Loss Account, *i.e.*, a net loss, will decrease it.

This is in accordance with the actual position, for if the business, regarded as distinct from its owner, has made a profit over the period, it owes this to its owner, and consequently its total indebtedness to the owner (indicated by the balance of Capital Account) is *increased*. On the contrary, if the business has made a loss, its indebtedness to its owner is correspondingly *reduced*, *i.e.*, the balance of Capital Account is less than it was prior to the ascertainment of the net loss.

There is no established order in which expenses should be set out in a Profit and Loss Account, but a sequence frequently adopted in practice and which is recommended for examination purposes is as follows :—

1. Charges common to all businesses, *e.g.*, office salaries, rent, rates, etc.
2. Charges common to all businesses of the particular class concerned, *e.g.*, travellers' salaries and commissions, etc.
3. Charges peculiar to the particular business, *e.g.*, staff bonuses.
4. Extraordinary expenses, *e.g.*, renewal charges, defalcations.
5. Finance charges, *e.g.*, loan interest.

The following is a specimen *pro forma* Profit and Loss Account :—

PROFIT AND LOSS ACCOUNT

Dr.   FOR THE YEAR ENDED 31ST DECEMBER, 19.....   *Cr.*

	£ s. d.		£ s. d.
To Office Salaries.		By Gross Profit transferred	
„ Rent and Rates.		from Trading Account.	
„ Insurance.		„ Discounts Received.	
„ Discounts Allowed.		„ Rent of Premises Sub-	
„ General Office Expenses.		let.	
„ Bad Debts.			
„ Provision for Bad Debts.			
„ Depreciation — Fixtures and Fittings.			
„ Balance, being Net Profit transferred to Capital Account.			
	£		£

It is not always an easy matter to decide whether an item of expense should be debited to the Trading Account or to the Profit and Loss Account and, of course, much depends upon the particular circumstances, so that it is impossible to lay down any hard and fast rule.

The main difference between a Trading Account and a Profit and Loss Account is that the former is concerned with the purchase or production of goods, whereas the latter is concerned with the distribution of goods. Thus the general rule that expenses which concern purchasing or production, and which vary directly with turnover, should be debited to the Trading Account will be found to be a fairly accurate guide. Carriage *inwards*, for example, is an item which varies directly with the amount of goods or raw materials purchased ; in other words, it is an addition to the cost price of the goods. Carriage *outwards*, on the other hand, concerns the distributive, not the productive or purchasing side of the business, and must therefore be debited to Profit and Loss Account.

Where two items are combined in one total, although one is a productive expense and the other a distributive expense, the total amount should be debited to Profit and Loss Account, and in fact this should be done in all cases of doubt. Thus, wages and salaries are sometimes given in one amount, and although the former usually applies to the Trading Account and the latter to the Profit and Loss Account, the combined figure would be debited to the latter account. Similarly, the item " Carriage " may appear in the Trial Balance, and although carriage inwards should appear in the Trading Account and carriage outwards in the Profit and Loss Account, the combined item of " Carriage " appears in the latter account.

Drawings of the proprietor should not appear in the Profit and Loss Account, but should be shown as a deduction from Capital Account in the Balance Sheet. Any goods withdrawn from the business by the trader for his personal use should be debited to his Capital Account and credited to Purchases Account (in preference to Sales Account) at cost price.

Opinions differ as to whether depreciation of plant and machinery and repairs to plant and machinery should be debited to Trading Account or Profit and Loss Account. It is considered that they are more correctly charged to Trading Account, for they are directly concerned in the production of goods which are to be sold but, for examination purposes, whichever method is adopted, a footnote should be added as to the alternative treatment.

To the credit of Profit and Loss Account should be placed such items of gain as interest received, discount received and similar items.

In practice, it is usual to show the Trading Account and the

G

Profit and Loss Account on one page of the ledger or on one sheet of paper, and to carry down the balance of the former to the latter. The whole is then headed :—

TRADING AND PROFIT AND LOSS ACCOUNTS
FOR THE YEAR ENDED 31ST DECEMBER, 19.....

Dr.   Cr.

The fact that the accounts are a record of the result of trading for a certain period ending on a specified date should always be included in the heading as shown above. It would *not* be correct to give the account as being " *at* 31*st December*, 19.....," for it does not represent a static position, but rather the result of a period's working, and the figures given in the account are those which have been collected day by day over the whole of the period.

Percentage Trading and Profit and Loss Accounts.

Percentages are frequently used in connection with Trading and Profit and Loss Accounts, and they afford a great advantage to the efficient trader who is not satisfied merely with making a profit but wishes to go further and ascertain the exact proportion of each item of income and expense to the whole.

There are several methods of using percentages for this purpose, the principal being :—

1. The percentage which each item of expense, etc., bears to the turnover ;
2. The percentage which each item bears to the cost price ; and
3. The percentage which each item bears to the gross profit.

The first method is the most satisfactory and convenient and that most frequently adopted in practice. The net sales figure is taken as the basis and each item is calculated as a percentage of this net figure. The percentage is obtained by multiplying each item by 100 and dividing the result by the total net sales.

The percentages arrived at may be useful for estimating purposes. They are not, however, primarily intended for use as the basis of estimates. The most useful end which percentages serve is probably that of enabling the trader to compare the figures thus arrived at with the corresponding figures of previous years. The advantage of this is apparent : it assists him in ascertaining which classes of expenses are increasing, in relation to the turnover, and which can, with economy, be reduced. The percentage of gross profit will also indicate whether the profits on the trading as a whole are sufficiently high ; and if not, whether the percentage could be increased by a greater turnover, or whether the prices charged should be increased. If this is impossible, in consequence of competition, then the question should be considered of decreasing the expenses, if possible, without detriment to the business as a whole.

EXAMPLE

From the following information prepare a Trading Account for the year ended 31st December, 19...., and show the percentage which each item bears to the turnover.

	£
Stock at beginning of year	8,750
Purchases	43,500
Sales	58,900
Wages	3,500
Returns Inwards	900
Returns Outwards	200
Stock at end of the year	11,550

TRADING ACCOUNT

Dr.   FOR THE YEAR ENDED 31ST DECEMBER, 19.....   *Cr.*

	£	%	£		£	%	£
To Stock.		15·09	8,750	By Sales.	58,900		
„ Purchases.	43,500			*Less* Re-			
Less Re-				turns.	900		
turns.	200					100·00	58,000
		74·65	43,300	„ Stock.		19·91	11,550
„ Wages.		6·03	3,500				
„ Balance, being							
Gross Profit.		24·14	14,000				
		119·91	£69,550			119·91	£69,550

When percentages are shown, however, it is usually preferable to adjust the closing stock on the debit side of the Trading Account in order to disclose the value and percentage of the *cost of the goods sold*. Thus the figures given in the previous example would appear as follows :—

TRADING ACCOUNT

Dr.   FOR THE YEAR ENDED 31ST DECEMBER, 19.....   *Cr.*

	%	£	£		%	£
To Cost of Goods				By Sales, *less*		
Sold :—				Returns.	100·00	58,000
Opening Stock.		8,750				
Purchases, *less*						
Returns.		43,300				
		52,050				
Less :						
Closing Stock.		11,550				
	69·83		40,500			
„ Wages.	6·03		3,500			
„ Balance, being						
Gross Profit.	24·14		14,000			
	100·00		£58,000		100·00	£58,000

Percentages may be utilized in a similar manner in connection with the Profit and Loss Account, the percentage of gross profit to turnover being brought down as the commencing item on the credit side.

THE BALANCE SHEET

When the Trading and Profit and Loss Accounts have been compiled, and the net profit or loss transferred to the Capital Account of the trader, there remains only one more step, and that is the drafting of a Balance Sheet.

It has been shown earlier in this chapter that all items of gain or loss, income or expense which relate to the current period, are gathered together and the net result is placed to the credit (or the debit) of the trader's personal account with the business. It follows, therefore, that all balances which partake of the nature of profit or loss have been disposed of, as far as the current period is concerned, and thus there remain only those balances which represent the possessions of the business and amounts owing to it, and the liabilities or debts owing by the business.

Thus, the only accounts open in the ledger will consist of :—

DEBIT BALANCES.	CREDIT BALANCES.
Personal Accounts, *i.e.*, Sundry Debtors. Real Accounts, *i.e.*, property, goods and cash. Adjustments, *i.e.*, expenses paid in advance, or income due but not received.	Personal Accounts, *i.e.*, Sundry Creditors. Provision Accounts, *i.e.*, expenses owing but not paid, or provision for possible bad debts, etc. Capital Account, *i.e.*, the amount owing by the business to the proprietor.

The *debit* balances represent *assets*, *i.e.*, possessions and debts owing to the business, while the *credit* balances represent *liabilities*, *i.e.*, debts owing by the business. In this sense Capital Account represents a liability, for it records a debt the business owes to the owner.

A Balance Sheet may be defined as a list of the assets and the liabilities of a business, arranged in a classified and orderly manner, so as to show the exact financial position of the business at the date to which the accounts are made up.

Form of the Balance Sheet.

A Balance Sheet is not an account, and does not form part of the general book-keeping system. It is a list of the balances of the ledger accounts, and is thus similar in nature to a Trial Balance, except that it is made *after* profits and losses have been dealt with, and also that it shows the balances in a carefully arranged form, not in the order in which they appear in the ledger, as in the case of the Trial Balance.

It is customary in England to show the liabilities on the left-hand side of the Balance Sheet and the assets on the right-hand side, a dividing line being ruled down the centre. The abbreviations *Dr.* or *Cr.*, and the prefixes *To* or *By* are not applicable to a Balance Sheet; the two sides being headed " Liabilities " and " Assets " respectively. Certain authorities contend, however, that the use of general headings for a Balance Sheet, such as " Liabilities " and " Assets," is unappropriate and unnecessary, but it is suggested that such headings should be retained at this stage of your study of the subject.

It should be noticed that, unlike the Trading and Profit and Loss Accounts, a Balance Sheet does not relate to a *period* of time but to one specified point of time. It shows the position of the business *at a particular date*. This difference is reflected in the heading of the Balance Sheet, for instead of being headed " *For the year ended* 31*st December*, 19....," it will appear as,

BALANCE SHEET

As at 31st December, 19.....

The Function of the Balance Sheet.

It must not be assumed from the above that because a Balance Sheet resembles a Trial Balance, every ledger account balance must be shown separately in the Balance Sheet. In a business of any size, this would be practically impossible, and in any case it would entirely defeat the main purpose of the Balance Sheet, which is to disclose the financial position of the business in a clear and concise statement.

It might almost be said that the object of a Balance Sheet is to give any interested person a " bird's-eye view " of the position of the business as a whole. For this purpose it is obviously both inconvenient and unnecessary for the balance of the account of every debtor and every creditor to be shown separately, and thus only the total of each class is given, under the title of " Sundry Debtors " and " Sundry Creditors " respectively.

Similarly, where separate Stock Accounts are kept for various kinds or classes of goods, it is sufficient if the balances are com-

bined and shown on the Balance Sheet in one amount as being the value of all stocks on hand at that particular date.

It will be realized that as the Balance Sheet consists of a list of all the debit and credit balances in the books, the two sides must exactly balance, provided there are no clerical errors in posting or in compiling the Trading and Profit and Loss Accounts.

It has already been explained that the balance of the Capital Account equals the difference between the total assets and the total liabilities of the business, for that is the amount which the business owes to the proprietor.

When the books are first opened the Capital Account is credited with the net amount which the owner advances to the business, and this figure must always equal the total possessions and debts receivable of the business less any debts payable.

The balance of the Capital Account is adjusted periodically to bring it into accord with the exact amount owing by the business to the owner (after the amount of the trader's drawings have been debited), by being credited with the net profit or debited with the net loss at the end of each trading period. Thus the credit balance of this account indicates the net worth of the business, *i.e.*, the amount by which it is *solvent*, as represented by the excess of assets over liabilities. If, on the other hand, the Capital Account shows a debit balance, the business is then *insolvent*, the deficiency being represented by the excess of the liabilities over the assets.

Thus the Balance Sheet shows the total assets and the total liabilities of the business and the difference between the two totals as represented by the balance of the Capital Account.

Assets and their Valuation.

Assets may conveniently be divided into the following main classes, *viz.* :—

1. FIXED ASSETS.
2. CURRENT ASSETS.
3. FICTITIOUS ASSETS.

FIXED ASSETS are those which are of a more or less permanent nature and are acquired for the purpose of enabling the trader to carry on his business.

Thus the factory to house the machines and the workpeople, the warehouse to store the finished goods, the plant and machinery to produce the commodities which are to be sold, the motor lorries to distribute the goods, are all examples of fixed assets. Assets of this nature are essential for the purposes of production and

they are kept more or less permanently, *i.e.*, they are not constantly bought and sold with a view to profit.

The fixed assets of the tradesman are his shop (if he owns his business premises), the shop fittings, the office furniture, and the delivery vans or horses and carts. These again are of a permanent nature, and are used constantly in order to enable him to carry on his business.

Fixed assets are valued, for balance sheet purposes, at their cost price less an allowance for depreciation sufficient to reduce their book values to scrap value by the end of their working life. Fluctuations in the market value of fixed assets are not usually provided for, unless the asset has become obsolete, as the earning capacity of the assets is not affected by these outside fluctuations. The distinction between fluctuation, obsolescence and depreciation has already been fully dealt with in the preceding chapter.

CURRENT ASSETS (alternatively termed " Floating Assets ") are cash and those assets which are not kept as agents of production but which are held for the purpose of being subsequently converted into cash. Assets of this class are, therefore, not of a fixed or permanent nature, but are constantly changing in the course of production or trading.

Thus the manufacturer purchases raw materials in order to manufacture them into commodities and in this form to re-sell them. The trader purchases goods from the wholesaler in order to sell them again to the public at a profit. Stock-in-trade is, therefore, an excellent example of a current asset.

Book debts are also current assets, for it is the intention of the trader to convert them into cash as soon as it is convenient. Bills receivable are similarly current assets, as they represent a stage further in the conversion of book debts into cash.

The basis of valuation of current assets is cost price or market price, whichever is the lower at the date of the Balance Sheet. If the Balance Sheet is to give a correct view of the financial position of the business, it is essential that no item should be shown therein at a value higher than that which it is actually worth at that particular date.

In the case of fixed assets, there is no intention of re-sale, for they are purchased for permanent use, and it is accordingly sufficient if they are valued at cost price and an adequate amount is written off in respect of depreciation each year.

Current assets, on the other hand, are acquired with the definite intention of re-sale, usually in the near future, and it is therefore important, as indicated above, that they should appear at a figure which is not in excess of the realizable value at the date of the Balance Sheet.

In the case of stock-in-trade, for example, if the market price

of goods has fallen below the price which they cost when they were bought, it is prudent to value them at the current market price, for the difference between these two prices is a possible loss which applies to the current period and should be provided for accordingly.   On the other hand, if the price has risen, it is not prudent to allow for a possible *gain*, for this may not materialize in the end, and the lower price, *i.e.*, the cost price, should be taken as the basis of valuation.   This basis of valuation is in accordance with the fundamental rule that anticipated losses should always be provided for as far as possible, while anticipated profits should be ignored until actually realized.

The valuation of book debts has already been dealt with in Chapter IX, and it will be recollected that the same principle was followed in regard to this type of current asset.   All debts which were estimated to be valueless were written off as irrecoverable while a provision was made for debts which were of doubtful value.   Thus the danger of giving too optimistic a view of the position in the Balance Sheet was avoided, and all possible losses were provided for.

It may be mentioned here that the difference between fixed and current assets is by no means as clearly defined as one might think at first sight.   The general distinction has been given above, but it is not possible to divide assets into these two classes with any degree of certainty, for much depends upon the individual circumstances of each business.

For example, the motor delivery van has been given as an example of a fixed asset, and in the majority of cases this is true, for it is an asset used permanently in the trader's business.   To the motor dealer who sold the van to the trader, however, the van was a current asset, but it was part of his stock-in-trade which was purchased, not to assist in carrying on the business, but in order to be re-sold.

Thus the same article was a fixed asset to one class of business and a current asset to another.   It will be found, however, that the true distinction in any particular case can always be made by applying carefully the definitions of each class of asset which have already been given.

Investments are usually valued, like stock-in-trade, at cost price or market price, whichever is the lower, although in this case ordinary day to day market fluctuations may be ignored. Where, however, investments are held more or less permanently they may be regarded as fixed assets and valued accordingly.   In any case it is usual to indicate the market price of the investments in the Balance Sheet.

FICTITIOUS ASSETS.—This term arises by reason of the fact that all debit balances that cannot be taken to the Trading and

Profit and Loss Accounts must be shown on the assets side of the Balance Sheet, although some of these balances may represent expenditure which, whilst of value to the business, has no separate realizable value. For example, it will be remembered that a provision for expenditure paid in advance results in a debit balance which must appear on the assets side of the Balance Sheet. Such expenditure cannot be regarded as a realizable asset of the business and is therefore a fictitious asset.

Assets may also be divided into :—

TANGIBLE.—Assets which can be handled, *e.g.*, cash, stock, plant.

INTANGIBLE.—Invisible assets, *e.g.*, goodwill, patent rights.

Order of Assets on Balance Sheet.

It is now necessary to consider the order in which the assets will be arranged in the Balance Sheet, for it is obvious that there must be some well-defined arrangement of the assets in order that the Balance Sheet may properly fulfil its functions.

If the various items are not given in any reasonable sequence, it is not possible for any one who is not actually acquainted with the business to obtain a clear idea of the financial position of the business. It should be remembered that the main purpose for which a Balance Sheet is usually studied by business men is in order to ascertain the net worth of the business, the realizability of the assets, the ratio of current assets to current liabilities, etc.

Thus, in order that the Balance Sheet may readily convey the desired information, the assets are arranged in a definite sequence dependent upon their order of realizability. There are two methods in practical use, one in which the most *permanent* assets are given first and the other in which the most *realizable* assets appear first.

There is no need to go into the relative merits of the two methods here. It is sufficient to point out that the former method is adopted by the great majority of commercial businesses and is the one that should be adopted by the reader; the latter method is used chiefly by banks and investment houses in order to give prominence to the liquid position of the concern.

In accordance with the general practice, the assets will appear in the following order :—

(1) Goodwill.
(2) Freehold Land and Buildings.
(3) Leasehold Land and Buildings.
(4) Plant and Machinery.
(5) Fittings and Fixtures.
(6) Stock.

(7) Sundry Debtors :
    (a) On Ledger Accounts.
    (b) On Bills Receivable.
(8) Cash at Bank :
    (a) On Deposit Account.
    (b) On Current Account.
(9) Office Cash and Petty Cash.
(10) Fictitious Assets and Adjustments.

Goodwill may be defined as " the probability that old customers will resort to the old place." That is, it is the value which the business has acquired in the course of time through having formed a " connection " amongst possible customers. A business which has been trading successfully for ten years will obviously be worth more, in case of sale as a going concern, than a business whose material assets are of equal value but which has not long been established. The difference between the two prices may be said to be attributed to the increased value of the goodwill of the older business.

Obviously so intangible an asset as goodwill is very unrealizable, for it would not be worth much in the case of a forced sale and it can be disposed of only in the event of the business being sold as a going concern. Thus, as it is the most unrealizable form of asset, it is shown as the first item.

Freehold land and buildings are shown as the next item as they are more permanent than leasehold property, while the latter is followed by the remaining fixed assets, which, owing to their nature, are less permanent than land and buildings. Then come the current assets, which, as their definition implies, are much less permanent than the aforementioned fixed assets.

Sundry debtors are less permanent, or more liquid, than stock, as the latter must be sold before it can become a " book-debt." Similarly, cash is shown after the debtors as it is the most liquid form of asset. Naturally, the fictitious items are given last, as they partake least of all of the true nature of assets.

It should be noted that it is customary to show the amount of depreciation written off any asset as a deduction from the value of such asset at the commencement of the trading period, the net amount then being extended into the money column. Also, additions to plant, buildings, etc., are usually shown separately as such, instead of one amount only being given for the particular asset.

Provisions for bad debts and for discounts on debtors should be shown as deductions from the gross figure of sundry debtors, the net amount being extended. It is also customary to distinguish between bills receivable and debtors' ledger balances, and

similarly between cash at bank on deposit account and on current account.

Nature and Order of Liabilities.

The arrangement of liabilities in the Balance Sheet presents little difficulty, for there are seldom more than two or three items to be considered in the case of a sole trader. The usual method adopted is to show the liabilities in the order in which they rank for payment.

The sundry creditors, consisting of the total of the creditors' ledger balances, are shown first on the liabilities side of the Balance Sheet, the provision for discounts, if any, being deducted, and the net amount extended into the money column.

The amount of the bills payable may be shown as a sub-division of sundry creditors, the combined total being extended.

Where there are any credit balances for adjustments, representing creditors for expenses which are due but have not yet been paid, they are usually shown together with, or immediately following, the item "Sundry Creditors."

The next item will consist of any loans made to the business by outside parties. For example, where a trader is in need of capital and obtains an advance from his banker in the form of a loan, his current account being kept in funds in the usual way, the debit balance of Cash at Bank Account, as shown in the cash book, will appear as an asset, while the amount of the loan or overdraft will appear as such on the liabilities side of the Balance Sheet.

The last item is the balance of Capital Account. Details of this are usually given on the Balance Sheet, the commencing balance being shown first, together with the amount of net profit earned during the period, less any drawings or net loss incurred during the period, the net amount being extended into the money column.

Thus, the liabilities will be arranged in the following order :—

      (1) Sundry Creditors :—
           (a) On Ledger Accounts.
           (b) On Bills Payable.
      (2) Creditors for Expenses.
      (3) Loans.
      (4) Capital Account.

The *working capital* of a business is represented by the excess of the current assets (*e.g.*, stock, sundry debtors, bills receivable, cash) over the external (or current) liabilities (*e.g.*, sundry creditors, bills payable).

Contingent Liabilities.

A contingent liability is one which may or may not arise at some future date. It is caused by some transaction, the result of which is not yet known, which is not *likely* to, but which *may* eventually, create a liability.

Thus, for example, when bills receivable are discounted with the bank, it has already been explained that, although for the present the trader ceases to have any direct interest in the bills and can pass entries to that effect through his books, it is nevertheless possible that he *may* become liable on these bills at some future date.

If the bills are not paid at maturity, the bank will have an immediate right of recourse against the trader, and his liability will then be revived.

Thus from the point of view of the trader, there is a contingent liability, for, although it is *unlikely* that the bills will not be paid, there is a *possible* liability which may or may not mature into an actual one.

In such cases a definite provision could be created, as is done with possible bad debts, but the method usually adopted in practice is to make a footnote on the Balance Sheet to the effect that the possibility of liability exists, as follows :—

"There is a contingent liability in respect of Bills
Receivable under discount amounting to £...."

It should be noted that where a memorandum note of this nature is made, no entries are required in the books in respect of the contingent liability.

Additional examples of contingent liabilities are law costs and possible damages in a court action in progress at the date of the Balance Sheet.

A further example of a contingent liability may arise where a trader purchases shares which are only partly paid up, as there is a contingent liability on him to pay up the balance if required. In this case, however, the shares should appear on the assets side of the Balance Sheet in such a way that the amount unpaid is apparent, *e.g.*, " 100 shares of £1 each in Traders, Ltd., 10s. 0d. paid up "; there is then no need for an explanatory footnote.

A Practical Example.

The reader should by this stage have gained a thorough knowledge of the method of preparing a trader's final accounts, so that no difficulty should be experienced in following the detailed example which will now be given.

It may be mentioned that in dealing with a Trial Balance, every item mentioned therein must appear *once*, either in the Trading Account or in the Profit and Loss Account or in the Balance Sheet. On the other hand, items referred to in footnotes, such as closing stock, depreciation, adjustments, provisions, etc., which do not at present appear in the accounts at all, will require to be entered both in the Trading or Profit and Loss Accounts *and* in the Balance Sheet.

EXAMPLE

The Trial Balance as set out below is extracted from the books of Arthur Lyons at 31st December, 19..... You are required to prepare Trading and Profit and Loss Accounts for the year ended 31st December, 19....., and a Balance Sheet as at that date.

TRIAL BALANCE

AS AT 31ST DECEMBER, 19.....

	Dr. £	Cr. £
Stock at 1st January	3,000	
Freehold Premises	2,000	
Bills Receivable	1,550	
Purchases	7,000	
Salaries	750	
Wages	1,100	
Sales		11,500
Furniture	250	
Discounts Allowed	680	
Discounts Received		395
Plant and Machinery	2,000	
Returns Inwards	80	
Rates and Taxes	160	
Insurance	100	
Sundry Debtors	3,200	
Carriage Inwards	162	
Bills Payable		510
Advertising	500	
General Office Expenses	640	
Sundry Creditors		2,800
Provision for Bad Debts		100
Returns Outwards		101
Cash at Bank	1,004	
Cash in Hand	30	
Drawings Account	200	
Capital Account		9,000
	£24,406	£24,406

Provide for depreciation on Freehold Premises at 2½ per cent., on Plant and Machinery at 10 per cent., and on Furniture and Fixtures at 10 per cent.   Increase the provision for bad debts to an amount equal to 5 per cent. on Sundry Debtors and make a provision of 2½ per cent. for discounts allowable, and a provision of 2½ per cent. on Sundry Creditors for discounts receivable.   Provide for £20 of Insurance as being premium paid in advance and £11 Rates due but not paid. The closing stock was valued at £3,000.

TRADING AND PROFIT AND LOSS ACCOUNTS

FOR THE YEAR ENDED 31ST DECEMBER, 19.....

Dr.   Cr.

	£		£	£
To Stock as at 1st Jan., 19.....	3,000	By Sales.	11,500	
£		Less Returns Inwards.	80	
,, Purchases. 7,000				11,420
Less Returns Outwards. 101		,, Stock as at 31st December, 19.....		3,000
	6,899			
,, Carriage Inwards.	162			
,, Wages.	1,100			
,, Depreciation of Plant and Machinery.	200			
,, Gross Profit c/d.	3,059			
	£14,420			£14,420
To Salaries.	750			
£		By Gross Profit b/d.		3,059
,, Rates and Taxes.[1] 160		,, Discounts Received.		395
Add amount due. 11		,, Provision for Discounts on Creditors.		70
	171			
,, Advertising.	500			
,, Insurance.[1] 100				
Less amount paid in advance. 20				
	80			
,, General Office Expenses.	640			
,, Discounts Allowed.	680			
,, Provision for Discounts on Debtors.	76			
,, Depreciation : £				
Freehold Premises. 50				
Furniture, etc. 25				
	75			
,, Provision for Bad Debts.	60			
,, Net Profit for Year transferred to Capital Account.	492			
	£3,524			£3,524

[1] In practice details of these adjustments would not be shown in the Profit and Loss Account, merely the net figures being extended, viz. :—Rates and Taxes, £171 ; Insurance, £80. For examination purposes, however, it is advisable to show full details as above.

NOTE.—The various provisions for outstanding expenses, etc., must not be collected under one heading in the Profit and Loss Account, but must be adjusted against the appropriate expense items, as in the above example.

BALANCE SHEET

AS AT 31ST DECEMBER, 19.....

Liabilities.		£	Assets.		£
Sundry Creditors :				£	
	£		Freehold Premises.	2,000	
On Trade Accounts.	2,800		Less Depreciation @		
Less Provision for			2½%.	50	
Discounts.	70				1,950
		2,730	Plant and Machinery.	2,000	
Bills Payable.		510	Less Depreciation @		
Sundry Creditor for Expenses.		11	10%.	200	
A. Lyons, Capital Account as at 1st Jan.,					1,800
19.....	9,000		Furniture and Fixtures.	250	
Add Net Profit for			Less Depreciation @		
Year.	492		10%.	25	
					225
	9,492		Stock on Hand.		3,000
Less Drawings.	200		Sundry Debtors :		
		9,292	On Trade Accounts.	3,200	
			Less Provision for Bad Debts.	160	
				3,040	
			Less Provision for Discounts.	76	
					2,964
			Bills Receivable.		1,550
			Cash at Bank.	1,004	
			Cash in hand.	30	
					1,034
			Insurance paid in advance.		20
		£12,543			£12,543

EXERCISE 10

A. With what objects are the Trading and Profit and Loss Accounts compiled ? Explain clearly how these accounts differ.

B. Explain briefly the nature of the items that are usually to be found in the Trading Account. Define the terms " gross profit " and " gross loss."

C. State briefly the items that are usually to be found in the Profit and Loss Account. How is the balance of this account treated ?

D. In what manner and for what reasons are percentages utilized in connection with Trading and Profit and Loss Accounts ?

E. Define a Balance Sheet. How is it compiled and what information does it give ?

F. How are Assets and Liabilities classified ? Explain the importance of distinguishing clearly between the different classifications.

G. From the following Trial Balance you are required to prepare Trading and Profit and Loss Accounts and a Balance Sheet.

TRIAL BALANCE, DECEMBER 31ST, 19.....

	£	£
Stock at the beginning of the year	224	
Purchases	742	
Sales		2,846
Creditors		249
Debtors	750	
Cash at Bank	587	
Salaries and Wages	649	
Office and Trade Expenses	201	
Rent and Rates	92	
Capital (G. McArthur)		800
Advertising Expenses	650	
	£3,895	£3,895

The Stock at the end of the year was valued at £304.

H. From the following Trial Balance taken from the books of Mark Middleton, a Merchant, prepare Trading and Profit and Loss Accounts for the half-year ended 30th June, 19...., and Balance Sheet as at that date :—

	£	£
Furniture and Fittings	500	
Interest		12
Stock, 1st January, 19.....	4,000	
Rates	600	
General Expenses	156	
Sundry Debtors and Creditors	3,685	170
Bills Receivable and Payable	685	100
Sales and Purchases	24,000	32,600
Returns Inwards and Outwards	300	1,000
Carriage Inwards	100	
Rent	1,500	
Insurance	75	
Discounts		96
Provision for Bad Debts		500
Travelling Expenses	131	
Audit Fee	52	
Printing and Stationery	97	
Drawings	925	
Advertising	102	
Salaries	2,240	
Capital Account, 1st January, 19...		6,195
Cash at Bank, Deposit Account	1,000	
Cash at Bank, Current Account	522	
Petty Cash Balance in Hand	3	
	£40,673	£40,673

The Stock on 30th June, 19...., was valued at £1,260. Depreciate Furniture and Fittings at 6%. Insurance unexpired—£15.

Indicate the percentage that (a) gross profit, and (b) net profit bear to the net turnover of the period.

J. From the following Trial Balance, taken from the books of Alfred Baker, a Merchant, on 31st December, 19...., prepare Trading and Profit and Loss Accounts for the year and Balance Sheet as at that date :—

	£	s.	d.	£	s.	d.
Capital Account				6,206	9	4
Opening Stock	8,560	0	0			
Discounts				35	1	4
Advertising	470	3	9			
Goodwill	950	0	0			
Provision for Bad Debts				180	0	0
Bills Payable				120	0	0
Carriage Inwards	330	0	0			
Returns Inwards	450	0	0			
Salaries	1,500	0	0			
National Insurance	31	2	6			
Income Tax	260	10	0			
Sales				36,000	0	0
Returns Outwards				190	0	0
Rent	75	0	0			
Purchases	26,270	0	0			
Bills Receivable	200	0	0			
Cash at Bank	666	1	9			
Cash in Hand	2	7	5			
Office Furniture	50	0	0			
Drawings Account	1,250	0	0			
Sundry Creditors				390	1	5
Rates	30	0	0			
Printing and Stationery	47	2	6			
Sundry Debtors	1,800	1	1			
General Expenses	136	13	1			
Insurance	42	10	0			
	£43,121	12	1	£43,121	12	1

The Closing Stock was valued at £3,980. The following adjustments are required :—

£25 Rent owing by Alfred Baker but not included in the accounts. Increase the Provision for Bad Debts to £250. Depreciate Office Furniture 7½%.

K. T. Johnson is in business as a Miller. The following Trial Balance was extracted from his books as on 31st December, 19.... :—

	£	s.	d.	£	s.	d.
Capital Account				25,000	0	0
Drawings Account	1,778	0	0			
H. Brown, Loan Account . . .				5,000	0	0
Purchases	26,220	0	0			
Purchases Returns				1,172	0	0
Sales				42,976	0	0
Sales Returns	84	0	0			
Freehold Mill	10,000	0	0			
Plant and Machinery (1st January) . .	8,740	0	0			
New Machinery Purchased . . .	1,296	0	0			
Motor Lorries	3,050	0	0			
Wages of Mill Hands	6,785	0	0			
Office Salaries	1,942	0	0			
Stock (1st January)	9,876	0	0			
Rates and Taxes (Mill, £172 ; Office, £19) .	191	0	0			
Sundry Debtors	12,860	0	0			
Sundry Creditors				5,112	0	0
Cash in Hand	276	0	0			
Bank Overdraft				5,000	0	0
Coal and Lighting (Mill)	398	0	0			
Office Expenses	321	0	0			
Travellers' Expenses and Commission . .	872	0	0			
Carriage Inwards	294	0	0			
Provision for Bad Debts (1st January) .				480	0	0
Discount Account (Balance) . . .				42	0	0
Bad Debts	384	0	0			
Cash Sales				1,296	0	0
Insurances	179	0	0			
Office Furniture	360	0	0			
Interest Account	172	0	0			
	£86,078	0	0	£86,078	0	0

You are required to prepare Trading and Profit and Loss Accounts for the year ended December 31st, 19...., and a Balance Sheet as at that date. In addition to the particulars given above, the following matters must be taken into consideration when preparing the above Accounts :—

(a) Depreciation is to be charged as follows :—Plant and Machinery (excluding the additions), 10% ; Motor Lorries, 20% ; Office Furniture, 5%.

(b) Make the Provision for Bad Debts up to £600.

(c) The Stock on hand, as on 31st December, 19...., was valued at £12,486.

(d) Unexpired insurance, as on 31st December, 19...., amounted to £38.

CHAPTER XI

THE ACCOUNTS OF A SOLE TRADER

In the preceding chapters the essential groundwork of the subject of book-keeping has been explained in detail. It is now proposed to consolidate the foregoing explanation by means of a complete example, showing the recording of the principal types of transactions in the various books of account. Thus the transactions of a sole trader will be shown as a whole, not merely by way of isolated examples of one type of transaction. The reader is emphatically advised to work through this example *in detail*, and to trace the double entry in respect of each transaction, as indicated by the reference folios.

In this connection it should be noted that folio references to the private ledger are denoted by the symbol " X " to distinguish them from references to the purchases ledger. Furthermore, in actual practice the various books of account would be continuous, but for simplicity it has been assumed in the case of the following example that a new set of books has been opened.

EXAMPLE

B. R. Tate is in business as a shirt and clothing manufacturer and on 1st December, 19...., his position is as follows :—

ASSETS :

Petty Cash, £20 ; Cash at Midland Bank : Current Account, £621 5s. 6d. ; Deposit Account, £1,000 ; Debtors :—A. M. Tyler, £150 ; B. T. Chatterton, £296 10s. 6d. ; R. Griffiths & Son, £102 ; N. L. Lawrence, £49 15s. 6d. ; S. Duncan & Co., £73 8s. 6d. ; Bills Receivable, £600 (N. L. Lawrence, £200, Hudson & Morton, £400) ; Stock in hand, £3,250 ; Motor Van, £150 ; Office Furniture, £200 ; Plant and Machinery, £1,500 ; Freehold Premises, £2,000.

LIABILITIES :

Sundry Creditors :—B. Hammond & Co., Ltd., £220 ; T. T. Smith, Ltd., £187 10s. ; H. N. Gregory, £305 10s. ; Bill Payable (T. T. Smith, Ltd.), £300.

Enter the following transactions in B. R. Tate's books of account. Close the books on 31st December and extract a Trial Balance as at that date, and prepare Trading and Profit and Loss Accounts for the month ending 31st December, 19...., and a Balance Sheet as at that date.

TRANSACTIONS

19.....

Dec. 1. Purchased from T. Lowe & Co., 100 pieces Skyteen Shirting @ 61s. per piece, less 5 per cent. trade discount.

„ „ Accepted B. Hammond & Co.'s draft for £220 at two months, payable at the Midland Bank.

„ „ Purchased, from Petty Cash : Ink, 10s. ; Envelopes, 9s. 6d. ; Soap, 2s.

„ 2. Paid Wages, £65, by cashing a cheque for this amount.

206

Dec. 2.   Sold to H. Hall & Co., 96 dozen Double Warp Flannelette Shirts @ 34s. 11d. per dozen.

,, ,,   Received from B. T. Chatterton, £250 on account, less 2½% cash discount.

,, 3.   Purchased from N. T. Supply Co., 24 pieces printed Repp @ 88s. 6d. per piece.

,, ,,   Paid H. N. Gregory £250 on account, less 2½% discount.

,, 5.   Paid N. L. Lawrence's bill receivable into bank for collection.

,, ,,   Sold to Norton & Son, 30 dozen heavy Union Shirts @ 50s. per dozen, and 50 dozen Overalls @ 10s. per dozen.

,, ,,   Drew upon them bill for £100 at 3 months.

,, ,,   Accepted N. T. Supply Co.'s bill for £106 4s. at 2 months.

,, 6.   Bank returned Lawrence's bill dishonoured. Notarial charges 3s. 6d.

,, ,,   Paid account of T. T. Smith, Ltd., less 2½% discount.

,, ,,   Paid from Petty Cash, Office Cleaning, £1 6s.; Postage Stamps, £3 10s.; Blotting Paper, 4s.

,, 7.   Discounted Norton & Son's acceptance with bank @ 5%.

,, ,,   Purchased from Box Supply Co., Ltd., 24 gross Cardboard Boxes @ 3s. 9d. per dozen.

,, ,,   Sold to H. & H. Harris, 12 dozen Cream Twill Tennis Shirts @ 37s. 6d. per dozen, less 5% trade discount.

,, 8.   N. L. Lawrence offered a cash payment of £100 and a new bill for £100 3s. 6d. at 3 months in place of the bill dishonoured. This offer was accepted.

,, ,,   Purchased 10 additional Stitching Machines @ £17 10s. each, and paid for them by cheque.

,, ,,   Received from H. Hall & Co., £100 on account, less 2½% discount.

,, 9.   Paid Wages, £65.

,, ,,   H. & H. Harris returned 8 Shirts as defective. Allowed them credit for full amount.

,, 10.   Sold to P. Featherstone, 20 dozen Handkerchiefs @ 5s. 3d. per dozen, and 12 dozen Washing Dresses @ 105s. per dozen.

,, ,,   Received £150, less 2½% discount, from A. M. Tyler.

,, ,,   Paid Carriage, £1 2s. 4d., from Petty Cash.

,, 12.   Sold to H. Hall & Co., 10 pieces Cream Twill @ 55s. per piece, and 20 pieces Longcloth @ 37s. 6d. per piece.

,, ,,   Drew cheque £50 for private purposes.

,, 13.   Bill payable (T. T. Smith, Ltd.) due this day, paid by Bank.

,, ,,   Received £102, less 2½% discount, by cheque from R. Griffiths & Son.

,, 14.   Purchased from H. N. Gregory, 60 gross Pearl Buttons @ 17s. 6d. per gross.

,, ,,   Paid T. Lowe & Co., £200 on account, less 2½% discount.

,, 16.   Paid Wages, £65.

,, ,,   Paid Insurance Premium, £30.

,, 17.   Sold to R. Hartley, 120 dozen boys' grey Flannelette Sports Shirts @ 12s. 6d. per dozen, and 60 dozen Bedford Cord Tunic Shirts @ 45s. per dozen.

,, ,,   Handed Hudson & Morton's bill to Bank for collection. This was duly paid.

,, 19.   Received cheque for balance of account from B. T. Chatterton.

,, ,,   Griffiths & Son's cheque returned by Bank dishonoured.

,, 20.   Paid, from Petty Cash: Office Cleaning, £1 6s.; Travelling Expenses, £3 5s. 6d.; Postage Stamps, £4 10s.

,, ,,   Paid £5 3s. 6d. for Repairs to Machinery.

,, 21.   Sold to A. M. Tyler, 18 dozen Grey Flannel Trousers @ 102s. 6d. per dozen, and 12 dozen Cream Tennis Trousers @ 181s. per dozen.

Dec. 21.   Griffiths & Son asked for cheque to be re-presented. Paid it into Bank again.

„   22.   Purchased from R. Fulwood & Son, 5 dozen reels Sewing Cotton @ 8s. 6d. per reel.

„   „   Received cheque, £20 3s. 9d., from H. & H. Harris.

„   „   Paid Carriage, £2 3s. 3d., from Petty Cash.

„   23.   Paid Wages, £65.

„   „   Sold to P. Featherstone, 24 dozen Vests @ 51s. 6d. per dozen, and 20 dozen Check Aprons @ 11s. 6d. per dozen.

„   „   S. Duncan & Co. became bankrupt. First and final payment of 10s. in £ made by Trustee.

„   28.   Purchased from H. Austin, Ltd., 20 pieces 28-in. Union Shirting @ 41s. 5d. per piece, and 10 pieces Check Gingham @ 21s. 2d. per piece, less 5% trade discount.

„   „   P. Featherstone returned 1 dozen Aprons as not up to sample. Allowed him full invoice price.

„   „   Paid H. N. Gregory's account, less 2½% discount.

„   29.   Returned to H. Austin, Ltd., 2 pieces Check Gingham as defective.

„   „   Received cheque, £49 15s. 6d., from N. L. Lawrence.

„   30.   Purchased from Petty Cash, 3 reams Letter Heading, 15s., and 1 dozen Filing Folders, 12s. 6d.

„   „   Paid Wages, £23 ; Salaries, £60.

„   „   Received P. Featherstone's acceptance for £100 at 2 months, and cheque for balance of his account.

„   31.   Drew cheque for Petty Cash disbursements for month.

„   „   Paid Lighting Bill for month, £15 7s. 8d.

„   „   Paid H. Austin, Ltd., by cheque, £47 7s. 9d.

NOTES

(1) The Stock at 31st December was valued at £3,700.

(2) £28 of the Insurance premium paid relates to the following year.

(3) Provisions for Discount amounting to £14 in the case of Debtors and £4 in the case of Creditors are to be made.

(4) One month's Depreciation should be written off at the following rates : Freehold Premises, 5% ; Plant and Machinery, 10% ; Office Furniture, 10% ; Motor Van, 20% (all per annum).

In order to record the position of B. R. Tate as at the 1st December, 19....., the first step is to make the opening entries in the Journal. The Purchases and Sales Day Books, Returns Books, Bill Books, Petty Cash and Bank Cash Books should then be opened and the transactions recorded therein in detail. If the transactions are recorded methodically the result will be that every individual transaction will be recorded in one or other of the books of original entry (the Cash Book being included in this term).

The next step is to open the ledger accounts, and to post thereto the opening balances from the Journal. Then, if the entries in the subsidiary books are posted to the appropriate personal ledger accounts in detail, and to the respective impersonal accounts in total, the principle of double entry will be maintained without error. The arithmetical accuracy of the books must then be proved by balancing all ledger accounts which are not affected by the Trading and Profit and Loss Accounts, and taking out a complete Trial Balance of all the ledger accounts.

When the Trial Balance is found to agree, the necessary steps must be taken to provide for the adjustments required, and the balances of all nominal accounts must then be transferred (*via* the Journal) and the Trading and Profit and Loss Accounts prepared.

When the net profit, or net loss, has been ascertained and transferred to the Capital Account of the proprietor the Balance Sheet may be prepared. The agreement of the two sides of the Balance Sheet is further evidence of the accuracy of the book-keeping records.

JOURNAL

Folio 1.

			Dr.			Cr.		
			£	s.	d.	£	s.	d.
19.....								
Dec. 1	Sundries *Dr.*							
	To Sundries							
	Petty Cash.	PCB1	20	0	0			
	Cash at Bank, Current Account.	CB1	621	5	6			
	,, ,, Deposit Account.	X8	1,000	0	0			
	Sundry Debtors :							
	A. M. Tyler.	SL1	150	0	0			
	B. T. Chatterton.	,, 2	296	10	6			
	R. Griffiths & Son.	,, 3	102	0	0			
	N. L. Lawrence.	,, 4	49	15	6			
	S. Duncan & Co.	,, 5	73	8	6			
	Bills Receivable.	X9	600	0	0			
	Stock in hand.	,, 7	3,250	0	0			
	Motor Van.	,, 6	150	0	0			
	Office Furniture.	,, 5	200	0	0			
	Plant and Machinery.	,, 4	1,500	0	0			
	Freehold Premises.	,, 3	2,000	0	0			
	Sundry Creditors :							
	B. Hammond & Co., Ltd.	PL1				220	0	0
	T. T. Smith, Ltd.	,, 2				187	10	0
	H. N. Gregory.	,, 3				305	10	0
	Bills Payable.	X10				300	0	0
	Capital Account.	,, 1				9,000	0	0
	Being assets, liabilities and capital at this date.							
,, 8	Plant and Machinery. *Dr.*	X4	175	0	0			
	To Bank.	CB1				175	0	0
	Being purchase of 10 *Stitching machines @* £17 10s. *each.* (*Memo. entry only—see CB1.*)							
,, 23	Bad Debts Account. *Dr.*	NL7	36	14	3			
	To S. Duncan & Co.	SL5				36	14	3
	Being bad debt written off.							
		c/f £	10,224	14	3	£10,224	14	3

SALES DAY BOOK

Date.	Particulars.	S.L. Folio.	Details.	Invoice Total.
			£ s. d.	£ s. d.
19..... Dec. 2	H. Hall & Co. 96 dozen Double Warp Flannelette Shirts @ 34s. 11d. per dozen.	6	167 12 0	167 12 0
„ 5	Norton & Son. 30 dozen Heavy Union Shirts @ 50s. per dozen. 50 dozen Overalls @ 10s. per dozen.	7	75 0 0 25 0 0	100 0 0
„ 7	H. & H. Harris. 12 dozen Cream Twill Tennis Shirts @ 37s. 6d. per dozen. *Less* 5% Trade Discount.	8	22 10 0 1 2 6	21 7 6
„ 10	P. Featherstone. 20 dozen Handkerchiefs @ 5s. 3d. per dozen. 12 dozen Washing Dresses @ 105s. per dozen.	9	5 5 0 63 0 0	68 5 0
„ 12	H. Hall & Co. 10 pieces Cream Twill @ 55s. per piece. 20 pieces Longcloth @ 37s. 6d. per piece.	6	27 10 0 37 10 0	65 0 0
„ 17	R. Hartley. 120 dozen boys' Grey Flannelette Sports Shirts @ 12s. 6d. per dozen. 60 dozen Bedford Cord Tunic Shirts @ 45s. per dozen.	10	75 0 0 135 0 0	210 0 0
„ 21	A. M. Tyler. 18 dozen Grey Flannel Trousers @ 102s. 6d. per dozen. 12 dozen Cream Tennis Trousers @ 181s. per dozen.	1	92 5 0 108 12 0	200 17 0
„ 23	P. Featherstone. 24 dozen Vests @ 51s. 6d. per dozen. 20 dozen Check Aprons @ 11s. 6d. per dozen.	9	61 16 0 11 10 0	73 6 0
			£	906 7 6
				NL14

PURCHASES BOOK

Date.	Particulars.	P.L. Folio.	Details.			Invoice Total.		
			£	s.	d.	£	s.	d.
19..... Dec. 1	T. Lowe & Co. 100 pieces Skyteen Shirting @ 61s. per piece.		305	0	0			
	Less 5% Trade Discount.	4	15	5	0	289	15	0
,, 3	N.T. Supply Co. 24 pieces Printed Repp @ 88s. 6d. per piece.	5	106	4	0	106	4	0
,, 7	Box Supply Co. 24 gross Cardboard Boxes @ 3s. 9d. per dozen.	6	54	0	0	54	0	0
,, 14	H. N. Gregory. 60 gross Pearl Buttons @ 17s. 6d. per gross.	3	52	10	0	52	10	0
,, 22	R. Fulwood & Son. 5 dozen reels Sewing Cotton @ 8s. 6d. per reel.	7	25	10	0	25	10	0
,, 28	H. Austin, Ltd. 20 pieces 28-in. Union Shirting @ 41s. 5d. per piece.		41	8	4			
	10 pieces Check Gingham @ 21s. 2d. per piece.		10	11	8			
			52	0	0			
	Less 5% Trade Discount.	8	2	12	0	49	8	0
					£	577	7	0
						NL13		

RETURNS INWARDS BOOK

Date.	Particulars.	S.L. Folio.	Details.	Total.
19.....			£ s. d.	£ s. d.
Dec. 9	H. & H. Harris.			
	8 Cream Twill Tennis Shirts @ 37s. 6d. per dozen.		1 5 0	
	Less 5% Trade Discount.	8	1 3	
	Defective in manufacture.			1 3 9
„ 28	P. Featherstone.			
	1 dozen Check Aprons @ 11s. 6d. per doz.	9	11 6	
	Not up to sample.			11 6
			£	1 15 3
				NL16

RETURNS OUTWARDS BOOK

Date.	Particulars.	P.L. Folio.	Details.	Total.
19.....			£ s. d.	£ s. d.
Dec. 29	H. Austin, Ltd.			
	2 pieces Check Gingham @ 21s. 2d. per piece.		2 2 4	
	Less 5% Trade Discount.	8	2 1	
				2 0 3
	Defective in manufacture.			
			£	2 0 3
				NL15

BILLS RECEIVABLE BOOK

No. of Bill	Date Received	From Whom Received	Drawer	Acceptor	Where Payable	Date of Bill	Term	Due Date	S.L. Fo.	Amount of Bill	Disposal
	19.....									£ s. d.	
93	Dec. 5	Norton & Son.	Self	Norton & Son.	—	Dec. 5	3 mos.	Mar. 8	7	100 0 0	Discounted 7th Dec.
94	„ 8	N. L. Lawrence.	„	N. L. Lawrence.	—	„ 8	3 mos.	Mar. 11	4	100 0 0	
95	„ 30	P. Featherstone.	„	P. Featherstone.	—	„ 30	2 mos.	Mar. 2	9	100 3 6	
										£300 3 6	
										X9	

BILLS PAYABLE BOOK

No. of Bill	Date Accepted	Drawer	To Whom Payable	Where Payable	Date of Bill	Term	Due Date	P.L. Fo.	Amount of Bill	How dealt with
	19.....								£ s. d.	
102	Dec. 1	B. Hammond & Co.	B. Hammond & Co.	Midland Bank.	Dec. 1	2 mos.	Feb. 4	1	220 0 0	
103	„ 5	N.T. Supply Co.	N.T. Supply Co.	Midland Bank.	Dec. 5	2 mos.	Feb. 8	5	106 4 0	
									£326 4 0	
									X10	

BANK CASH BOOK

Dr.   RECEIPTS

Date.	Particulars.	Fo.	Discount.	Bank.
19....			£ s. d.	£ s. d.
Dec. 1	To Balance.	J1		621 5 6
,, 2	,, B. T. Chatterton.	SL2	6 5 0	243 15 0
,, 5	,, Bills Receivable.	X9		200 0 0
,, 7	,, Bills Receivable.	,,9		100 0 0
,, 8	,, N. L. Lawrence.	SL4		100 0 0
,, 8	,, H. Hall & Co.	,,6	2 10 0	97 10 0
,, 10	,, A. M. Tyler.	,,1	3 15 0	146 5 0
,, 13	,, R. Griffiths & Son.	,,3	2 11 0	99 9 0
,, 17	,, Bills Receivable.	X9		400 0 0
,, 19	,, B. T. Chatterton.	SL2		46 10 6
,, 21	,, R. Griffiths & Son.	,,3		99 9 0
,, 22	,, H. & H. Harris.	,,8		20 3 9
,, 23	,, S. Duncan & Co. (Trustee).	,,5		36 14 3
,, 29	,, N. L. Lawrence.	,,4		49 15 6
,, 30	,, P. Featherstone.	,,9		40 19 6
			£15 1 0	£2,301 17 0
			NL8	
Dec. 31	To Balance	b/d		288 7 3

PAYMENTS   *Cr.*

Date.	Particulars.	Fo.	Discount.	Bank.
19.....			£ s. d.	£ s. d.
Dec. 2	By Wages.	NL1		65 0 0
,, 3	,, H. N. Gregory.	PL3	6 5 0	243 15 0
,, 6	,, N. L. Lawrence (Dishonoured Bill).	SL4		200 0 0
,,	,, do. (Notarial Charges).	,,4		0 3 6
,,	,, T. T. Smith, Ltd.	PL2	4 13 9	182 16 3
,, 7	,, Bank Charges.	NL2		1 5 0
,, 8	,, Plant and Machinery.	X4		175 0 0
,, 9	,, Wages.	NL1		65 0 0
,, 12	,, Drawings.	X2		50 0 0
,, 13	,, Bills Payable.	,,10		300 0 0
,, 14	,, T. Lowe & Co.	PL4	5 0 0	195 0 0
,, 16	,, Wages.	NL1		65 0 0
,,	,, Insurance.	,,3		30 0 0
,, 19	,, R. Griffiths & Son (Cheque returned).	SL3		99 9 0
,, 20	,, Repairs.	NL4		5 3 6
,, 23	,, Wages.	,,1		65 0 0
,, 28	,, H. N. Gregory.	PL3	2 14 0	105 6 0
,, 30	,, Wages.	NL1		23 0 0
,, 31	,, Salaries.	,,5		60 0 0
,,	,, Petty Cash.	PCB		19 16 1
,,	,, Lighting.	NL6		15 7 8
,,	,, H. Austin, Ltd.	PL8		47 7 9
,,	,, Balance	c/d		288 7 3
			£18 12 9	£2,301 17 0
			NL9	

Dr.   PETTY CASH BOOK   **Cr.**

Amount Reed. £ s. d.	C.B. Folio.	Date.	Details.	Vou. No.	Total. £ s. d.	Stationery. £ s. d.	Travelling. £ s. d.	Cleaning. £ s. d.	Carriage. £ s. d.	Postages. £ s. d.	Led. Fol.	Ledger A/cs. £ s. d.
20 0 0	J1	19..... Dec. 1	To Balance.									
		„ 1	By Ink.	1	0 10 0	10 0						
			„ Envelopes.	2	0 9 6	9 6						
			„ Soap.	3	0 2 0			2 0				
		„ 6	„ Office Cleaning.	4	1 6 0			1 6 0				
			„ Postage Stamps.	5	3 10 0					3 10 0		
			„ Blotting Paper.	6	0 4 0	4 0						
			„ Carriage.	7	1 2 4				1 2 4			
		„ 10	„ Office Cleaning.	8	1 6 0			1 6 0				
		„ 20	„ Travelling Expenses.	9	3 5 6		3 5 6					
			„ Postage Stamps.	10	4 10 0					4 10 0		
			„ Carriage.	11	2 3 3				2 3 3			
		„ 22	„ Letter Heading.	12	0 15 0	15 0						
		„ 30	„ Filing Folders.	13	0 12 6	12 6						
					19 16 1	2 11 0	3 5 6	2 14 0	3 5 7	8 0 0		
19 16 1	CB1	„ 31	To Cash.			NL12	NL12	NL12	NL10	NL11		
		„ 31	By Balance c/d		20 0 0							
£39 16 1					£39 16 1							
20 0 0		Dec. 31	To Balance b/d									

Private Ledger.

Dr. CAPITAL ACCOUNT *Cr.*

19.....			£	s.	d.	19.....			£	s.	d.
Dec. 31	To Draw-					Dec. 1	By Balance.	J1	9,000	0	0
	ings.	J3	50	0	0	„ 31	„ Profit				
„ „	„ Balance.	c/d	9,274	10	9		and Loss				
							Account.	J3	324	10	9
			£9,324	10	9				£9,324	10	9
						Dec. 31	By Balance.	b/d	9,274	10	9

Dr. DRAWINGS ACCOUNT *Cr.*

19.....			£	s.	d.	19.....			£	s.	d.
Dec. 12	To Bank.	CB1	50	0	0	Dec. 31	By Capital Ac-				
							count.	J3	50	0	0

Dr. FREEHOLD PREMISES *Cr.*

19.....			£	s.	d.	19.....			£	s.	d.
Dec. 1	To Balance.	J1	2,000	0	0	Dec. 31	By Profit				
							and Loss				
							Account.	J3	8	6	8
						„ „	„ Balance.	c/d	1,991	13	4
			£2,000	0	0				£2,000	0	0
Dec. 31	To Balance.	b/d	1,991	13	4						

Dr. PLANT AND MACHINERY *Cr.*

19.....			£	s.	d.	19.....			£	s.	d.
Dec. 1	To Balance.	J1	1,500	0	0	Dec. 31	By Profit				
„ 8	„ Bank.	CB1	175	0	0		and Loss				
							Account.	J3	12	10	0
						„ „	„ Balance.	c/d	1,662	10	0
			£1,675	0	0				£1,675	0	0
Dec. 31	To Balance.	b/d	1,662	10	0						

Folio 5.

Dr.   OFFICE FURNITURE   Cr.

19.....			£ s. d.	19.....			£ s. d.
Dec. 1	To Balance.	J1	200 0 0	Dec. 31	By Profit and Loss Account.	J3	1 13 4
				,, ,, ,, Balance.	c/d	198 6 8
			£200 0 0				£200 0 0
Dec. 31	To Balance.	b/d	198 6 8				

Folio 6.

Dr.   MOTOR VAN   Cr.

19.....			£ s. d.	19.....			£ s. d.
Dec. 1	To Balance.	J1	150 0 0	Dec. 31	By Profit and Loss Account.	J3	2 10 0
				,, ,, ,, Balance.	c/d	147 10 0
			£150 0 0				£150 0 0
Dec. 31	To Balance.	b/d	147 10 0				

Folio 7.

Dr.   STOCK ACCOUNT   Cr.

19.....			£ s. d.	19.....			£ s. d.
Dec. 1	To Balance.	J1	3,250 0 0	Dec. 31	By Trading Account.	J2	3,250 0 0
Dec. 31	To Trading Account.	J2	3,700 0 0				

Folio 8.

Dr.   CASH ON DEPOSIT ACCOUNT   Cr.

19.....			£ s. d.				
Dec. 1	To Balance.	J1	1,000 0 0				

Folio 9.

Dr.   BILLS RECEIVABLE ACCOUNT   *Cr.*

19.....			£	s.	d.	19.....			£	s.	d.
Dec. 1	To Balance.	J1	600	0	0	Dec. 5	By Bank.	CB1	200	0	0
„ 31	„ Sundries.	BRB1	300	3	6	„ 7	„ do.	„	100	0	0
						„ 17	„ do.	„	400	0	0
						„ 31	„ Balance.	c/d	200	3	6
			£900	3	6				£900	3	6
Dec. 31	To Balance.	b/d	200	3	6						

Folio 10.

Dr.   BILLS PAYABLE ACCOUNT   *Cr.*

19.....			£	s.	d.	19.....			£	s.	d.
Dec. 13	To Bank.	CB1	300	0	0	Dec. 1	By Balance.	J1	300	0	0
„ 31	„ Balance.	c/d	326	4	0	„ 31	„ Sundries.	BPB1	326	4	0
			£626	4	0				£626	4	0
						Dec. 31	By Balance.	b/d	326	4	0

Sales Ledger.

Folio 1.

Dr.   A. M. TYLER   *Cr.*

19.....			£	s.	d.	19.....			£	s.	d.
Dec. 1	To Balance.	J1	150	0	0	Dec. 10	By Bank and				
„ 21	„ Sales.	SDB1	200	17	0		Discount.	CB1	150	0	0
						„ 31	„ Balance.	c/d	200	17	0
			£350	17	0				£350	17	0
Dec. 31	To Balance.	b/d	200	17	0						

Folio 2.

Dr.   B. T. CHATTERTON   *Cr.*

19.....			£	s.	d.	19.....			£	s.	d.
Dec. 1	To Balance.	J1	296	10	6	Dec. 2	By Bank and				
							Discount.	CB1	250	0	0
						„ 19	„ Bank.	„	46	10	6
			£296	10	6				£296	10	6

Folio 3.

Dr. R. GRIFFITHS & SON **Cr.**

19.....			£	s.	d.	19.....			£	s.	d.
Dec. 1	To Balance.	J1	102	0	0	Dec. 13	By Bank and				
„ 19	„ Bank						Discount.	CB1	102	0	0
	(Cheque					„ 21	„ Bank.	„	99	9	0
	Dishon-										
	oured).	CB1	99	9	0						
			£201	9	0				£201	9	0

Folio 4.

Dr. N. L. LAWRENCE **Cr.**

19.....			£	s.	d.	19.....			£	s.	d.
Dec. 1	To Balance.	J1	49	15	6	Dec. 8	By Bank.	CB1	100	0	0
„ 6	„ Bank					„ „	„ Bills Re-				
	(Bill Dis-						ceivable.	BRB1	100	3	6
	honoured).	CB1	200	0	0	„ 29	„ Bank.	CB1	49	15	6
„ „	„ do. (No-										
	tarial										
	Charges).	CB1		3	6						
			£249	19	0				£249	19	0

Folio 5.

Dr. S. DUNCAN & CO. **Cr.**

19.....			£	s.	d.	19.....			£	s.	d.
Dec. 1	To Balance.	J1	73	8	6	Dec. 23	By Bank (Trus-				
							tee).	CB1	36	14	3
						„ „	„ Bad Debts				
							Account.	J1	36	14	3
			£73	8	6				£73	8	6

Folio 6.

Dr. H. HALL & CO. **Cr.**

19.....			£	s.	d.	19.....			£	s.	d.
Dec. 2	To Sales.	SDB1	167	12	0	Dec. 8	By Bank and				
„ 12	„ do.	SDB1	65	0	0		Discount.	CB1	100	0	0
						„ 31	„ Balance.	c/d	132	12	0
			£232	12	0				£232	12	0
Dec. 31	To Balance.	b/d	132	12	0						

H

Folio 7.

Dr. NORTON & SON *Cr.*

19..... Dec. 5	To Sales.	SDB1	£	s.	d.	19..... Dec. 5	By Bills Receivable.	BRB1	£	s.	d.
			100	0	0				100	0	0

Folio 8.

Dr. H. & H. HARRIS *Cr.*

19..... Dec. 7	To Sales.	SDB1	£	s.	d.	19..... Dec. 9 „ 22	By Returns. „ Bank.	RIB1 CB1	£	s.	d.
			21	7	6				1 20	3 3	9 9
			£21	7	6				£21	7	6

Folio 9.

Dr. P. FEATHERSTONE *Cr.*

19..... Dec. 10 „ 23	To Sales. „ do.	SDB1 SDB1	£	s.	d.	19..... Dec. 28 „ 30 „ „	By Returns. „ Bills Receivable. „ Bank.	RIB1 BRB1 CB1	£	s.	d.
			68 73	5 6	0 0				100 40	11 0 19	6 0 6
			£141	11	0				£141	11	0

Folio 10.

Dr. R. HARTLEY *Cr.*

19..... Dec. 17	To Sales.	SDB1	£	s.	d.						
			210	0	0						

Purchases Ledger.

Folio 1.

Dr. B. HAMMOND & CO. *Cr.*

19..... Dec. 1	To Bills Payable.	BPB1	£	s.	d.	19..... Dec. 1	By Balance.	J1	£	s.	d.
			220	0	0				220	0	0

Folio 2.

Dr. T. T. SMITH, LTD. *Cr.*

19..... Dec. 6	To Bank and Discount.	CB1	£	s.	d.	19..... Dec. 1	By Balance.	J1	£	s.	d.
			187	10	0				187	10	0

Folio 3.

Dr.   H. N. GREGORY   Cr.

19.....			£	s.	d.	19.....			£	s.	d.
Dec. 3	To Bank and					Dec. 1	By Balance.	J1	305	10	0
	Discount.	CB1	250	0	0	„ 14	„ Purchases.	PB1	52	10	0
„ 28	„ do.	CB1	108	0	0						
			£358	0	0				£358	0	0

Folio 4.

Dr.   T. LOWE & CO.   Cr.

19.....			£	s.	d.	19.....			£	s.	d.
Dec. 14	To Bank and					Dec. 1	By Purchases.	PB1	289	15	0
	Discount.	CB1	200	0	0						
„ 31	„ Balance.	c/d	89	15	0						
			£289	15	0				£289	15	0
						Dec. 31	By Balance.	b/d	89	15	0

Folio 5.

Dr.   N.T. SUPPLY CO.   Cr.

19.....			£	s.	d.	19.....			£	s.	d.
Dec. 5	To Bills Pay-					Dec. 3	By Purchases.	PB1	106	4	0
	able.	BPB1	106	4	0						

Folio 6.

Dr.   BOX SUPPLY CO.   Cr.

						19.....			£	s.	d.
						Dec. 7	By Purchases.	PB1	54	0	0

Folio 7.

Dr.   R. FULWOOD & SON   Cr.

						19.....			£	s.	d.
						Dec. 22	By Purchases.	PB1	25	10	0

Folio 8.

Dr.　　　　　　　　　　H. AUSTIN, LTD.　　　　　　　　　*Cr.*

19.....			£	s.	d.	19.....			£	s.	d.
Dec. 29	To Returns.	ROB1	2	0	3	Dec. 28	By Purchases.	PB1	49	8	0
„ 31	„ Bank.	CB1	47	7	9						
			£49	8	0				£49	8	0

Nominal Ledger.

Folio 1.

Dr.　　　　　　　　　　WAGES ACCOUNT　　　　　　　　　*Cr.*

19.....			£	s.	d.	19.....			£	s.	d.
Dec. 2	To Bank.	CB1	65	0	0	Dec. 31	By Trading				
„ 9	„ do.	„	65	0	0		Account.	J2	283	0	0
„ 16	„ do.	„	65	0	0						
„ 23	„ do.	„	65	0	0						
„ 30	„ do.	„	23	0	0						
			£283	0	0				£283	0	0

Folio 2.

Dr.　　　　　　　　　　BANK CHARGES ACCOUNT　　　　　　　*Cr.*

19.....			£	s.	d.	19.....			£	s.	d.
Dec. 7	To Bank.	CB1	1	5	0	Dec. 31	By Profit and Loss Account.	J2	1	5	0

Folio 3.

Dr.　　　　　　　　　　INSURANCE ACCOUNT　　　　　　　　*Cr.*

19.....			£	s.	d.	19.....			£	s.	d.
Dec. 16	To Bank.	CB1	30	0	0	Dec. 31	By Provision.	c/d	28	0	0
						„ „	„ Profit and Loss Account.	J2	2	0	0
			£30	0	0				£30	0	0
Dec. 31	To Provision.	b/d	28	0	0						

Folio 4.

Dr.　　　　　　　　　　REPAIRS ACCOUNT　　　　　　　　　*Cr.*

19.....			£	s.	d.	19.....			£	s.	d.
Dec. 20	To Bank.	CB1	5	3	6	Dec. 31	By Profit and Loss Account.	J2	5	3	6

Folio 5.

Dr.   SALARIES ACCOUNT   Cr.

19.....			£	s.	d.	19.....			£	s.	d.
Dec. 30	To Bank.	CB1	60	0	0	Dec. 31	By Profit and Loss Account.	J2	60	0	0

Folio 6.

Dr.   LIGHTING ACCOUNT   Cr.

19.....			£	s.	d.	19.....			£	s.	d.
Dec. 31	To Bank.	CB1	15	7	8	Dec. 31	By Profit and Loss Account.	J2	15	7	8

Folio 7.

Dr.   BAD DEBTS ACCOUNT   Cr.

19.....			£	s.	d.	19.....			£	s.	d.
Dec. 23	To S. Duncan & Co.	J1	36	14	3	Dec. 31	By Profit and Loss Account.	J2	36	14	3

Folio 8.

Dr.   DISCOUNTS ALLOWED ACCOUNT   Cr.

19.....			£	s.	d.	19.....			£	s.	d.
Dec. 31	To Sundries.	CB1	15	1	0	Dec. 31	By Profit and Loss Account.	J2	29	1	0
,, ,,	,, Provision.	c/d	14	0	0						
			£29	1	0				£29	1	0
						19.....					
						Dec. 31	By Provision.	b/d	14	0	0

Folio 9.

Dr.   DISCOUNTS RECEIVED ACCOUNT   Cr.

19.....			£	s.	d.	19.....			£	s.	d.
Dec. 31	To Profit and Loss Account.	J2	22	12	9	Dec. 31	By Sundries.	CB1	18	12	9
						,, ,,	,, Provision.	c/d	4	0	0
			£22	12	9				£22	12	9
19.....											
Dec. 31	To Provision.	b/d	4	0	0						

Folio 10.

Dr.   CARRIAGE ACCOUNT   Cr.

19.....			£	s.	d.	19.....			£	s.	d.
Dec. 31	To Petty Cash.	PCB1	3	5	7	Dec. 31	By Profit and Loss Account.	J2	3	5	7

Folio 11.

Dr.   POSTAGES ACCOUNT   Cr.

19.....			£	s.	d.	19.....			£	s.	d.
Dec. 31	To Petty Cash.	PCB1	8	0	0	Dec. 31	By Profit and Loss Account.	J2	8	0	0

Folio 12.

Dr.   GENERAL EXPENSES   Cr.

19.....			£	s.	d.	19.....			£	s.	d.
Dec. 31	To Petty Cash : Stationery.	PCB1	2	11	0	Dec. 31	By Profit and Loss Account.	J2	8	10	6
	Travelling Expenses.		3	5	6						
	Cleaning.		2	14	0						
			£8	10	6				£8	10	6

Folio 13.

Dr.   PURCHASES ACCOUNT   Cr.

19.....			£	s.	d.	19.....			£	s.	d.
Dec. 31	To Sundries.	PB1	577	7	0	Dec. 31	By Trading Account.	J2	577	7	0

Folio 14.

Dr.   SALES ACCOUNT   Cr.

19.....			£	s.	d.	19.....			£	s.	d.
Dec. 31	To Trading Account.	J2	906	7	6	Dec. 31	By Sundries.	SDB1	906	7	6

Folio 15.

Dr. RETURNS OUTWARDS ACCOUNT Cr.

19.....			£	s.	d.	19.....			£	s.	d.
Dec. 31	To Trading Account.	J2	2	0	3	Dec. 31	By Sundries.	ROB1	2	0	3

Folio 16.

Dr. RETURNS INWARDS ACCOUNT Cr.

19.....			£	s.	d.	19.....			£	s.	d.
Dec. 31	To Sundries.	RIB1	1	15	3	Dec. 31	By Trading Account.	J2	1	15	3

TRIAL BALANCE
As at 31st December, 19....

Folio.		Dr. £	s.	d.	Cr. £	s.	d.
X1	Drawings.	50	0	0			
,, 2	Capital Account.				9,000	0	0
,, 3	Freehold Premises.	2,000	0	0			
,, 4	Plant and Machinery.	1,675	0	0			
,, 5	Office Furniture.	200	0	0			
,, 6	Motor Van.	150	0	0			
,, 7	Stock Account.	3,250	0	0			
,, 8	Cash on Deposit Account.	1,000	0	0			
,, 9	Bills Receivable.	200	3	6			
,, 10	Bills Payable.				326	4	0
SL1	A. M. Tyler.	200	17	0			
,, 6	H. Hall & Co.	132	12	0			
,, 10	R. Hartley.	210	0	0			
PL4	T. Lowe & Co.				89	15	0
,, 6	Box Supply Co.				54	0	0
,, 7	R. Fulwood & Son.				25	10	0
NL1	Wages.	283	0	0			
,, 2	Bank Charges.	1	5	0			
,, 3	Insurance.	30	0	0			
,, 4	Repairs.	5	3	6			
,, 5	Salaries.	60	0	0			
,, 6	Lighting.	15	7	8			
,, 7	Bad Debts.	36	14	3			
,, 8	Discounts Allowed.	15	1	0			
,, 9	Discounts Received.				18	12	9
,, 10	Carriage.	3	5	7			
,, 11	Postages.	8	0	0			
,, 12	General Expenses.	8	10	6			
,, 13	Purchases.	577	7	0			
,, 14	Sales.				906	7	6
,, 15	Returns Outwards.				2	0	3
,, 16	Returns Inwards.	1	15	3			
PCB1	Petty Cash.	20	0	0			
CB1	Cash at Bank (C/A).	288	7	3			
		£10,422	9	6	£10,422	9	6

JOURNAL (contd.)

Folio 2.

			Dr.			Cr.		
			£	s.	d.	£	s.	d.
19.....		b/f	10,224	14	3	10,224	14	3
Dec. 31	Trading Account. Dr.	—	4,112	2	3			
	To Sundries.							
	Stock Account.	X7				3,250	0	0
	Purchases.	NL13				577	7	0
	Wages.	,, 1				283	0	0
	Returns Inwards.	,, 16				1	51	3
	Being balances transferred.							
,, ,,	Sundries. Dr.	—						
	To Trading Account.					908	7	9
	Sales.	NL14	906	7	6			
	Returns Outwards.	,, 15	2	0	3			
	Being balances transferred.							
,, ,,	Stock Account. Dr.	X7	3,700	0	0			
	To Trading Account.	—				3,700	0	0
	Being value of stock at end of month.							
,, ,,	Trading Account. Dr.	—	496	5	6			
	To Profit and Loss Account.	—				496	5	6
	Being gross profit for month.							
,, ,,	Profit and Loss Account. Dr.	—	140	6	6			
	To Sundries.							
	Bank Charges.	NL2				1	5	0
	Insurance.	,, 3				2	0	0
	Repairs.	,, 4				5	3	6
	Salaries.	,, 5				60	0	0
	Lighting.	,, 6				15	7	8
	Bad Debts.	,, 7				36	14	3
	Carriage.	,, 10				3	5	7
	Postages.	,, 11				8	0	0
	General Expenses.	,, 12				8	10	6
	Being balances transferred.							
,, ,,	Profit and Loss Account. Dr.	—	29	1	0			
	To Discounts Allowed Account.	NL8				29	1	0
	Being balance transferred.							
,, ,,	Discounts Received Account. Dr.	NL9	22	12	9			
	To Profit and Loss Account.	—				22	12	9
	Being balance transferred.							
		c/f	£19,633	10	0	£19,633	10	0

JOURNAL (*contd.*)

			Dr.			Cr.		
19.....			£	s.	d.	£	s.	d.
		b/f	19,633	10	0	19,633	10	0
Dec. 31	Profit and Loss Account. Dr.	—	25	0	0			
	To Sundries.							
	Freehold Premises.	X3				8	6	8
	Plant and Machinery.	,, 4				12	10	0
	Office Furniture.	,, 5				1	13	4
	Motor Van.	,, 6				2	10	0
	Being depreciation for month, *viz. :—Freehold Premises,* 5%; *Plant and Machinery,* 10%; *Furniture,* 10%; *and Motor Van,* 20% (*all per annum*).							
,, ,,	Insurance prepaid. Dr.	NL3	28	0	0			
	To Insurance Account.	,, 3				28	0	0
	Being amount of insurance paid in advance.							
,, ,,	Profit and Loss Account. Dr.	—	324	10	9			
	To Capital Account.	X1				324	10	9
	Being net profit for month.							
,, ,,	Capital Account. Dr.	X1	50	0	0			
	To Drawings.	,, 2				50	0	0
	Being drawings for month transferred.							
			£20,061	0	9	£20,061	0	9

In actual practice the balances of the nominal accounts would probably be transferred direct to the Trading and Profit and Loss Accounts, without journal entries; the latter have here been set out in full in order that the student may obtain a clear idea of the double entry involved.

TRADING AND PROFIT AND LOSS ACCOUNTS

Dr.   FOR THE MONTH ENDED 31ST DECEMBER, 19.....   *Cr.*

	£ s. d.		£ s. d.
To Stock as at 1st December.	3,250 0 0	By Sales. 906 7 6	
£ s. d.		*Less* Returns. 1 15 3	904 12 3
,, Purchases. 577 7 0			
Less Returns. 2 0 3			
	575 6 9	,, Stock as at 31st December, 19.....	3,700 0 0
,, Wages.	283 0 0		
,, Gross Profit. c/d	496 5 6		
	£ 4,604 12 3		£ 4,604 12 3
To Bank Charges.	1 5 0	By Gross Profit. b/d	496 5 6
,, Insurance.	2 0 0	,, Discounts Received.	22 12 9
,, Repairs.	5 3 6		
,, Salaries.	60 0 0		
,, Lighting.	15 7 8		
,, Bad Debts.	36 14 3		
,, Carriage.	3 5 7		
,, Postages.	8 0 0		
,, General Expenses.	8 10 6		
,, Discounts Allowed.	29 1 0		
,, Depreciation.			
Freehold £ s. d.			
Premises. 8 6 8			
Plant. 12 10 0			
Office Furniture. 1 13 4			
Motor Van 2 10 0			
	25 0 0		
,, Net Profit for month transferred to Capital Account.	324 10 9		
	£518 18 3		£518 18 3

NOTE.—The above illustration shows the usual method of presentation but, in practice, ledger accounts would be prepared for both the Trading Account and the Profit and Loss Account for the purpose of showing the various transfers from the nominal accounts.

BALANCE SHEET

AS AT 31ST DECEMBER, 19.....

Liabilities.	£ s. d.	£ s. d.	£ s. d.	Assets.	£ s. d.	£ s. d.	£ s. d.
Sundry Creditors.	169 5 0			Freehold Premises	2,000 0 0		
Less Provision for				*Less* Depreciation.	8 6 8		
Discounts	4 0 0						1,991 13 4
		165 5 0		Plant and Machin-			
Bills Payable.		326 4 0		ery.	1,500 0 0		
B. R. Tate's Capital				*Add* Additions.	175 0 0		
Account as at 1st							
December. 19...	9,000 0 0				1,675 0 0		
Add Net Profit for				*Less* Depreciation.	12 10 0		
month.	324 10 9						1,662 10 0
				Office Furniture.	200 0 0		
	9,324 10 9			*Less* Depreciation.	1 13 4		
Less Drawings.	50 0 0						198 6 8
		9,274 10 9		Motor Van.	150 0 0		
				Less Depreciation.	2 10 0		
							147 10 0
				Stock in Hand.			3,700 0 0
				Sundry Debtors.	543 9 0		
				Less Provision for			
				Discounts.	14 0 0		
							529 9 0
				Bills Receivable.			200 3 6
				Cash on Deposit			
				Account.	1,000 0 0		
				Cash on Current			
				Account.	288 7 3		
				Cash in Hand.	20 0 0		
							1,308 7 3
				Insurance Prepaid.			28 0 0
	£	9,765 19 9			£	9,765 19 9	

EXERCISE 11

A. At the 30th November, 19...., my books showed the following balances : Bank (overdraft), £56; Goods on Hand, £1,500; Bills Receivable, £410; Bills Payable, £135. I owed R. Chambers £210, and A. Glover £54. N. Dickens owed me £300. My business premises were valued at £3,000.

All payments are made by cheque and all amounts received are paid into the bank upon receipt.

My transactions during December were as follows :—

19.....		£
Dec. 2.	R. Chambers bought goods	124
„ 7.	My acceptance fell due and was paid . . .	40
„ 10.	I discounted draft for £200, receiving cash . .	196
„ 16.	R. Horne bought goods	79
„ 18.	N. Dickens paid cash	100
	And was allowed discount	10
„ 20.	R. Horne returned goods (not according to sample)	25
„ 22.	Bought goods from A. Glover	209
„ 23.	Received acceptance from R. Horne for . .	54
„ 28.	Sundry Cash sales	270
„ 30.	Paid Salaries	20
„ 30.	Office Rent due, not paid	45

£

Dec. 31. Wrote off 10% of value of Business Premises as
depreciation.

„ 31. Examined my pass book and found I had been
charged interest on overdraft at the bank . . 2

„ 31. Stock of Goods on hand valued at . . . 1,450

Open the necessary accounts in the ledger as on 1st December, 19....,
and pass the transactions given through the proper subsidiary books to
the ledger. Balance the ledger accounts as on 31st December, 19...., and
extract a Trial Balance. Make out Trading and Profit and Loss Accounts
for the period and draw up a Balance Sheet as at 31st December, 19.....

B. On 1st May, 19...., W. Clark re-opened his books with the following balances,
in addition to his Capital Account :—

	£	s.	d.
Cash	18	10	6
Bank	297	14	9
C. Carr (*Dr.*)	115	3	3
T. Crone (*Cr.*)	163	17	0
Rent owing	25	0	0
Stock on hand	357	8	6

During the month his transactions were as follows :—

		£	s.	d.
May 3.	Paid rent by cheque	25	0	0
„ 5.	Bought of T. Crone :—			
	15 cwt. Canadian cheese at 11d. per lb.			
	4½ cwt. N.Z. butter at 1s. 5d. per lb.			
„ 7.	Received of C. Carr, cheque . . .	113	0	0
	Discount allowed him	2	3	3
„ 10.	Paid cheque into bank	113	0	0
„ 13.	Sold to C. Carr :—			
	9½ cwt. Canadian cheese at 1s. 2d. per lb.			
	3¾ cwt. N.Z. butter at 1s. 9d. per lb.			
„ 14.	Paid T. Crone's account to 1st inst. by cheque	160	0	0
	Discount received	3	17	0
„ 18.	C. Carr returned 56 lb. butter.			
„ 19.	Sold same for cash	1	10	0
„ 21.	Cash purchases to date . . .	6	13	9
„ 24.	Received from C. Carr, cheque on account			
	(banked)	80	0	0
„ 26.	Carr's cheque returned dishonoured.			
„ 27.	Cash sales to date	37	17	7
„ 28.	Drew from bank for self . . .	35	0	0
„ 29.	Expenses for month paid in cash . .	4	10	9
	Wages paid in cash . . .	19	3	0
„ 31.	One month's rent accrued . .	25	0	0
	Stock on hand valued at . . .	403	10	4

Open the necessary ledger accounts as at 1st May and pass these transactions through the proper subsidiary books to the ledger. Take out a
Trial Balance, close the ledger accounts, make out Trading and Profit and
Loss Accounts for the period and draw up a Balance Sheet as at 31st May,
19.....

C. On 1st May, 19....., C. Campbell re-opened his books with the following balances, in addition to his Capital Account :—

Cash, £35 10s. ; Bank, £409 ; P. Payne (*Dr.*), £201 10s. ; B. Barnett (*Cr.*), £269 15s. 6d. ; Bills Receivable, £250 ; Bills Payable (of 7th April at one month), £400 ; Stock, £573 15s. 6d.

During the month his transactions were :—

May 3. Discounted Bill Receivable (£250) ; discount charged, £2 8s.

„ 5. Paid B. Barnett by cheque, £265 in full settlement of his account.

„ 6. Purchased of B. Barnett :—

    7,800 cub. ft. oak at 11½d. per cub. ft.

    2,400 cub. ft. elm at 8d. per cub. ft.

    12,600 cub. ft. deals at 6d. per cub. ft.

„ 10. Renewed Bill Payable this day, with £2 2s. interest added for further month's accommodation.

„ 12. Cash sales (proceeds banked), £89 17s. 10d.

„ 15. Sold to P. Payne :—

    1,800 cub. ft. oak at 1s. 2d. per cub. ft.

    2,300 cub. ft. ash at 10d. per cub. ft.

    6,000 cub. ft. deal at 8d. per cub. ft.

„ 18. Received from P. Payne his bill of exchange at two months for £500 and cheque £98. Discount allowed, £4 6s. 8d.

„ 20. Issued Credit Note to P. Payne for ash returned, valued at £40.

„ 21. Accepted B. Barnett's draft at 1 month for £500.

    And sent him cheque on account for £200.

„ 25. Cash purchases to date, £11 14s.

„ 27. Drew for self from bank, £30.

„ 28. Sold to P. Payne, sundry timber for cash, £37 3s. 10d.

„ 29. Paid wages for month by cheque, £44 11s. 6d.

    Paid expenses in cash, £12 7s. 4d.

„ 31. One month's rent accrued, £25.

    Stock on hand valued at £1,066 6s. 2d.

Open the necessary ledger accounts as at 1st May and pass the above transactions through the proper subsidiary books to the ledger. Take out a Trial Balance, close the ledger accounts, make out Trading and Profit and Loss Accounts for the period and draw up a Balance Sheet as at 31st May, 19.....

D. K. Pippin started in business as a wholesale fruit dealer on 1st September, 19..... At that date his assets were as follows :—

Cash at Bank, £1,000 ; Cash in Hand, £12 ; Stock of Fruit, etc., £175 ; Fittings, Baskets, etc., £21. He had no liabilities.

You are required to open his ledger as on 1st September, 19....., from the above particulars, and to post thereto, through the proper subsidiary books, the following transactions :—

19.....

Sept. 1. Drew and cashed cheque for £25, for office cash.

„ 2. Bought for cash, 50 bushels of " Cox's Orange " apples, at 9s. per bushel.

„ 3. Sold, on credit, to B. Brown, 20 bushels " Worcester Pearmain " apples at 8s. 6d. per bushel.

„ 4. Paid wages, in cash, £5 7s. 6d.

„ 5. Bought, on credit, from R. Robinson & Co., 30 bushels " William " pears, at 10s. per bushel.

„ 6. Paid in cash, carriage, £3 17s. 2d.

„ 8. Sold, on credit, to S. Smith, 10 bushels of " Cox's Orange " apples, at 10s. 9d. per bushel.

Sept. 9. Bought, on credit, from J. Jones & Son, 56 bushels of " James Grieve " apples, at 8s. 10d. per bushel.

„ 9. S. Smith returned half a bushel of apples sold him on the 8th inst. as not up to sample.

„ 10. Paid, by cheque, to R. Robinson & Co., the amount of their account, less 5% discount.

„ 10. Drew and cashed cheque for £20 for office cash.

„ 11. B. Brown & Co. paid their account by cheque. Paid cheque into bank.

„ 12. Purchased, by cheque, from H. Pound & Co., new weighing machine for £9 10s.

„ 13. Paid in cash, wages £6 10s.

„ 13. Stock in hand valued at £235.

Balance the Cash Book and Ledger as on 13th September, 19...., and extract a Trial Balance. Prepare Trading and Profit and Loss Accounts for the period, and draw up a Balance Sheet as at 13th September, 19.....

E. Martin Ravary carries on business as a wholesale ladies' costume and cloth merchant. On the 1st January, 19...., his assets and liabilities were as follows :—

	£ s. d.	£ s. d.
Assets.		
Furniture and Fixtures		258 0 0
Sundry Debtors :—		
H. Lyons	104 0 0	
B. Bryce	158 0 0	
C. Allen	17 0 0	
P. Wilson	21 0 0	
		300 0 0
Stock on Hand		1,029 0 0
Bills Receivable :—		
B. Bryce (due 15th January, 19....) . .		62 0 0
Cash in Hand		15 0 0
Cash at Bank		256 0 0
Liabilities.		
Sundry Creditors :—		
M. Herriott	129 0 0	
C. Testout	241 0 0	
H. Dickson	36 0 0	
		406 0 0
Bills Payable :—		
H. Dickson (due 12th January, 19....) . .		150 0 0

Open the necessary accounts in the ledger, and post to it, through the proper subsidiary books, the following transactions :—

19.....

Jan. 1. Drew and cashed cheque for £100 for office cash.

Bought for cash 16 Paris model ladies' coats for £47.

„ 2. Sold, on credit, to George Dawson, 56 yards velvet at 30s. 6d. per yard.

„ 3. B. Bryce paid, by cheque, £120 on account.

„ 3. H. Lyons gave a bill for three months for the amount of his account.

Bought, on credit, 2 rolls of Scotch tweed at £56 per roll from Robert McGredy & Co.

George Dawson returned 5 yards of velvet sold him on the 2nd instant—damaged.

Jan. 5. Sold, for cash, two costumes at £6 and £5 10s. respectively.
Paid, in cash, wages £12 and office expenses £2 1s.

„ 8. Bought on credit, 100 yards lining silk at 21s. 6d. per yard from C. Testout.

„ 9. Paid, by cheque, M. Herriott's account, less 2½% discount.

„ 10. Cash sales to date, £38.
Sold, on credit, 24 costumes at £4 4s. each to P. Wilson, less 5% trade discount.

„ 12. H. Dickson's bill, due this day, was duly met through the bank.
Paid wages, in cash, £14, and office expenses, £3 4s.

„ 14. Paid, in cash, carriage, £8 16s.

„ 15. B. Bryce's bill, due this day, was duly met through the bank.

„ 16. Bought, on credit, 150 yards blue serge at £1 per yard, from M. Herriott, less 5% trade discount.
Gave M. Herriott a cheque on account, £50.

„ 17. Cash sales for week, £92.

„ 20. Martin Ravary drew cash, £50, for private purposes.

„ 21. Purchased, for cash, 8 dozen coat hangers at 24s. per dozen (charge to Furniture and Fixtures).
Returned 10 yards blue serge, purchased on the 16th inst., to M. Herriott, as faulty.
B. Bryce paid balance of account by cheque. Paid cheque into bank.

„ 22. Paid cash into bank, £100.

„ 22. Stock on hand valued at £1,243.

Balance the Ledger Accounts as on 22nd January, and extract a Trial Balance. Prepare Trading and Profit and Loss Accounts for the period, and draw up a Balance Sheet as at 22nd January, 19.....

CHAPTER XII

ACCOUNTS CURRENT AND CONSIGNMENT ACCOUNTS

Accounts Current.

An Account Current may be defined as a statement of account, in debit and credit form, between two persons, in which interest is charged or allowed on the various transactions recorded in the account. It is a copy of the ledger account of the first named person as that account appears in the ledger of the second person, and records the transactions between the two persons, *with the addition of a provision for interest*. Thus an Account Current headed " *J. Jones, London,* in Account Current with *B. Thomas, Cardiff,*" would be a copy of Jones's account in the ledger of B. Thomas and would normally be rendered by Thomas to Jones. The Account Current might for convenience, even though rendered by Thomas to Jones, be headed " *B. Thomas, Cardiff,* in Account Current with *J. Jones, London,*" and would then be a copy of the account of Thomas in Jones's ledger.

The account current is chiefly used between merchants engaged in foreign trade and others, where considerable balances are outstanding between them for varying periods. By charging interest on the fluctuating balance the merchant is compensated for the temporary loss of the use of the money owing to him.

A form of account current is also used between banker and customer, as when the balance of the customer's account fluctuates constantly, it is essential that there should be some effective method of calculating the amount of interest due to or by the customer.

Calculating Interest : Banking Method.

The most elementary method of arriving at the amount of interest payable would be to work out a sum in simple interest on the amount of each balance for its respective period. Thus, in the specimen account of A. Bates in the banker's ledger on page 235, it will be observed that there is a balance of £500 standing to Bates's credit for 5 days, a balance of £490 for 1 day, and a balance of £540 for 3 days.

If interest were calculated on each balance for the period it remained unchanged, and this were repeated for each fresh balance up to 31st December, the total of all these items would represent the amount of interest due to Bates for the half-year.

Obviously such a system would be extremely inconvenient in modern business, and a very much simpler method has therefore been devised for dealing with the calculation of interest.

It will be remembered that, in explaining how the discount upon a bill of exchange is calculated, it was stated that

$$\text{Interest} = \frac{\text{Amount} \times \text{Rate of Interest} \times \text{Number of Years}}{100}$$

or

$$\text{Interest} = \frac{\text{Amount} \times \text{Rate of Interest} \times \text{Number of Days}}{365 \times 100}$$

It follows, therefore, that if the balance of the account is multiplied by the number of days for which it stands, and the resulting product is multiplied by the rate per cent. and divided by 36,500, the result will represent the amount of interest for that balance.

To go a step further, the same result will be achieved if each balance during the half-year is multiplied by the number of days for which it remains stationary, and all the products are added together first, only the total result being multiplied by the rate per cent. and divided by 36,500. Thus, this multiplication and division has to be done once only instead of every time the balance of the account changes. This is the method adopted by banks, and the following example of an account in the bank ledger will illustrate the working of this particular system.

Furniture Dealer.	ARNOLD BATES					9, Morton Street Bristol.
19.....		Dr.	Cr.	Bal.	Days.	Products
June 30	By Balance.		£500	Cr. £500	5	2,500
July 5	To Smith.	£10		Cr. £490	1	490
,, 6	By Cash.		£50	Cr. £540	3	1,620
,, 9	To Lawrence.	£14				
	To Jackson.	£20		Cr. £506		

Each balance is multiplied by the number of days for which it stands, *e.g.*, £500 remains from 30th June to 5th July = 5 days ; £490 remains from 5th July to 6th July = 1 day ; and so forth. The process will be continued until the end of the half-year, when the products will be added up and the grand total, multiplied by the rate of interest and divided by 36,500, will be the amount of interest due to Bates for the half-year.

It will be noticed that the ruling of the account is quite different from that adopted in ordinary commercial practice, there being only one column for details, the debit and credit columns being placed side by side, and the balance of the account being ascertained and extended every time an entry is made in the account, or daily where more than one transaction takes place on any particular day.

This illustration is given in order to enable the reader to gain an understanding of the general principle of interest calculation by means of products, but it must not be thought that the above method of display is to be adopted for ordinary commercial practice.

In banking the calculation of the balance of the account every time an entry is made is essential, in order to guide the banker in paying, or refusing, cheques drawn by the customer. In commercial practice generally, no such necessity arises, and the constant calculation of the balance would result in a considerable amount of unnecessary work.

Calculating Interest : Commercial Method.

The same principle is adopted in commercial practice, but it is applied in another manner. The usual form of account ruling is retained, debit items being given on the left-hand side and credit items on the right-hand side, but additional columns are also provided on each side of the account for the " Number of Days " and for the " Products."

Instead of multiplying the fluctuating balance by the number of days as it stands, the actual debit and credit entries are multiplied by the number of days from the commencing date, known as the *zero date*, in each case, and each individual result is extended into the products column. This zero date is usually either the date of the earliest transaction or a date prior to this, while the amounts are taken *to the nearest* £ for the purposes of multiplication by the number of days. Interest is not usually charged or allowed for the day upon which the transaction takes place, and in calculating the number of days the starting date (zero date) *or* the date of the transaction must be omitted.

The balance of the money columns at the end of the period is similarly multiplied by the number of days from the zero date to the end of the account, and the total debit products are then subtracted from the total credit products. This balance of products is then converted into £ s. d. by multiplying by the rate of interest and dividing by 36,500 as before ; the result represents the amount of interest for the period. The amount of interest ascertained in this way is inserted in the money column on the *same* side of the account current as the product balance appears, and the account is finally balanced off, thus disclosing the total amount of the customer's indebtedness, inclusive of interest.

To take the example already given, if the transactions between Bates and the bank were to be recorded in an account current, as would be the case between two merchants, the zero date would be 30th June. The first debit entry, £10, is made 5 days after the zero date (30th June to 5th July), so the product will be 10 × 5 = 50. The second debit entry (£14) is made 9 days from the zero date

(30th June to 9th July), so the product will be $14 \times 9 = 126$. The credit entry on 6th July is 6 days from the zero date, so the product, *on the credit side*, will be $50 \times 6 = 300$. This process would be continued until 31st December, when the balance of the account at that date would be multiplied by 184 (*i.e.*, the number of days from 30th June to 31st December), the total credit products and the total debit products would be ascertained, and the one would be subtracted from the other. This result can then be readily converted into money by the aforementioned formula. The formula for converting the balance of products into sterling can best be memorized if it is remembered that it represents interest at the given rate for one day on an amount equivalent to the balance of products in pounds. For example, in the illustration given on page 238, the calculation is :—

$$\frac{5 \ (5\%)}{100} \times \frac{1 \ (1 \ day)}{365} \times \frac{\pounds 83,355 \ (\text{Balance of products in pounds})}{1}$$

The result would then be exactly the same as that which would have been arrived at under the former, *i.e.*, the banking method of calculation. (The reader can easily prove this for himself by working out an imaginary example under the two methods and comparing the results.)

An actual example of an account current worked out in detail will now be given, and if this is studied carefully the method of calculating interest should be perfectly clear.

EXAMPLE

Messrs. Horton & Sons, of London, export to Lewis and Lewis of Cape Town, on the undermentioned dates, goods to the values indicated :—

7th July, £1,210 5s. 3d. ; 10th August, £710 9s. ; 18th September, £805 3s. 2d. ; 30th September, £620 5s. 6d. ; 4th November, £241 9s. 8d. ; 1st December, £430 4s. 1d.

They receive cash on account thereof as follows :—

21st July, £1,200 ; 1st September, £605 15s. ; 30th September, £750 ; 15th October, £700 ; 28th November, £200 9s. ; 28th December, £500 5s.

Draft an account current, submitted by the exporters, recording these transactions, and showing the position as at 31st December, interest being calculated at 5% per annum.

(*For worked solution see next page.*)

The balance of products is inserted on the appropriate side of the account, so that the debit and the credit products can be balanced in the same way as the money columns.

The abbreviation E. & O. E. (Errors and Omissions Excepted) is invariably used on accounts current, and also on account sales,

Messrs. *Lewis & Lewis, Cape Town.*
In ACCOUNT CURRENT with

HORTON & SONS

LONDON
31st December, 19.....

Interest to 31st December, 19...., at 5% per annum.

Dr.

Date.	Particulars.	Amount. £ s. d.	Days.	Products.
19....				
July 7	To Goods.	1,210 5 3	7	8,470
Aug. 10	,,	710 9 0	41	29,110
Sept. 18	,,	805 3 2	80	64,400
,, 30	,,	620 5 6	92	57,040
Nov. 4	,,	241 9 8	127	30,607
Dec. 1	,,	430 4 1	154	66,220
,, 31	,, Balance of Products.			83,355
,, 31	,, Interest.	11 8 5		
		£ 4,029 5 1		339,202
Dec. 31	To Balance *brought down.*	72 16 1		
	E. & O.E.			

Cr.

Date.	Particulars.	Amount. £ s. d.	Days.	Products.
19....				
July 21	By Cash.	1,200 0 0	21	25,200
Sept. 1	,,	605 15 0	63	38,178
,, 30	,,	750 0 0	92	69,000
Oct. 15	,,	700 0 0	107	74,900
Nov. 28	,,	200 9 0	151	30,200
Dec. 28	,,	500 5 0	181	90,500
,, 31	,, Balance of Principal (£61 7s. 8d.),			
,, 31	,, Balance *carried down.*	72 16 1	184	11,224
		£ 4,029 5 1		339,202

NOTE.—The zero date is 30th June.

$$\text{Interest} = \frac{£83,355 \times 5}{36,500} = £11 \text{ 8s. 5d.}$$

which will be explained shortly, and indicates that the right is reserved to make any alterations necessary through clerical errors in the preparation of the statement. It is merely a custom, and is of no *legal* value—*i.e.*, the right to correct errors, etc., is not lost if it is omitted.

There are other methods of calculating interest on accounts current, one being to take *the last day of the period* as the zero date, but the method described above is that most frequently used and is recommended to the reader as being the most suitable for his purpose.

The student may wonder why interest is added to the account on the side which shows the smaller total of products, but the reason will be apparent if the first two items in this example are considered. Clearly, the net effect of the sale of goods, value £1,210, on the 7th July and the remittance of £1,200 on the 21st July is that Horton has lent Lewis and Lewis £1,210 for 14 days —hence interest must be *debited* to their account. The same principle can be applied right through the account. The final balance must be included and the products thereon added to the credit side, thereby increasing the debit interest, because this amount is still needed to clear the account.

When goods are bought or sold and the invoice in respect thereof is dated forward, the calculation of interest will commence as from the due date of the invoice, *i.e.*, if goods are received on 2nd April on an invoice dated two months forward, interest will run from 2nd June.

CONSIGNMENTS

When a trader forwards goods to an agent, either in this country or abroad, for the latter to sell on his behalf, he is said to make a *consignment*. The person sending the goods is known as the *consignor* and the agent to whom the goods are sent as the *consignee*.

A *consignment* must be clearly distinguished from a *sale*. In the latter case the ownership of the goods passes to the buyer when the sale is completed, whether payment is made at the time or at some future date. In the case of a consignment, however, the ownership in the goods never actually passes to the agent or consignee ; he sells the goods on behalf of the consignor and remits to him the net proceeds of the sale, less expenses and commission.

As the consignee never becomes the owner he does not take any risk or responsibility, except in special circumstances, when he is paid an additional commission for doing so. If the goods are damaged, or are destroyed by fire, or for some reason prove unsaleable, it is the consignor who must stand the loss. If the agent guarantees that no bad debts will be incurred in respect of

the consignment, *i.e.*, if he undertakes to indemnify the consignor against loss, he is then termed a *del credere* agent, and receives an additional commission (known as *del credere* commission) for doing so.

This primary relationship between consignor and consignee is important, because it explains the whole of the book-keeping method of recording consignments in the books of both parties. This will be referred to again shortly.

The necessity for sending consignments generally arises where a merchant wishes to sell goods at some distant place to which it is impossible to send any one actually in his employ, and there is no specific person or firm at that place who is in direct touch with the merchant and is willing to purchase the goods from him. If there were any such person, a direct sale would be effected and the need for a consignment would not arise.

For this reason, a consignment is sent to some agent, who acts entirely independently, except that he undertakes to dispose of the goods for an agreed commission, usually by way of a percentage upon the gross proceeds of the sale. For example, a farmer growing large quantities of potatoes in Lincolnshire may have several tons which he wishes to sell through Covent Garden Market in London. He does not wish to go to London himself to sell them, and it would probably not pay him to do so ; on the other hand, Covent Garden is a market, not a firm who will buy the potatoes from him. The difficulties may, in this event, be overcome by making a consignment. The farmer consigns the potatoes to a produce broker in London, who accepts delivery of them, arranges for their storage and for their sale on the market, and remits to the grower the net proceeds after deducting his expenses and agreed commission.

Similarly goods are often consigned to foreign places where there is a known demand for them, agents actually on the spot undertaking to sell them at the best price they can get, either immediately or in course of time according to the circumstances.

When the consignee has disposed of the goods he sends to the consignor an *Account Sales*, which is a statement of the result of the transaction, setting out the gross proceeds, the various expenses and charges which have been incurred by the consignee in connection with the consignment, the agent's commission, and the net proceeds.

An Account Sales usually appears in the following form :—

ACCOUNT SALES OF
1,000 Barrels of Flour
For Account of *Messrs. Horton & Sons*

Mark.	Particulars.	Price.	Amount.					
			£	s.	d.	£	s.	d.
	Prompt. 10th May, 19.....							
L T	1,000 Barrels of Flour.	24/-	1,200	0	0			
B	Discount 2½%.		30	0	0			
A X						1,170	0	0
	Less Charges.							
	Landing and Cartage.		1	17	0			
	Fire Insurance.			10	0			
	Warehousing.			10	6			
E. & O.E.	Commission 5% on £1,170.		58	10	0			
						61	7	6
	Note : Bill £600 accepted against above consignment due 10th June.							
					£	1,108	12	6

Cape Town, 5th May, 19.....
Lewis and Lewis.

This statement records a consignment of 1,000 barrels of flour which Messrs. Horton and Sons, of London, sent to Lewis and Lewis of Cape Town. The latter sold the flour for £1,200, less cash discount, and had to pay £1 17s. for landing and cartage, 10s. for fire insurance, and 10s. 6d. for warehousing. The consignee's commission is calculated as 5% on the proceeds *less* cash discount, *i.e.*, 5% on £1,170. Thus the total deductions amount to £61 7s. 6d., and the net amount which Lewis and Lewis owe to Horton and Sons is therefore £1,108 12s. 6d.

The "Prompt" date is the date upon which it is agreed that the account shall be settled by the buyer. The "mark" in the margin refers to the distinguishing mark which has been stamped on the barrels to identify them during transit and on landing. The abbreviation E. & O. E. has already been explained on page 237.

The settlement of the amount due is generally effected by means of a bill of exchange or banker's draft. It often happens that the consignor does not wish to wait for his money until the consignment has been sold and settlement effected, especially when the goods have been consigned to a far distant country. In such cases it is usual for the consignor to draw a bill upon the consignee for a certain proportion of the value of the goods as soon as the consignment is made. The bill can then be discounted with a banker, and the necessity of waiting some considerable time before any part of the proceeds of the transaction is received is avoided.

As far as the consignee is concerned, it is very probable that by the time the bill falls due for payment the goods will have been sold and he will be in possession of the proceeds ; thus payment of the bill will serve to discharge a greater part of his liability to the consignor. The amount of the bill will then be taken into consideration when a final settlement takes place between the two parties.

Entries in Consignor's Books.

It was stated that the essential point to be remembered in connection with consignments is that the goods remain the property of the *consignor* until they are actually sold, and that the consignee does not at any time become their owner, but merely acts as the consignor's agent.

This principle naturally affects the method of treatment of consignments in the books of account. The consigning of the goods is regarded as a separate trading venture, quite distinct from the ordinary sales of the business, and it is recorded accordingly. The consignee's account is not debited until the account sales is received, indicating that the goods have been sold and that the consignee is responsible to the consignor for the proceeds.

Where consignments are numerous, a special Consignments Journal and Consignments Ledger are kept, but otherwise the entries are passed through the ordinary books. A special account, headed "Consignment to——" (giving the consignee's name) is opened for each consignment and is closed upon its completion, the net profit or loss on each individual consignment being, therefore, recorded separately.

The entries made in the consignor's books may be summarized as follows :—

1. UPON DESPATCH OF THE CONSIGNMENT :—

Debit the Consignment to —— Account and credit a Consignment Outwards Account with the cost price of the goods. The latter account records goods sent out of the business, and the balance thereof is credited to Trading Account when the accounts are balanced.

It is quite usual for the consignor to despatch a *pro forma* invoice to the consignee with a view to indicating the minimum prices at which the consignor desires the goods to be sold, and also to prevent disclosure of the profit on the goods to the consignee. This is done only for purposes of convenience, and the entries to Consignments Account should be made at cost price, as otherwise profits may be anticipated.

2. UPON PAYING ANY EXPENSES.

When any expenses are incurred by the consignor in connection

with the consignment, they are debited to the Consignment to —— Account, and credited to cash (or to a personal account if the expenses are not actually paid, but are *owed*).

3. On Drawing a Bill on the Consignee.

When a bill is drawn upon the consignee for a part of the value of the goods before receipt of the Account Sales, the transaction affects the personal account of the consignee and *not* the Consignment to —— Account. This is because the bill is really drawn upon the consignee *in anticipation of his becoming liable for the proceeds*, and does not at the moment affect the consignment itself, for the goods may be lost at sea or may never be sold.

Bills Receivable Account is therefore debited, *via* the Bills Receivable Book, and the consignee's personal account is credited.

4. On Discounting a Bill drawn in Advance.

If a bill drawn in this way is discounted, the ordinary procedure is followed. Bank Account, *i.e.*, the Cash Book, is debited and Bills Receivable Account is credited with the face value of the bill, and Bank Charges (or Interest) Account is debited and (Bank) Cash Book is credited with the amount of the discount.

The amount of discount is sometimes debited to the Consignment to —— Account, instead of to the Bank Charges Account, but this is not strictly correct, as it is not a true consignment expense, but an expense that results from the general financial operations of the consignor.

5. On Receipt of the Account Sales.

The personal account of the consignee is debited with the gross proceeds of the consignment and is credited with all expenses incurred by the consignee on behalf of the consignor, including his commission. Consignment to —— Account is credited with the gross proceeds of the consignment and is debited with all expenses incurred, the balance being transferred to Profit and Loss Account. Alternatively the personal account of the consignee can be debited, and the Consignment to —— Account credited, with the net proceeds of the consignment, but the former method is recommended in that full details of the expenses incurred by the consignee will be shown in the accounts.

6. On Payment by the Consignee.

When a remittance is received from the consignee in respect of the balance outstanding, his personal account is credited and Cash or Bills Receivable Account will be debited, according to the nature of the remittance. The amount of the remittance will either be for the net proceeds, or, where a bill has been drawn in advance by the consignor, for the net proceeds less the amount of the bill already drawn. Thus, in either case, the personal

account will be closed as far as the particular consignment is concerned.

At the close of the trading period, any goods on consignment which have not been sold must be credited to the Consignment to —— Account and brought down as a debit balance just as stock on hand is credited to a Trading Account. Thus unsold stock must be included in the Balance Sheet at cost price, which will include a fair proportion of any charges already incurred by the consignor in respect of them.

If the goods have been sent on consignment at *pro forma* invoice prices above the actual cost prices and recorded at such prices in the Consignment Accounts, it is necessary to make an adjustment at the balancing date in order to reduce the value of the goods out on consignment to cost price. It is, however, unnecessary to go into this in detail in the present work, and the reader is recommended to utilize cost price as the basis of the entries in the various accounts wherever possible.

Entries in the Consignee's Books.

The essential principle of consignments also affects the records made in the books of the consignee. As the consignee does not *purchase* the goods, he will not pass any entries through his books until he has himself sold them. It then becomes necessary to record the fact that he has sold goods and is responsible for their value to his principal, the consignor.

The usual entries in the books of the consignee may be summarized as follows :—

1. On Receipt of the Goods.

As the goods are not the property of the consignee, no entries are required in his books of account on receipt of a consignment. It is, however, business-like to keep some record of the fact that goods belonging to another have been received, and this is usually effected by means of an entry in some statistical or memorandum book, merely for purposes of reference. This entry may be made in the Goods Inwards Book, described on page 70, or in a special Consignments Inwards Book.

2. Bill Drawn in advance by Consignor.

If the consignor draws a bill in advance, the consignee, when it is presented to him for acceptance, enters it in his Bills Payable Book, whence its amount is eventually transferred to the credit of Bills Payable Account, the personal account of the consignor being debited.

3. On Paying Expenses.

When any expenses in connection with the consignment, such as cartage, warehousing, etc., are incurred by the consignee, the

personal account of the consignor is debited and Cash (or a personal account, if the expense is owed and not paid) is credited.

4. On Selling the Goods.

When the goods are sold the purchaser's account (or the Cash Book if they are sold for cash) is debited, and the consignor's personal account is credited with the gross proceeds.

5. On Calculating the Commission.

When the goods have been sold, the amount of the agreed commission is calculated. This is debited to the consignor's personal account, and credited to Commission Account. The balance on Commission Account is transferred to the credit of Profit and Loss Account at the end of the accounting period.

6. On Remitting the Balance.

When the consignment is disposed of, it remains only to remit the balance of the amount outstanding to the consignor. This will ordinarily be the balance of the consignor's personal account, which will therefore be debited ; Cash, or Bills Payable Account, as the case may be, being credited with the amount of such remittance.

When making up his accounts at the end of the trading period, any balance outstanding on the consignor's personal account will be included in the total of Sundry Debtors, or of Sundry Creditors, in the Balance Sheet, according to whether the account is in debit or credit respectively.

It need hardly be added that, as the goods received on consignment do not belong to the consignee, any unsold portion of the consignment must *not* be included with the consignee's own stock when computing its value for Balance Sheet purposes.

The following example illustrates the practical application of the foregoing methods in the books of both the consignor and the consignee.

EXAMPLE

Horton & Co., of London, consigned 1,000 barrels of flour to Lewis & Lewis of Cape Town, on 7th March, 19...., invoicing them at cost, *i.e.*, 15s. 6d. per barrel. They paid freight £25 16s., and insurance £6, and drew a bill upon Lewis & Lewis for £600 at 3 months' *date* which they discounted with their bankers on 12th March at 5%. The bill was duly met at maturity. On 1st June, Horton & Co. received an Account Sales showing that the goods were sold for £1,200, less 2½% cash discount, and that Landing and Cartage Expenses amounted to £1 17s., Fire Insurance to 10s., and Warehousing to 10s. 6d. Commission at 5% on the proceeds (less discount) had been deducted, and a banker's draft for the balance was enclosed.

Show the necessary ledger entries in the books of both the consignor and the consignee.

It will be noted that the Account Sales given on page 241 agrees with that referred to in the above example.

A bank draft indicates a bill drawn upon a banker by a banker and payable on demand. It is therefore treated in the books like a cheque, *i.e.*, as if it were cash.

Consignor's Books.

Dr.	CONSIGNMENT TO LEWIS & LEWIS						Cr.		
	(1,000 Barrels of Flour)								
19.....		£	s.	d.	19.....		£	s.	d.
Mar. 7	To Consignment Outwards.	775	0	0	June 1	By Lewis & Lewis:— Proceeds of Consignment.	1,170	0	0
,, ,,	,, Cash, Freight.	25	16	0					
,, ,,	,, Cash, Insurance.	6	0	0					
June 1	,, Lewis & Lewis:— Landing etc. Expenses.	1	17	0					
	Fire Insurance.		10	0					
	Warehousing.		10	6					
	Commission, 5% on £1,170.	58	10	0					
,, 30	,, Profit and Loss Account.	301	16	6					
		£ 1,170	0	0			£1,170	0	0

Dr.	CONSIGNMENT OUTWARDS						Cr.		
19.....		£	s.	d.	19.....		£	s.	d.
June 30	To Trading Account.	775	0	0	Mar. 7	By Consignment to Lewis & Lewis.	775	0	0

Dr.	BILLS RECEIVABLE						Cr.		
19.....		£	s.	d.	19.....		£	s.	d.
Mar. 7	To Lewis & Lewis.	600	0	0	Mar.12	By Cash.	600	0	0

Dr.   [EXTRACTS FROM] CASH BOOK   Cr.

19.....		£	s.	d.	19.....		£	s.	d.
Mar. 12	To Bills Receivable.	600	0	0	Mar. 7	By Consignment to Lewis & Lewis, Freight.	25	16	0
June 1	,, Lewis & Lewis.	508	12	6	,, ,,	,, do., Insurance.	6	0	0
					,, 12	,, Bank Charges.	7	7	11

Dr.   BANK CHARGES   Cr.

19.....		£	s.	d.	19.....		£	s.	d.
Mar. 12	To Cash.	7	7	11	June 30	By Profit and Loss Account.	7	7	11

Dr.   LEWIS & LEWIS   Cr.

19.....		£	s.	d.	19.....		£	s.	d.
June 1	To Consignment Account.	1,170	0	0	Mar. 7	By Bills Receivable.	600	0	0
					June 1	,, Consignment Account : Landing, etc. Expenses.	1	17	0
						,, Fire Insurance.		10	0
						,, Warehousing.		10	6
						,, Commission.	58	10	0
					,,	,, Cash.	508	12	6
		£ 1,170	0	0			£ 1,170	0	0

Consignee's Books.

Dr.   HORTON & Co.   *Cr.*

19.....		£	s.	d.	19.....		£	s.	d.
Apr. 5	To Bills Payable.	600	0	0	May 5	By Cash— Proceeds of Consignment.	1,170	0	0
„ 15	„ Cash— Landing and Cartage.	1	17	0					
„ „	„ do. Insurance.		10	0					
„ „	„ do. Warehousing.		10	6					
May 5	„ Commission, 5% on £1,170.	58	10	0					
„ „	„ Cash.	508	12	6					
		£ 1,170	0	0			£ 1,170	0	0

Dr.   BILLS PAYABLE   *Cr.*

19......		£	s.	d.	19.....		£	s.	d.
June 10	To Cash.	600	0	0	April 5	By Horton & Co.	600	0	0

Dr.   COMMISSION   *Cr.*

19.....		£	s.	d.	19.....		£	s.	d.
June 30	To Profit and Loss Account.	58	10	0	May 5	By Horton & Co.	58	10	0

Dr.   [EXTRACTS FROM] CASH BOOK   *Cr.*

19.....		£	s.	d.	19.....		£	s.	d.
May 5	To Horton & Co.	1,170	0	0	April 15	By Horton & Co.—Landing and Cartage.	1	17	0
					„ „	„ do. Insurance.		10	0
					„ „	„ do. Warehousing.		10	6
					May 5	„ Horton & Co.	508	12	6
					June 10	„ Bills Payable.	600	0	0

In the preceding example, the whole of the consignment had been sold before the consignor closed his accounts. It may happen, however, that when the consignor closes his books part of the consignment remains unsold. The procedure which then becomes necessary will be appreciated if the Consignment to —— Account is regarded as a separate Trading Account for that particular activity. The cost of the consignment and expenses in connection therewith are debited to the account, and proceeds from that part of the consignment which has been sold are credited. To complete the account, after the manner of a Trading Account, it will be necessary to credit the value of the unsold stock ; the corresponding debit will be the first entry in the Consignment to —— Account for the succeeding period in which the balance of the consignment will be sold.

The expenses incurred by the consignor and certain items of expenditure incurred by the consignee will have been incurred in respect of the consignment as a whole, and not merely in respect of that part of the consignment which has been sold. Consequently, the value of the unsold portion of the consignment which is credited to Consignment to —— Account must include not only its proper proportion of the cost price of the consignment, but also its fair proportion of those expenses which have been incurred in respect of the whole consignment.

Suppose in the previous example that Lewis and Lewis had sold only 800 barrels of flour for £1,200 (less 2½% discount), that their payments for Landing and Cartage Expenses and Fire Insurance were in respect of the whole consignment, but that the charge for Warehousing referred only to the barrels which had been sold. The Consignment to Lewis and Lewis Account in the consignor's books would then appear as follows :—

Dr.   CONSIGNMENT TO LEWIS & LEWIS   Cr.
                            (1,000 Barrels of Flour)

19.....		£	s.	d.	19.....			£	s.	d.
Mar. 7	To Goods on Consignment.	775	0	0	June 1	By Lewis & Lewis— Proceeds of				
,, ,,	,, Cash— Freight.	25	16	0		Consignment.		1,170	0	0
,, ,,	,, Insurance.	6	0	0	June 30	,, Balance				
June 1	,, Lewis & Lewis— Landing and Cartage.	1	17	0		unsold. c/d		161	16	7
	Fire Insurance.		10	0						
	Warehousing.		10	6						
	Commission.	58	10	0						
June 30	,, Profit and Loss Account.	463	13	1						
		£ 1,331	16	7				£ 1,331	16	7
July 1	To Balance. b/d	161	16	7						

The value of the 200 barrels remaining unsold is arrived at as follows:—

		£	s.	d.
Cost of 1,000 barrels consigned		775	0	0

Expenditure in respect of the whole consignment:—

		£	s.	d.			
Consignor :	Freight	25	16	0			
	Insurance . . .	6	0	0			
Consignee :	Landing and Cartage . .	1	17	0			
	Fire Insurance . . .		10	0			
					34	3	0
				5)	809	3	0

Proportionate value of 200 barrels £161 16 7

NOTE.—As the Commission and Warehousing Charges refer solely to the goods sold they are *not* included in computing the value of the stock in hand.

EXERCISE 12

A. What is the object of an account current ? Illustrate your answer with an actual example of a pro-forma account current.

B. What are the principal methods of calculating interest in accounts current ?

C. Distinguish between sales and consignments, and explain the principal features of each.

D. Define the terms :—" Consignor," " Consignee," " Account Sales " and " *Del credere* commission."

E. What entries in the books of the consignor are necessary to record a consignment (*a*) on dispatch of the goods ; (*b*) on receipt of the account sales ; and (*c*) on receipt of the net proceeds ?

F. Draw up a specimen account sales for 50 cases of White Shirtings consigned by a Manchester cloth merchant to a firm of Chinese commission agents.

G. Calculate interest at 5% by means of the product method on the following account current :—

Herring Bros.   In Account with J. SPRAT.

Dr.		£	19.....		Cr. £
19.....			Feb. 28.	By Returns.	200
Dec. 31.	To Balance.	2,000	Mar. 14.	,, Cash.	1,600
19.....			,, 31.	,, Balance c/d.	2,800
Jan. 31.	,, Goods.	1,200			
Mar. 31.	,, ,,	1,400			
		£4,600			£4,600
Mar. 31.	To Balance b/d.	2,800			

H. The undermentioned transactions took place between Chesham & Co., Ltd., of Bradford, and Jansenn & Co., of Tientsin :—

		£	s.	d.
19.....				
Dec. 31.	Balance owing by Jansenn & Co., to Chesham & Co., Ltd.	1,200	0	0
19.....				
Jan. 7.	Chesham & Co., Ltd., shipped goods to Jansenn & Co.	850	0	0
May 10	Sight draft received by Chesham & Co., Ltd., from Jansenn & Co. . .	1,500	0	0
,, 25.	Chesham & Co., Ltd., paid freight and insurance charges on behalf of Jansenn & Co.	250	0	0

Prepare the account current, bearing interest at 5%, to be rendered by Chesham & Co., Ltd., to Jansenn & Co., as on 30th June, 19.....

J. On 12th November, Clarke Bros., of Glasgow, shipped to J. Saxby, of Lagos, 40 cases of mixed drapery goods, which were invoiced *pro forma* at £27 15s. per case. The payments made by Clarke Bros. in connection with this consignment were :—Insurance, £14 7s. ; Freight, £34 5s. ; Sundry Charges, £4 2s. The payments made by Saxby in Africa were :—Warehousing, £12 ; Insurance, £1 15s. ; Landing Charges, etc., £5 9s. 6d. On 14th January Saxby sold 23 cases of goods at £30 per case, and the remainder on 27th January at £37 per case. All these sales were effected for prompt cash. A commission of 3% on all sales, plus 1¾% *del credere*

I

commission, is payable to Saxby. On 20th November, Clarke Bros. drew a bill of exchange on Saxby for £800, which was duly accepted.

Prepare an Account Sales showing the result of the above consignment, and state the amount of Saxby's indebtedness to Clarke Bros.

K. On 22nd June, Brown Brothers, of Sheffield, shipped to Begum & Chattergee, of Calcutta, 40 cases of mixed cutlery. The goods were invoiced *pro forma* at £50 per case, the cost price being £40 per case. The Sheffield payments in connection with this consignment were :—Insurance, £11 10s. ; Freight, £46 ; Sundry Charges, £2 10s. The payments made by Begum & Chattergee, in Calcutta, were :—Landing Charges, £8 10s. ; Insurance, £1 10s.

On 30th August, Begum & Chattergee sold 20 cases at £60 per case, and on 6th September 20 cases at £57 10s. per case. Cash was received by them in respect of both sales. A commission of $3\frac{1}{4}$% is payable to Begum & Chattergee. The balance of the account was remitted by banker's draft on 10th September. Prepare an Account Sales showing the result of the above consignment, and show how the transactions would appear in the books of Brown Bros.

L. Eller & Co., of London, consigned goods to the value of £750 to their agent, A. Cain, in Spain ; they paid Freight, Insurance, etc., £32, and drew a bill of exchange on Cain at two months for £600 ; this bill was discounted by them with their bankers, the charge therefore being £7 10s. In due course Cain rendered an Account Sales showing that the goods were sold for £795. He deducted his commission, which is 5%, and expenses paid by him of £17 12s. 6d., and remitted a banker's draft for the balance. Show the necessary ledger accounts in the books of both Ellis & Co. and A. Cain.

CHAPTER XIII

RECEIPTS AND PAYMENTS ACCOUNTS : INCOME AND EXPENDITURE ACCOUNTS

The preceding chapters have dealt with the methods of recording transactions, ascertaining the profits, and presenting the financial position, of trading concerns alone, and no reference has been made to the accounts of institutions of a non-trading nature.

It is evident that the greater portion of the methods and principles which have been described hitherto are applicable only in a very small degree to the accounts of clubs, societies, charities, etc., for in these the vital element of trading and profit-making is absent. In these cases it is chiefly a question of balancing income against expenditure and of discovering the surplus, or the deficiency, for the period.

The form of account generally made use of by non-trading concerns is the Receipts and Payments Account or the Income and Expenditure Account.

The Receipts and Payments Account.

A Receipts and Payments Account may be defined as a statement of the cash actually received and paid during a given period.

It is, in effect, a summary of the cash book, and shows the amount of cash in hand at the beginning of the period as its opening balance and the amount of the cash in hand at the end of the period as its closing balance.

It differs from the cash book in that it is a *statement*, prepared at the end of a period, in order to show the monetary transactions of the period in a clear and concise form. Thus, the various cash book entries are combined according to their nature, the items of each class being shown in one amount on the statement, just as the balances of the various debtors' accounts are given in one amount on the Balance Sheet of a trading concern.

It sometimes happens that the Receipts and Payments Account of an institution will also be a record of the actual true income and expenditure for the period. This state of affairs will arise where all items of income actually received in cash and all items of expenditure paid in cash relate solely to the period under review, and no receipts and payments of a capital nature have been made during the period.

As, however, a Receipts and Payments Account records the actual cash transactions for the period and nothing more, it is

253   I*

very unusual to find that it also shows a complete statement of the period's work. The account will probably include items which are not properly applicable to the period, *e.g.*, subscriptions received in advance, and on the other hand will omit some items which are applicable, *e.g.*, expenses incurred but not paid. Furthermore, this form of account often conveys a wrong impression of the financial position of the particular concern, as usually no distinction is made between capital receipts and payments, *e.g.*, those in connection with the sale or purchase of fixed assets, and receipts and payments on revenue account, *i.e.*, the *ordinary* items of income and expenditure.

A Receipts and Payments Account is similar to the cash book in that incoming cash is recorded on the left-hand side and outgoing cash on the right-hand side of the statement. In practice it is usually found that a columnar Cash Book with suitable analysis columns for the main items of receipts and payments will facilitate the preparation of the final account.

The following example shows the usual form of a Receipts and Payments Account :—

EXAMPLE

An analysis of the cash book of the " Union of Engineers " for the year ended 31st December, 19...., gives the following information : Balance at 1st January, £19 5s. 4d. ; Subscriptions Received : Fellows £210, Associates £509 5s. ; Examination Fees, £300 10s. ; Interest on Investments, £22 9s. 8d. ; Office Expenses, £187 6s. 10d. ; Salaries, £505 ; Printing and Stationery, £93 2s. 3d. ; Examiners' Fees, £120 10s. ; Purchase of Furniture for Reading Room, £110.

Prepare a Receipts and Payments Account for the year ended 31st December, 19......

RECEIPTS AND PAYMENTS ACCOUNT

Dr.   FOR THE YEAR ENDED 31ST DECEMBER, 19.....   Cr.

	£	s.	d.		£	s.	d.
To Balance at 1st January.	19	5	4	By Office Expenses.	187	6	10
„ Subscriptions :				„ Office Salaries.	505	0	0
£ s. d.				„ Printing and Stationery.	93	2	3
Fellows. 210 0 0				„ Examiners' Fees.	120	10	0
Associates. 509 5 0				„ Furniture for Reading Room.	110	0	0
	719	5	0	„ Balance *carried down*.	45	10	11
„ Examination Fees.	300	10	0				
„ Interest on Investments.	22	9	8				
£	1,061	10	0	£	1,061	10	0
To Balance *brought down*.	45	10	11				

The Income and Expenditure Account.

An Income and Expenditure Account is a further form of account that is also adopted by non-trading concerns, but it differs

essentially from a Receipts and Payments Account, and must not be confused with the latter form of account.

An Income and Expenditure Account is prepared to show *all* the revenue income for the period, whether actually received or accrued and not yet received, and *all* the revenue expenditure for the period, whether actually paid or accrued and not yet paid. The balance of the account, therefore, shows the surplus (profit) of the total income over the total expenditure or the deficiency (loss) for the period under review.

The Income and Expenditure Account of a society or institution corresponds to the Profit and Loss Account of a trader. It requires to be adjusted in a similar manner in order to include outstanding items and to exclude inapplicable items.

It is also similar in that expenditure is shown on the left-hand, or debit, side, and income on the right-hand, or credit, side. In this respect the procedure is the reverse to that followed in the case of a Receipts and Payments Account.

Capital items, *i.e.*, those which relate to actual assets or liabilities and not to revenue income or expenditure, must be excluded from the account. Thus, for example, if additional furniture is purchased by a club the outlay is of a capital nature, and does not concern the ordinary expenses of the club. It will consequently be excluded from the Income and Expenditure Account, although if cash is paid for it, it would be included in a Receipts and Payments Account.

An Income and Expenditure Account should be accompanied by a Balance Sheet showing the assets and liabilities of the under-taking in the ordinary manner.

Differences between the two Forms of Account.

It should by now be clear that there are a number of points of difference between a Receipts and Payments Account and an Income and Expenditure Account. These differences, which are tabulated below, arise from the fact that the former account is merely a summary of the cash book, whilst the latter is designed to show the excess of income over expenditure or *vice versa* over a period.

A Receipts and Payments Account includes :—

    (1) Receipts or payments of a capital nature ;

    (2) Income received or expenses paid in advance, which, therefore, relate to the succeeding period ; and

    (3) Income received or expenses paid in arrear, *i.e.*, in respect of a preceding period.

A Receipts and Payments Account does not *include :*—

    (4) Income relating to the current period which has not actually been received ;

(5) Expenditure relating to the current period which has not yet been paid ; or

(6) Any provisions for depreciation, bad debts, etc.

On the other hand, an Income and Expenditure Account will not include any items under (1) to (3) above, while it will include any items which may come under (4) to (6) above.

Furthermore, an Income and Expenditure Account forms an essential part of the double entry system in the same way as a Profit and Loss Account, whereas a Receipts and Payments Account is, as a general rule, merely a memorandum statement.

If it is desired to convert a Receipts and Payments Account into an Income and Expenditure Account for the same period, it is necessary to exclude therefrom any items which come under the first three headings given above, and also to obtain the necessary information in order to be able to include in the account items under (4) to (6) above.

EXAMPLE

In addition to the information given in the previous example on page 254 the books of the "Union of Engineers" showed the following balances as at 1st January of the same year :—

	£	s.	d.
Capital Account (Entrance Fees, etc.)	2,000	0	0
Value of Premises	1,330	0	0
Furniture	140	0	0
Investments	543	0	0
Income and Expenditure Account (*Cr.* Balance brought forward)	24	0	4

There is an item of £9 3s. 6d. outstanding for Printing, and the Austin Company, Ltd., owe £7 7s. for the hire of the hall. The figure given for Office Expenses includes a payment of £8 5s. in respect of the previous year. Depreciation is to be allowed on Furniture at the rate of 5% exclusive of additions during the year. Construct the Income and Expenditure Account for the year ended 31st December, 19...., and Balance Sheet at that date.

INCOME AND EXPENDITURE ACCOUNT

Dr.　　　　FOR THE YEAR ENDED 31ST DECEMBER, 19....　　　　*Cr.*

Expenditure.	£	s.	d.	Income.	£	s.	d.	£	s.	d.
To Office Expenses.	179	1	10	By Subscriptions :—						
„ Office Salaries.	505	0	0		£	s.	d.			
„ Printing and Stationery	102	5	9	Fellows. 210	0	0				
„ Examiners' Fees.	120	10	0	Associates. 509	5	0				
„ Depreciation on Furniture.	7	0	0					719	5	0
				„ Examination Fees.				300	10	0
„ Balance—Surplus of income over expenditure.	135	14	1	„ Interest on Investments.				22	9	8
				„ Letting of Hall.				7	7	0
	£ 1,049	11	8					£ 1,049	11	8

BALANCE SHEET OF THE UNION OF ENGINEERS
AS AT 31ST DECEMBER, 19.....

Liabilities.		£	s.	d.	Assets.		£	s.	d.
Capital Account.		2,000	0	0	Premises.		1,330	0	0
Income and Expenditure						£			
Account :— £ s. d.					Furniture.	140			
Brought					*Less* Depreciation.	7			
Forward. 24 0 4						—			
Add Surplus						133			
for year to					Additions during				
date 135 14 1					year.	110			
						—			
		159	14	5			243	0	0
Sundry Creditors.		9	3	6	Sundry Debtors.		7	7	0
					Investments.		543	0	0
					Cash at Bank.		45	10	11
	£	2,168	17	11		£	2,168	17	11

EXERCISE 13

A. What is the purpose of a Receipts and Payments Account ?

B. How does a Receipts and Payments Account differ from an Income and Expenditure Account ?

C. For what type of concern is an Income and Expenditure Account suitable ? Why are Trading and Profit and Loss Accounts not suitable for such concerns ?

D. What are the steps necessary to convert a Receipts and Payments Account into an Income and Expenditure Account ?

E. From the following particulars, construct the Income and Expenditure Account for the year ended 31st December, 19...., of the Brenttown Literary and Dramatic Society :—
Subscriptions paid, £24 ; Net Proceeds received from lectures, £10 ; Net proceeds from plays produced, £150 ; Rent, £34 ; Sundry expenses, £5 ; Advertising paid, £24 ; Printing expenses paid, £7 10s. As on 31st December the Society owed £17 for rent ; £15 for printing ; and is owed £10 for subscriptions.

F. The Receipts and Payments Account of the Tresham Rowing Club for the year ended 31st December, 19...., is as follows :—

RECEIPTS AND PAYMENTS ACCOUNT
Dr.　　　　FOR THE YEAR ENDED 31st DECEMBER, 19.....　　　　*Cr.*

	£	s.	d.		£	s.	d.
To Balance at Bank at 1st				By Boat House Rent.	200	0	0
January.	60	5	0	„ Wages of Waterman.	240	0	0
„ Subscriptions.	350	0	0	„ Printing and Sta-			
„ Entrance Fees.	150	0	0	tionery.	54	0	0
„ Proceeds of Gala, etc.	220	0	0	„ Postage and Sundries.	12	4	0
				„ Balance at Bank at			
				31st December.	274	1	0
	£780	5	0		£780	5	0

The other ledger balances of the Club are :—

	£	s.	d.
Capital Account (Donations, etc.)	1,747	0	0
Club House (as per valuation) . . .	1,500	0	0
Furniture and Fixtures	175	0	0
Income and Expenditure Account (*Dr.* Balance brought forward)	11	15	0

Charge 10% depreciation on Furniture and Fixtures. Construct Income and Expenditure Account for the year, and Balance Sheet as at 31st December, 19...

G. An analysis of the Cash Book of the Sports Social Club for the year ended 31st March, 19...., gives the following information :—

Balance overdrawn at 1st April, 19...., £15 7s. 11d. ; Entrance Fees, £42 2s. ; Members' Subscriptions received, including arrears, £175 10s. ; Donations, £10 10s. ; Interest on Investments, £7 14s. ; Receipts from Canteen, £84 13s. 9d. ; Sale of Tennis Balls, etc., £15 15s. 6d. ; Upkeep of Grounds, £95 7s. ; Wages of Groundsman, £125 ; Printing and Stationery, £6 12s. ; Postages, etc., £3 2s. 7d. ; Stores for Canteen, £51 18s. ; Purchase of New Mower, £45 ; Bank Charges, £3 7s. 7d.

Prepare a Receipts and Payments Account from the above particulars for the year ended 31st March, 19.....

H. From the following Trial Balance of the " Progressive " Club as at 31st December, 19...., prepare Income and Expenditure Account and Balance Sheet.

TRIAL BALANCE.

	£	s.	d.	£	s.	d.
Printing and Stationery	79	17	2			
Newspapers	27	8	0			
Repairs	70	10	0			
Purchase of Billiard Table . . .	100	0	0			
Wines and Spirits	305	0	2			
Cigars	50	0	0			
Decoration of Premises	900	0	0			
Cash in Hand	60	17	9			
Cash at Bank	640	0	0			
Salary of Secretary	150	0	0			
Sundry Debtors	146	2	10			
Stock of Wines, Spirits and Cigars (1st January)	84	0	0			
Wages of Caretakers . . .	352	0	0			
Rent	200	0	0			
Rates and Taxes	70	0	0			
Sundry Expenses	20	3	6			
Lighting and Heating . . .	100	10	0			
Furniture and Fixtures . . .	679	11	3			
Subscriptions				1,489	18	6
Sundry Creditors				365	13	6
Sale of Wines, Spirits and Cigars . .				581	16	7
Capital Account (1st January) . .				1,308	5	5
Donations				290	6	8
	£4,036	0	8	£4,036	0	8

Allow 10% depreciation on Furniture and Fixtures (excluding additions) ; write £500 off Decoration of Premises. Stock of Wines, Spirits and Cigars on 31st December, £90 10s.

CHAPTER XIV

SINGLE ENTRY BOOK-KEEPING

The chief aim of the preceding chapters has been to instruct the reader in the principles and methods of book-keeping in accordance with the double entry system. In every instance it has been insisted that the basic principle of double entry must be complied with, *i.e.*, that for every debit there must be a corresponding credit, and *vice versa*.

It has been shown that the whole system of book-keeping depends upon the assumption that there is a twofold aspect to every transaction which takes place in business, some one, or something, always gaining while some one, or something, else loses to a corresponding extent.

The foregoing principles are fully observed in every sound system of keeping books of account. The Single Entry system of book-keeping, on the other hand, refers to any system which does *not* completely recognize the twofold aspect of every transaction. It is *not*, therefore, a sound system, and in fact it is doubtful whether it can strictly be called a system at all, as it follows no essential principles, as in the case of the double entry system.

It is thought, however, that this text-book would be incomplete unless some reference were to be made to Single Entry methods, particularly as they are still adopted, unfortunately, in many small retail businesses, and a short description of them will therefore be given in this concluding chapter.

What is Single Entry ?

As has already been stated, Single Entry Book-keeping may be defined as that system of keeping books of account which does not fully recognize the twofold aspect of every transaction.

Pure Single Entry recognizes only the personal aspect of transactions, and consequently requires no books of account, other than personal ledgers, to record dealings with debtors and creditors. Thus only one entry is made in the personal account of the person dealt with, that entry being made at the time of the transaction. In practice, however, a Cash Book is invariably kept, but this is done in order to be able to check the cash position at any time, rather than with any idea of recording the impersonal aspect of transactions.

Generally, however, the term Single Entry is used in its broader sense so as to include the many systems of book-keeping which are based upon a *partial* use of double entry principles. Naturally, such systems cannot be governed by any basic principles or any fixed rules, the book-keeping records being kept in each case in accordance with the individual opinions of the owner. These indefinite systems are at their best a compromise and are usually very unsatisfactory.

The most elementary of the so-called single entry systems is one in which the Cash Book is the only book of account, credit sales being recorded in a memorandum book and the entries being cancelled as and when the amounts owing are paid. A " daily takings " book is kept to record the amount of each day's cash sales, while invoices in respect of purchases are kept on a file until they are paid, when they are transferred to a " paid " file.

This is so elementary a method that it requires but passing mention, and it is usually met with only in very small retail businesses. A development, particularly where credit sales are numerous, is to replace the " memorandum book " by a Sales Day Book, from which items are posted to a Sales Ledger containing the debtors' accounts.

A method which may be taken as being more fairly representative of Single Entry book-keeping, however, is one in which a Cash Book and Debtors' and Creditors' Ledgers are kept. All cash transactions are recorded in the Cash Book. Those which concern debtors or creditors are posted to the respective personal accounts in the ledgers, but no such action is taken in regard to transactions affecting real or nominal accounts. Purchases and sales on credit are entered in the personal ledger accounts direct from the purchases invoices and copies of the sales invoices. Discounts allowed and received are also entered direct in the Debtors' and Creditors' Ledgers ; they may be noted in the Cash Book.

This system thus applies the principles of double entry to *cash* transactions which affect debtors or creditors and it also provides for a complete record of all transactions affecting personal accounts. It is inadequate, however, in that it does not provide for the keeping of any real or nominal accounts, nor does it recognize the twofold aspect of transactions other than those which concern cash, debtors and creditors.

It will at once be obvious to the reader that a serious and fundamental defect of any such system is that there is no possible means of preparing Trading and Profit and Loss Accounts or a Balance Sheet at any particular time. As an efficient system of book-keeping, therefore, any such method is a complete failure, for one of its chief functions should be to provide all the informa-

tion necessary to enable the trader to ascertain his income and his expenditure, the gross and the net profit (or loss) for any period, and the exact financial position of the business at any time.

Disadvantages of Single Entry.

The various systems of single entry book-keeping possess many disadvantages compared with the double entry method, which is the only satisfactory system. The chief of these disadvantages may be summarized as follows :—

(1) Apart from the Cash Book, no record is kept of the impersonal aspect of every transaction, the personal aspect alone being recorded in the books of account.

(2) As there is no equalizing debit entry for every credit entry, or *vice versa*, it is not possible to check the arithmetical accuracy of the books by preparing a Trial Balance.

(3) As no nominal accounts are kept, there is no material for the preparation of Trading and Profit and Loss Accounts. Not only is it impossible to ascertain the profit or loss for a given period with any degree of accuracy, but in addition there is no information as to the *sources* of profits or losses, so that detailed comparisons with previous trading periods are also impossible.

(4) The absence of any real accounts renders the preparation of a statement of the financial position of the business a difficult task, and detailed accuracy is impossible. There is no means of proving the accuracy of the accounts by the agreement of the two sides of the Balance Sheet, as is possible under the double entry system.

(5) The danger of clerical error and inaccuracy and the risk of fraud are considerably increased owing to the impossibility of the periodical balancing of the books.

Whereas double entry book-keeping is an efficient, convenient and accurate system of recording business transactions, single entry is not a definite system, but a haphazard record incapable of expansion to any real extent and completely unsatisfactory as a factor in modern commercial practice.

The Ascertainment of Profits from Single Entry Records.

It has already been pointed out that under the single entry system of book-keeping there is no provision for the preparation of Trading and Profit and Loss Accounts, and it therefore appears as though a trader who keeps his books in this manner is unable to gain any idea as to the success or otherwise of his business. An approximate estimate of the profit or loss for the period can

be obtained, however, by means of a comparison of the net value of the assets at the beginning and at the end of the period, after allowing for additions to or withdrawals from capital during the period under review.

It will be remembered that where books of account are kept under double-entry principles, the net profit or loss at the end of a trading period is credited or debited respectively to the trader's Capital Account. Thus, if no extra capital has been put into the business during the period and no withdrawals of capital have been made, the difference between the balance of the Capital Account at the beginning of the period and that at the end of the period will represent the net profit or loss for the period according to the increase or decrease in the Capital Account balance.

The balance of a trader's Capital Account is, however, always equal to the difference between the total assets and the total liabilities of the business, for the insertion of the balance of the account is necessary in order that the two sides of the Balance Sheet may agree. It follows, therefore, that if the capital at the beginning of the period is compared with the capital at the end of the particular period, the difference will represent the net profit or loss of the business for the period, providing there have been no additions to or withdrawals from capital during the period.

Where books are kept by single entry the preparation of detailed final accounts is often impossible, but it is possible to prepare a statement of assets and liabilities, with the aid of the trader's memoranda and, if necessary, his memory.

This statement is usually termed a STATEMENT OF AFFAIRS, and is prepared from the information which the books supply in regard to the balance of cash, of sundry debtors and of sundry creditors, and from any memoranda, etc., which the trader may possess in regard to the value of the fixed assets, e.g., premises, plant and machinery, motor vans, etc. The stock on hand at any given date is, of course, ascertained in the usual way by means of an inventory.

In the event of any adjustments being necessary in respect of depreciation, bad debts, etc., the value of the assets concerned must be adjusted at the end of the period to the required extent, thereby reducing the total value of the assets at that date. Thus the excess of assets over liabilities is reduced to the extent of these provisions, the net profit or loss being correspondingly affected.

It will at once be realized that this method of ascertaining profits is very unsatisfactory for many reasons. The preparation of the statement of affairs may possibly depend upon information which is not supplied by the books of account, and often undue reliance must be placed upon the trader's memory. The slightest error in the value of any asset at once causes a corresponding error in the estimated amount of profit or loss, and there is no sound

method available of checking the working or of preventing the most hopeless inaccuracy.

Unlimited fraud can be committed by employees without any indication being given by the books and accounts. Finally, there is no explanation or detailed information given as to how the result of the trading period has arisen. If the comparison of the two statements of affairs discloses an apparent loss when the trader was under the impression that he was making a profit, there is no detailed information available which will enable him to investigate the position, nor will he be able to discover whether the loss is accounted for by a clerical error, by fraud, or by a trading loss of some kind or another.

EXAMPLE

L. Hirst, trading as a baker and confectioner, keeps his books by single entry. On 31st December, 1950, he valued his shop and bakehouse at £1,000, his bakehouse plant at £250, and his stock at £500, while his books showed the total debtors to be £900, total creditors £1,020, and the balance of cash in hand £220. At the 31st December, 1951, his books gave the total debtors as £1,200, total creditors as £940 and cash as £76. His stock was valued at £640, and he had bought a delivery van for £150, but his premises and plant were valued as before. His drawings for the year were £300. Prepare statements showing his profit for the year ended 31st December, 1951, and a Statement of Affairs at the close of the year.

STATEMENT OF AFFAIRS
AS AT 31ST DECEMBER, 1950

Liabilities.	£	Assets.	£
Sundry Creditors.	1,020	Premises.	1,000
Capital Account.	1,850	Plant.	250
		Stock.	500
		Sundry Debtors.	900
		Cash.	220
	£2,870		£2,870

STATEMENT OF AFFAIRS
AS AT 31ST DECEMBER, 1951

Liabilities.	£	Assets.	£
Sundry Creditors.	940	Premises.	1,000
Net Value of Assets.	2,376	Plant.	250
		Motor Van.	150
		Stock.	640
		Sundry Debtors.	1,200
		Cash.	76
	£3,316		£3,316

STATEMENT OF PROFITS

Dr.   FOR THE YEAR ENDED 31ST DECEMBER, 1951   Cr.

	£		£	£
To Net Profit for the year.	826	By Net Assets at 31st December, 1951		2,376
		Less value at 31st December, 1950		1,850
		Net Increase.		526
		„ Cash Withdrawn.		300
	£826			£826

Thus, after making the necessary adjustments for profits and drawings the statement of affairs at the close of the year would appear as follows :—

STATEMENT OF AFFAIRS

AS AT 31ST DECEMBER, 1951

Liabilities.	£	£	Assets.	£
Sundry Creditors.		940	Premises.	1,000
Capital Account as at 1st January, 1951	1,850		Plant.	250
Add Net Profit for Year.	826		Motor Van.	150
	2,676		Stock.	640
Less Drawings.	300		Sundry Debtors.	1,200
		2,376	Cash.	76
		£3,316		£3,316

Final Accounts from Single Entry Records.

In some cases the information available from single entry records is sufficient to enable Trading and Profit and Loss Accounts and Balance Sheet to be prepared, and this method of ascertaining the profit and the financial position should always be adopted where possible.

The position at the commencement of the period must first be ascertained by means of a Statement of Affairs or Balance Sheet and a cash summary together with details of debtors, creditors and other outstandings at the end of the period is all the further information necessary. The following example will illustrate the procedure.

EXAMPLE

From the following particulars prepare Trading and Profit and Loss Accounts for the year ended 31st March, 1951, and a Balance Sheet as at that date.

BALANCE SHEET as at 31st March, 1950

Liabilities.	£	Assets.		£
Sundry Creditors.	16,262	Plant and Machinery.		18,250
Bank Overdraft.	2,168	Stock.		27,750
Capital.	37,200	Sundry Debtors.	£10,700	
		Less Provision for		
		Bad Debts.	1,070	
				9,630
	£55,630			£55,630

Dr.	CASH SUMMARY for year ended 31st March, 1951			Cr.
	£			£
To Cash Sales.	10,626	By Bank Overdraft.	b/f	2,168
„ Debtors.	81,004	„ Creditors.		52,636
		„ Wages.		9,700
		„ Salaries.		3,007
		„ Trade Expenses.		15,206
		„ Bank Balance.	c/d	8,913
	£91,630			£91,630
To Balance	b/d 8,913			

The books disclosed the fact that Discounts Allowed totalled £2,202, and Discounts Received £1,506. Stock at 31st March, 1951, was valued at £30,100, Debtors at £11,250 and Creditors at £17,205.

Depreciation is to be written off Plant and Machinery at 10% and a Provision of 10% on Debtors outstanding is to be made against Bad Debts. Insurance premiums of £62 have been paid in advance and included in Trade Expenses.

The Purchases and Sales can be ascertained by drafting the following Accounts :—

Dr.	PURCHASES ACCOUNT				Cr.
1951		£	1950		£
Mar. 31	To Cash paid to		Mar. 31	By Balance. b/d	16,262
	Creditors.	52,636	1951		
	„ Discounts		Mar. 31	„ Purchases.[1]	55,085
	Received.	1,506			
	„ Balance. c/d	17,205			
		£71,347			£71,347
			1951		
			April 1	By Balance. b/d	17,205

[1] This is the "missing link" in the account and reveals the Purchases for the year.

Dr.   CREDIT SALES ACCOUNT   Cr.

1950			£	1951			£
Mar. 31	To Balance.	b/d	10,700	Mar. 31	By Cash received from Debtors.		81,004
1951					,, Discounts Allowed.		2,202
Mar. 31	,, Sales.[1]		83,756		,, Balance.	c/d	11,250
			£94,456				£94,456
1951							
April 1	To Balance.	b/d	11,250				

[1] This is the "missing link" in the account and reveals the Credit Sales for the year.

TRADING AND PROFIT AND LOSS ACCOUNTS

Dr.   FOR THE YEAR ENDED 31ST MARCH, 1951   Cr.

		£			£	£
To Opening Stock.		27,750	By Sales—			
,, Purchases.		55,085		Credit.	83,756	
,, Wages.		9,700		Cash.	10,626	
,, Gross Profit.	c/d	31,947				94,382
			,, Closing Stock.			30,100
		£124,482				£124,482
To Salaries.		3,007	By Gross Profits.	b/d		31,947
,, Trade Expenses.		15,144	,, Discounts Received.			1,506
,, Discounts Allowed.		2,202				
,, Provision for Bad Debts.		55				
,, Depreciation on Plant.		1,825				
,, Balance—Net Profit.		11,220				
		£33,453				£33,453

BALANCE SHEET
AS AT 31ST MARCH, 1951

Liabilities.		£	Assets.		£	£
Sundry Creditors.		17,205	Plant and Machinery.	18,250		
	£		Less 10% Depreciation.	1,825		
Capital as at 31.3.50.	37,200					16,425
Add Profit for Year.	11,220		Stock.			30,100
		48,420	Sundry Debtors.		11,250	
			Less Provision for Bad Debts.		1,125	
						10,125
			Cash at Bank.			8,913
			Insurance paid in advance.			62
		£65,625				£65,625

Conversion of Single Entry into Double Entry System.

When a trader who has kept his books by single entry is desirous of improving his system by the installation of a complete double entry system the process of conversion must be effected at a given date. The method to be adopted in this case may be summarized as follows :—

(1) A complete set of new account books must be obtained, including :—

(a) Private Ledger }
    Nominal Ledger } or General Ledger.
(b) Purchases Ledger.
(c) Sales Ledger.
(d) Purchases Day Book.
(e) Sales Day Book.
(f) Returns Inwards and Outwards Books.
(g) Bills Receivable and Payable Books.
(h) Journal.
(i) Petty Cash Book.
(j) Cash Book.

Some traders may not require all the above-mentioned books, e.g., Bill Books and Returns Books may not be necessary.

It is obvious that where a Cash Book has been correctly kept a new book need not be obtained, nor will Purchases and Sales Ledgers be required if these have already been kept. In the majority of cases, however, it is usually found advisable to obtain a complete set of new books.

(2) The next step is to prepare a Statement of Affairs, if this has not already been done, at the date upon which the conversion is to be effected.

(3) The opening Journal entry is then made from this Statement of Affairs, the balance of the trader's capital being of course included.

(4) The Sales and Purchases Ledgers will be opened by debiting the debtors' balances and crediting the creditors' balances respectively as shown by the Schedules prepared when compiling the Statement of Affairs. Where these ledgers have previously been correctly kept, it is not necessary to take any further action in this connection.

(5) The amount of the cash balance will form the opening entry in the Cash Book, unless this is already in use, and the Petty Cash imprest amount will be debited as an opening entry in the Petty Cash Book.

(6) Real accounts will be opened in the General Ledger or

Private Ledger, as the case may be, in respect of the assets, and for any other items, such as a provision for bad debts, etc. The nominal accounts in the General Ledger (or Nominal Ledger) will be opened as and when they are required.

(7) To complete the process of conversion a Trial Balance should be taken out so as to ensure that the books have been correctly opened in accordance with double entry principles.

If every subsequent transaction is thereafter recorded in such a way that every debit has its corresponding credit and *vice versa*, the books will then be kept in accordance with double entry principles and all the advantages and benefits of this system will be obtained.

The opening Journal entry for the conversion of the books of L. Hirst (see page 263) into the double entry system would be as follows :—

JOURNAL

			Dr.	Cr.
1951			£	£
Jan. 1	Sundries	Dr.		
	To Sundries			
	Premises.		1,000	
	Plant.		250	
	Motor Van.		150	
	Stock.		640	
	Sundry Debtors.		1,200	
	Cash.		76	
	Sundry Creditors.			940
	Capital Account.			2,376
	Being assets, liabilities and capital as at this date.			
			£3,316	£3,316

EXERCISE 14

A.   Define Single Entry book-keeping.

B.   Describe an elementary system of Single Entry book-keeping.

C.   What are the disadvantages of Single Entry book-keeping as compared with the double entry system ?

D.   How are profits ascertained for a given period by a trader who keeps his books by Single Entry ?

E.   Explain the steps that must be taken in order to convert at any given date books kept upon the Single Entry system to the double entry system.

F. H. Richards keeps his books by single entry. As on 31st December, 1950 and 1951, his financial position was as follows :—

	31st Dec., 1950. £	31st Dec., 1951. £
Stock in Trade	2,471	1,948
Sundry Creditors	1,871	2,014
Sundry Debtors	1,047	1,126
Cash in hand	27	59
Bank Overdraft	2,101	1,746
Bills Receivable	1,014	1,006
Fixtures and Fittings	200	190
Motor Van	240	170

The drawings during the year amounted to £320. Ignore depreciation and provisions.

Prepare a statement from the above particulars, showing H. Richards's profit or loss for the year ended 31st December, 1951.

G. At 1st January, 19...., W. Penn's Capital was £1,400. At 31st December of the same year he possessed the following assets :—

Cash in Hand, £20 ; Cash at Bank, £350 ; Sundry Debtors, £800 ; Stock-in-Trade, £1,500 ; Horses and Carts, £200 ; Fixtures and Fittings, £100. His liabilities were : Trade Creditors, £1,200. He had drawn out during the year £360.

Prepare a Statement of Profit and a Statement of Affairs, providing 5% on Debtors for Bad Debts ; also, depreciate Horses and Carts by 10% and Fixtures and Fittings by 8%.

H. At the 31st March, 19...., H. Morton prepared a Statement of Affairs of his business which disclosed the following information :—

Stock on Hand, £1,030 7s. 6d. ; Sundry Debtors, £2,176 10s. ; Sundry Creditors, £1,171 ; Bills Payable, £350 ; Bank Overdraft, £730 9s. ; Petty Cash in Hand, £25 ; Freehold Premises, £4,500 ; Plant and Machinery, £1,275 15s. ; Fixtures and Fittings, £220.

He decides to convert his books to the double entry system as at 31st March, 19...., after making a provision for Bad Debts of 5% on the Sundry Debtors, and writing off depreciation on Plant and Machinery at 10%, and Fixtures and Fittings at 7½%. You are required to show the opening journal entry necessary to effect the desired conversion.

J. J. Hawkins had not kept proper books of account, but from the following details you are required to ascertain the profit and loss for the year ended 30th June, 1952, and also to show in what manner the available records may be kept on a double entry basis, as and from the 1st July, 1952.

	30th June, 1951.	30th June, 1952.
	£	£
Cash at Bank	228	60
Cash in hand	18	15
Sundry Debtors	621	1,050
Sundry Creditors	1,801	2,100
Bills Payable	*Nil*	150
Bills Receivable	340	200
Private Drawings	*Nil*	200
Stock	963	1,425
Plant and Machinery	1,360	1,525
Office Furniture	124	130

Depreciate Plant and Machinery by 10%, and Office Furniture by 5%. Make a provision for Bad Debts of 5% on the Sundry Debtors, after writing off £40 as irrecoverable.

ANSWERS TO EXERCISES

Exercise 1.

F. Journal Totals : £92 16s. (Debits—H. Scott, £30 5s., Cash, £25, Cash, £12 12s., H Scott, £9 17s., Cash, £15 2s. ; Credits—Stock of Goods, £30 5s., H. Scott, £25, Stock of Goods, £12 12s., Stock of Goods, £9 17s., H. Scott, £15 2s.) ; Ledger Accounts : H. Scott, Balance, Nil : (Debits—£30 5s., £9 17s. ; Credits—£25, £15 2s., Cash, Balance (*Dr.*) : £52 14s. (Debits—£25, £12 12s., £15 2s.), Stock of Goods, Balance (*Cr.*) : £52 14s. Credits—£30 5s., £12 12s., £9 17s.). **G.** G. Ridge, Balance (*Dr.*) : £19 19s. 6d. (Debits —£20 15s. 9d., £16 17s. 4d. ; Credits—£15 10s., £2 3s. 7d.). **H.** Trial Balance : £1,018 12s. (Debits—Cash, £799 16s. 6d., Stock of Goods, £32 14s., J. Field, £113 7s. 6d., Carriage, £4 3s. 6d., Wages, £13, F. Lawn, £33 2s. 9d., Rent, £9, M. Lowe, £13 7s. 9d., ; Credits—Capital, £1,000, H. Heat, £18 12s.). **J.** Trial Balance : £1,645 (Debits—Cash, £879 16s. 6d., Stock of Goods, £510 11s., J. Hignett, £172 10s., Wages, £4, Rent, £2, Postages, £1 2s. 6d., J. Dewar, £75 ; Credits—Capital, £1,570, W. Sparrow, £75).

Exercise 2.

E. Journal Totals : £7,977 (Debits—Freehold Premises, £2,400, Motor and Cycle Stock, £3,200, Plant and Tools, £321, R. Browne, £200, P. Premier, £128, E. Elswick, £100. Office Furniture, £100, Cash, £1,528 ; Credits—Rudge-Whitworth Co., Ltd., £428, Raleigh, Ltd., £814, Capital, £6,735). **F.** Trial Balance : £2,059 12s. 9d. (Debits— Cash, £236 8s. 6d., Fixtures and Fittings, £200, Stock, £1,450 14s. 4d., O. Jay, £127 18s. 8d., Purchases, £26 11s., Wages £16 13s. 11d., Office Expenses, £1 6s. 4d. ; Credits—L. Polsen, £66 16s. 10d., R. Turtle, £40 15s. 8d., Capital, £1,872 9s. 3d., Sales, £79 11s.). **G.** Trial Balance, £4,740 5s. 1d. (Debits—Cash, £1,094 17s. 5d., Stock, £2,050, Fixtures, £490, Motor Vans, £625, J. Beeton, £144 12s. 6d., D. Hunt, £15 7s. 8d., Rent, £100, Packing Materials, £7 7s. 6d., Purchases, £150 10s., Wages, £55, Postages, £4 2s. 3d., Carriage, £3 7s. 9d. ; Credits—R. Ballard, £215, F. Shaw, £258, Capital, £4,000, Sales, £267 5s. 1d.) ; Trading Account, Totals : £2,367 5s. 1d. (Debits—Opening Stock, £2,050, Purchases, £150 10s., Gross Profit, £166 15s. 1d. ; Credits—Sales, £267 5s. 1d., Closing Stock, £2,100) ; Profit and Loss Account, Totals : £169 17s. 6d. (Debits—Rent, £100, Packing Materials, £7 7s. 6d., Wages, £55, Postages, £4 2s. 3d., Carriage, £3 7s. 9d. ; Credits—Gross Profit, £166 15s. 1d., Net Loss, £3 2s. 5d.) ; Balance Sheet Totals, £4,469 17s. 7d. (Liabilities—R. Ballard, £215, F. Shaw, £258, Capital £3,996 17s. 7d. ; Assets—Fixtures, £490, Motor Van, £625, Stock, £2,100, J. Beeton, £144 12s. 6d., D. Hunt, £15 7s. 8d., Cash, £1,094 17s. 5d.). **H.** Trading Account, Totals : £2,543 (Debits—Opening Stock, £326, Purchases, £879, Gross Profit, £1,338 ; Credits—Sales, £2,248, Closing Stock, £295) ; Profit and Loss Account, Totals : £1,338 (Debits— Salaries and Wages, £596, Office Expenses, £98, Carriage, £87, Rent, £157, Net Profit, £400 ; Credits—Gross Profit, £1,338) ; Balance Sheet Totals : £1,321 (Liabilities— Creditors, £321, Capital Account, £1,000 ; Assets—Stock, £295, Debtors, £777, Cash, £249).

Exercise 3.

E. Journal Totals : £7,520 18s. 10d. (Debits—R. Bartley, £231 7s. 9d., C. Crossley, £174 8s. 4d., I. Cooks, £31 11s. 10d., Cash, £760 5s., Stock, £1,171 2s. 5d., Fixtures and Fittings, £427 3s. 6d., Freehold Buildings, £4,250, Motor Vehicles, £475 ; Credits— F. Larking, £477 16s., H. Teal, £823 1s. 7d., Capital, £6,220 1s. 3d.). **F.** Sales Day Book : £174 9s. 6d. (£55 10s., £49 5s. 8d., £52, £12 4s. 2d., £5 9s. 8d.). **G.** Sales Day Book : £237 1s. 5d. (£156, £16 4s., £10 1s., £14 16s., £38 17s., £1 3s. 5d.). **H.** Sales Day Book—Total : £1,155 9s. 6d. ; Motor Cars, £769 2s. 6d. (£182 10s., £401 12s. 6d., £185) ; Motor Cycles, £365 5s. (£65 5s., £300) ; Accessories : £21 2s. (£2 10s., £3 15s., £12,

£2 17s.).). **J.** Sales Day Book—Total : £183 3s. 5d. ; Flour : £53 18s. 7d. (£24 10s., £4 14s. 4d., £2 4s. 6d., £2 6s., £20 3s. 9d.) ; Wheat, £84 14s. 7d. (£3 15s., £80 19s. 7d.); Oats : £18 13s. 1d. (£13 8s. 3d., £5 4s. 10d.) ; Barley : £12 1s. 6d. ; Maize, £13 15s. 8d.

Exercise 4.

E. Purchases Book : £216 12s. 1d. (£28 4s. 4d., £51 15s. 11d., £10 17s. 6d., £4 17s. 4d., £120 17s.). **F.** Purchases Book—Total : £2,237 15s. 4d. ; House Coal, £1,683 16s. 8d. (£237 10s., £532 16s. 8d., £913 10s.) ; Slack Coal : £108 0s. 4d. (£48 14s., £59 6s. 4d.) ; Coke : £39 13s. 4d. ; Anthracite : £406 5s. (£211 5s., £195). **G.** Returns Outwards Book : £54 8s. 3d. (£20 5s., £2 5s., £2, £22 7s. 6d., £7 10s. 9d.). **H.** Purchases Book : £85 8s. 10d. (£19 15s. 9d., £19 2s. 6d., £46 10s. 7d.) ; Sales Day Book : £15 15s. 3d. (£2 5s., £10 3s. 3d., £3 7s.) ; Returns Outwards Book : £10 6s. 9d. (£3 5s. 3d., £7 1s. 6d.) ; Returns Inwards Book : 19s. 6d. (4s. 6d., 15s.).

Exercise 5.

G. Cash Balance (*Dr.*) : £69 0s. 9d. (Debits—£123 7s., £71 5s., £12 7s. 11d., £46 4s. 3d., £14 8s. 4d., £9 10s. 4d. ; Credits—£3 7s., £30, £106 5s., £4 10s., £37 10s., £4 7s. 10d., £16 17s. 3d., £4 10s., 15s., £69 0s. 9d.) ; Discounts (*Dr.*) : £4 18s. 9d. (£3 15s., £1 3s. 9d.) ; Discounts (*Cr.*) : £11 12s. 9d. (£4 2s. 9d., £7 10s.). **H.** Bank Balance (*Dr.*) : £328 13s. 9d. (Debits—£235 6s. 2d., £62 4s. 6d., £159 13s. 5d. ; Credits—£72 10s. 4d., £56, £328 13s. 9d.) ; Cash Balance (*Dr.*) : £10 (Debits—£86 4s. 10d., £100, 15s. ; Credits —£17 6s. 5d., £159 13s. 5d., £10) ; Discounts (*Dr.*) : £3 5s. 6d. ; Discounts (*Cr.*) : £3 16s. 4d. **J.** Bank Balance (*Dr.*) : £101 3s. 4d. (Debits—£150, £71 5s., £10 ; Credits —£50, 16s. 8d., £25, £25, £29 5s., £101 3s. 4d.) ; Cash Balance (*Dr.*) : £34 5s. (Debits— £50, £25, £22 10s., £8 5s., £18, £25 ; Credits—£2 10s., £32, £15, £15, £10, £15, £15, £10, £34 5s.) ; Discounts (*Dr.*) : £3 15s. ; Discounts (*Cr.*) : 15s. **K.** Bank Balance (*Dr.*) : £719 19s. (Debits—£820 6s. 10d., £64 9s. 9d., £160 15s. 6d., £19 1s. 8d. ; Credits—£130, £19 8s. 4d., £8 10s. 5d., £7 5s., £149 18s. 6d., £29 12s. 6d., £719 19s.) ; Discounts (*Dr.*) : £2 11s. 5d. (£1 0s. 3d., £1 11s. 2d.) ; Discounts (*Cr.*) : 7s. 6d. **L.** (*a*) Pass Book Balance (*Cr.*) : £1,281 1s. 10d. (£1,250 + £248 10s. 9d. − £217 8s. 11d.) ; (*b*) Pass Book Balance (*Dr.*) : £1,218 18s. 2d. (£1,250 − £248 10s. 9d. + £217 8s. 11d.).

Exercise 6.

F. Petty Cash Expenditure : £8 19s. 5d.   **G.** Petty Cash Expenditure : £3 5s. 2d. (Postages, £1 10s., Stationery, 10s. 7d., Travelling Expenses, 12s., Carriage, 2s. 9d., Sundry Expenses, 2s. 6d., Ledger Accounts, 7s. 4d.). **H.** Petty Cash Expenditure : £21 10s. 5d. (Stationery, £1 3s. 4d., Postages and Telegrams, £4 11s. 9d., Carriage, 10s. 10d., Travelling Expenses, £2 15s., Sundries, 1s., Cleaning 5s., Ledger Accounts, £12 3s. 6d.).

Exercise 7.

G. Bill Stamp : 4s. ; Due Date : 6th December. **H.** Bills Receivable Book : £979 1s. 6d. (£750, £175 12s. 6d., £53 9s.) ; Due Dates : 23rd June, 14th April, 28th June. **J.** Bills Payable Book : £863 13s. (£350, £37 18s., £475 15s.) ; Due Dates : 7th September, 9th December, 10th August. **K.** Bill Receivable : £200 ; Due Date : 4th August ; Banker's Discount (60 days) : £1 12s. 11d. ; Ledger Balances : Sales (*Cr.*), £300, Cash Book (*Dr.*), £298 7s. 1d., Banker's Discount (*Dr.*), £1 12s. 11d. **L.** Due Date (First Bill) : 24th November ; Banker's Discount (105 days) : £11 5s. 3d. ; New Bill Receivable : £570 10s. 3d. ; Due Date (New Bill) : 27th January ; Ledger Balances : Sales (*Cr.*), £870, Cash Book (*Dr.*), £288 4s. 6d., Bills Receivable (*Dr.*), £570 10s. 3d., Banker's Discount (*Dr.*), £11 5s. 3d. **M.** New Bill Payable : £253 18s. 9d. (Dishonoured Bill, £250, Notarial Charges, 3s. 9d., Interest, £3 15s. ; Due Dates : 7th April, 10th July ; Ledger Balances : Purchases (*Dr.*), £250, Cash Book (*Cr.*), £253 18s. 9d., Notarial Charges (*Dr.*), 3s. 9d., Interest (*Dr.*), £3 15s.)

Exercise 8.

F. Trial Balance : £764 6s. (Debits—G. Dartmouth, £22 8s., Stock, £342 19s., Fixtures and Fittings, £143 8s., Purchases, £28 16s., Wages, £23 11s., Trade Expenses, £5 3s. 6d., Discount, £5, Cash in Hand, £10 15s. 6d., Cash at Bank, £182 5s. ; Credits— Capital, £400, Totnes & Co., £304 8s., H. Gilbert, £23 17s. 11d., Sales, £31 2s., Returns Outwards, £4 18s. 1d.). **G.** Trial Balance : £1,291 11s. 6d. (Debits—R. Alexander &

Co., £28 9s., Stock, £280, Purchases, £147 4s. 6d., Postages, 10s., Stationery, £1 10s., Wages, £16 5s., Carriage, £1 2s. 6d., Petty Cash, £5 12s. 6d., Cash at Bank, £810 18s.; Credits—Capital, £1,000, Chatenay & Co., £72, D. Barton, £64 8s. 6d., Sales, £135 9s., Returns Outwards, £10 16s., Discount, £8 18s.). **H.** Trial Balance: £1,392 12s. 9d. (Debits—Fixtures and Fittings, £42 10s., Drawings, £20, Purchases, £557 14s. 9d., Returns Inwards, £22 10s., Bank Charges, 16s. 8d., Stationery, £11, Salaries, £72, Discount, £2 2s. 9d., Cash in Hand, £8 13s., Cash at Bank, £655 5s. 7d.; Credits— Capital, £750, Hope & Co., £202, Sales, £434 18s., Returns Outwards, £5 14s. 9d.). **J.** (a) Under-statement of Sundry Creditors by £20; (b) Under-statement of Net Profit (or over-statement of Net Loss) by £100; (c) No effect on accounts but personal accounts of both customers incorrect; (d) Under-statement of Net Profit (or over-statement of Net Loss) by £20. **K.** (a) Debit Carriage Inwards, Credit Purchases, £10; (b) Debit Purchases, Credit Supplier, £10.

Exercise 9.

E. Suspense Account, Totals: £37 19s. (Debits—H. Jones, £1 19s., Sales, £36; Credits —Balance, £18 9s. 6d., Returns Inwards, £10, Sundry Creditors, £4 3s. 4d., W. Robinson, £5 6s. 2d.); (a) Debit Suspense, Credit H. Jones, £1 19s.; (b) Debit Suspense, Credit Sales, £36; (c) Debit Returns Inwards, Credit Suspense, £10; (d) Credit Suspense (single entry), £4 3s. 4d.; (e) Debit W. Robinson Credit Suspense, £5 6s. 2d. **F.** (i) Annual Deprecia- tion, £2,250; (ii) Depreciation, £5,000, £3,333 6s. 8d., £2,222 4s. 5d., £1,481 9s. 8d., £987 13s. 1d., £475 6s. 2d. (adjusted). **G.** Discounts Account Totals: £140 3s. (Debits —Discounts Allowed, £79 10s. 6d., Closing Provision, £60 12s. 6d.; Credits—Opening Provision, £85 17s. 6d., Profit and Loss Account, £54 5s. 6d.); Journal Entry: Debit Profit and Loss Account, Credit Discounts Account, £54 5s. 6d. **H.** Debit Profit and Loss Account, Credit Provision for Bad Debts, £15; Debit Profit and Loss (or Trading) Account, Credit Machinery, £337 10s.; Debit Profit and Loss (or Trading) Account, Credit Wages, £17 10s.; Debit Rent, Credit Profit and Loss Account, £19 10s.; Debit Profit and Loss Account, Credit Provision for Discounts, £87 10s., Debit Provision for Dis- counts, Credit Profit and Loss Account, £21; Debit Trading Account (deduction from closing stock), Credit Stock Account, £105, Net Decrease in Profit: £522 (Decreases— £15, £337 10s., £17 10s., £87 10s., £105; Increases—£19 10s., £21). **J.** Trading Account Totals: £16,231 (Debits—Opening Stock, £1,146, Purchases (net), £4,797, Carriage Inwards, £231, Manufacturing Wages, £3,913, Factory Fuel, £759, Factory Expenses, £724, Depreciation of Plant and Machinery, £240, Gross Profit £4,421; Credits—Sales (net), £14,802, Closing Stock, £1,429); Profit and Loss Account Totals: £4,439 (Debits —Salaries, £628, Rent, Rates and Insurance, £626, Carriage Outwards, £324, Travellers' Salaries and Commission, £987, Office Expenses, £228, Provision for Bad Debts, £76, Depreciation of Office Furniture, £17 10s., Net Profit, £1,552 10s.; Credits—Gross Profit, £4,421, Discounts, £18); Balance Sheet Totals: £11,607 10s. (Liabilities— Sundry Creditors, £1,698, Accrued Wages, £57, Capital, £9,852 10s.; Assets—Lease- hold Factory, £2,500, Plant and Machinery, £2,160, Office Furniture, £332 10s., Stock, £1,429, Sundry Debtors, £3,497, Bills Receivable, £60, Cash in Hand, £221, Cash at Bank, £1,240, Insurance in Advance, £68).

Exercise 10.

G. Trading Account Totals: £3,150 (Debits—Opening Stock, £224, Purchases, £742, Gross Profit, £2,184; Credits—Sales, £2,846, Closing Stock, £304); Profit and Loss Account Totals: £2,184 (Debits—Salaries and Wages, £649, Rent and Rates, £92, Office and Trade Expenses, £201, Advertising Expenses, £650, Net Profit, £592; Credits —Gross Profit, £2,184); Balance Sheet Totals: £1,641 (Liabilities—Sundry Creditors, £249, Capital, £1,392; Assets—Stock, £304, Sundry Debtors, £750, Cash at Bank, £587). **H.** Trading Account Totals: £33,560 (Debits—Opening Stock, £4,000, Purchases (net), £23,000, Carriage Inwards, £100, Gross Profit, £6,460; Credits—Sales (net), £32,300, Closing Stock, £1,260); Profit and Loss Account Totals: £6,568 (Debits—Salaries, £2,240, Rent, £1,500, Rates, £600, Insurance, £60, General Expenses, £156, Travelling Expenses, £131, Printing and Stationery, £97, Audit Fee, £52, Advertising, £102, Depreciation of Furniture and Fittings, £30, Net Profit, £1,600; Credits—Gross Profit, £6,460, Interest, £12, Discounts, £96); Balance Sheet Totals: £7,140 (Liabilities— Sundry Creditors, £170, Bills Payable, £100, Capital, £6,870; Assets—Furniture and Fittings, £470, Stock, £1,260, Sundry Debtors, £3,185, Bills Receivable, £685, Cash at Bank Deposit Account, £1,000, Cash at Bank Current Account, £522, Petty Cash, £3,

Insurance in Advance, £15); Gross Profit, 20%; Net Profit, 4·95%. **J.** Trading Account Totals : £39,530 (Debits—Opening Stock, £8,560, Purchases (net), £26,080, Carriage Inwards, £330, Gross Profit, £4,560 ; Credits—Sales (net), £35,550, Closing Stock, £3,980); Profit and Loss Account Totals : £4,595 1s. 4d. (Debits—Salaries, £1,500, National Insurance, £31 2s. 6d., Rent, £100, Rates, £30, Insurance, £42 10s., Advertising, £470 3s. 9d., Printing and Stationery, £47 2s. 6d., General Expenses, £136 13s. 1d., Income Tax, £260 10s., Provision for Bad Debts, £70, Depreciation of Office Furniture, £3 15s., Net Profit, £1,903 4s. 6d. ; Credits—Gross Profit, £4,560, Discounts, £35 1s. 4d.); Balance Sheet Totals : £7,394 15s. 3d. (Liabilities—Sundry Creditors, £390 1s. 5d., Bills Payable, £120, Accrued Rent, £25, Capital, £6,859 13s. 10d. ; Assets— Goodwill, £950, Office Furniture, £46 5s., Stock, £3,980, Sundry Debtors, £1,550 1s. 1d., Bills Receivable, £200, Cash at Bank, £666 1s. 9d., Cash in Hand, £2 7s. 5d.). **K.** Trading Account Totals : £56,674 (Debits—Opening Stock, £9,876, Purchases (net), £25,048, Carriage Inwards, £294, Wages of Mill Hands, £6,785, Mill Rates and Taxes, £172, Coal and Lighting, £398, Depreciation of Plant and Machinery, £874, Gross Profit, £13,227 ; Credits—Credit Sales (net), £42,892, Cash Sales, £1,296, Closing Stock, £12,486); Profit and Loss Account Totals : £13,269 (Debits—Office Salaries, £1,942, Office Rates and Taxes, £19, Insurance, £141, Office Expenses, £321, Travellers' Expenses and Commission, £872, Bad Debts, £384, Provision of Bad Debts, £120, Interest, £172, Depreciation of Motor Lorries, £610, Depreciation of Office Furniture, £18, Net Profit, £8,670 ; Credits —Gross Profit, £13,227, Discounts, £42) ; Balance Sheet Totals : £47,004 (Liabilities— Sundry Creditors, £5,112, Bank Overdraft, £5,000, Loan, £5,000, Capital, £31,892; Assets—Freehold Mill, £10,000, Plant and Machinery, £9,162, Motor Lorries, £2,440, Office Furniture, £342, Stock, £12,486, Sundry Debtors, £12,260, Cash in Hand, £276, Insurance in Advance, £38).

Exercise 11.

A. Trial Balance Totals : £5,672 (Debits—Bank, £450, Stock, £1,500, Bills Receivable, £264, A. Dickens, £190, Premises, £3,000, Purchases, £209, Banker's Discount, £4, Discount, £10, Returns Inwards, £25, Salaries, £20 ; Credits—Bills Payable, £95, R. Chambers, £86, A. Glover, £263, Capital, £4,755, Sales, £473) ; Trading Account Totals : £1,898 (Debits—Opening Stock, £1,500, Purchases, £209, Gross Profit, £189 ; Credits— Sales (net), £448, Closing Stock, £1,450); Profit and Loss Account Totals : £381 (Debits— Salaries, £20, Rent, £45, Discount, £10, Bank Interest, £2, Banker's Discount, £4, Depreciation of Premises, £300 ; Credits—Gross Profit, £189, Net Loss, £192) ; Balance Sheet Totals : £5,052 (Liabilities—Sundry Creditors, £349, Bills Payable, £95, Accrued Rent, £45, Capital, £4,563 ; Assets—Premises, £2,700, Stock, £1,450, Sundry Debtors, £190, Bills Receivable, £264, Bank, £448). **B.** Trial Balance Totals : £854 14s. 11d. (Debits—C. Carr, £93 18s. 4d., Stock, £357 8s. 6d., Purchases, £119 7s. 9d., Returns Inwards, £4 18s., Drawings, £35, Expenses, £4 10s. 9d., Wages, £19 3s., Discount Allowed, £2 3s. 3d., Cash at Bank, £190 14s. 9d., Cash in Hand, £27 10s. 7d. ; Credits— T. Crone, £112 14s., Capital, £600, Sales, £138 3s. 11d., Discount Received, £3 17s.) Trading Account Totals : £536 16s. 3d. (Debits—Opening Stock, £357 8s. 6d., Purchases, £119 7s. 9d., Gross Profit, £60 ; Credits—Sales, (net) £133 5s. 11d., Closing Stock, £403 10s. 4d.); Profit and Loss Account Totals : £63 17s. (Debits—Rent, £25, Wages, £19 3s., Expenses, £4 10s. 9d., Discount Allowed, £2 3s. 3d., Net Profit, £13 ; Credits— Gross Profit, £60, Discounts Received, £3 17s.); Balance Sheet Totals : £715 14s. (Liabilities—Sundry Creditors, £112 14s., Accrued Rent, £25, Capital £578 ; Assets— Stock, £403 10s. 4d., Sundry Debtors, £93 18s. 4d., Cash at Bank, £190 14s. 9d., Cash in Hand, £27 10s. 7d.). **C.** Trial Balance Totals : £2,343 10s. 10d. (Debits—Bills Receivable, £500, Stock, £573 15s. 6d., Drawings, £30, Purchases, £780 9s., Returns Inwards, £40, Wages, £44 11s. 6d., Expenses, £12 7s. 4d., Discount Allowed, £4 6s. 8d., Banker's Discount, £2 8s., Interest, £2 2s., Cash at Bank, £292 11s., Cash in Hand, £60 19s. 10d. ; Credits—C. Payne, £40, B. Barnett, £68 15s., Bills Payable, £902 2s., Capital, £800, Sales, £527 18s. 4d., Discount Received, £4 15s. 6d.) ; Trading Account Totals : £1,554 4s. 6d. (Debits—Opening Stock, £573 15s. 6d., Purchases, £780 9s., Gross Profit, £200 ; Credits—Sales (net), £487 18s. 4d., Closing Stock, £1,066 6s. 2d.) ; Profit and Loss Account Totals : £204 15s. 6d. (Debits—Wages, £44 11s. 6d., Rent, £25, Expenses, £12 7s. 4d., Discount Allowed, £4 6s. 8d., Interest, £2 2s., Banker's Discount, £2 8s., Net Profit, £114 ; Credits—Gross Profit, £200, Discounts Received, £4 15s. 6d.); Balance Sheet Totals : £1,919 17s. (Liabilities—Sundry Creditors, £108 15s., Bills Payable, £902 2s., Accrued Rent, £25, Capital, £884 ; Assets—Stock, £1,066 6s. 2d., Bills Receivable, £500, Cash at Bank, £292 11s., Cash in Hand, £60 19s. 10d.). **D.** Trial

Balance Totals : £1,247 7s. 2d. (Debits—Stock, £175, Fittings, Baskets, etc., £30 10s., S. Smith, £5 2s. 2d., Purchases, £62 4s. 8d., Returns Inwards, 5s. 4d., Wages, £11 17s. 6d., Carriage, £3 17s. 2d., Cash at Bank, £939 15s., Cash in Hand, £18 15s. 4d. ; Credits—Capital, £1,208, J. Jones & Sons, £24 14s. 8d., Sales, £13 17s. 6d., Discount Received, 15s.) ; Trading Account Totals : £248 12s. 2d. (Debits—Opening Stock, £175, Purchases, £62 4s. 8d., Gross Profit, £11 7s. 6d. ; Credits—Sales (net), £13 12s. 2d., Closing Stock, £235) ; Profit and Loss Account Totals : £15 14s. 8d. (Debits—Wages, £11 17s. 6d., Carriage, £3 17s. 2d. ; Credits—Gross Profit, £11 7s. 6d., Discount Received, 15s., Net Loss, £3 12s. 2d.) ; Balance Sheet Totals : £1,229 2s. 6d. (Liabilities—Sundry Creditors, £24 14s. 8d., Capital, £1,204 7s. 10d. ; Assets—Fittings, Baskets, etc., £30 10s., Stock, £235, Sundry Debtors, £5 2s. 2d., Cash at Bank, £939 15s., Cash in Hand, £18 15s. 4d.).
E. Trial Balance Totals : £2,278 17s. 8d. (Debits—C. Allen, £17, P. Wilson, £116 15s. 2d., G. Dawson, £77 15s. 6d., Furniture and Fittings, £267 12s., Stock, £1,029, Bills Receivable, £104, Drawings, £50, Purchases, £409, Returns Inwards, £7 12s. 6d., Wages, £26, Expenses, £5 5s., Carriage, £8 16s., Cash at Bank, £150 4s. 6d., Cash in Hand, £9 17s.; Credits—M. Herriott, £83, C. Testout, £348 10s., H. Dickson, £36, R. McGredy & Co., £112, Capital, £1,364, Sales, £322 13s. 2d., Returns Outwards, £9 10s., Discount Received, £3 4s. 6d.) ; Trading Account Totals : £1,558 0s. 8d. (Debits—Opening Stock, £1,029, Purchases (net), £399 10s., Gross Profit, £129 10s. 8d. ; Credits—Sales (net), £315 0s. 8d., Closing Stock, £1,243) ; Profit and Loss Account Totals : £132 15s. 2d. (Debits—Wages, £26, Expenses, £5 5s., Carriage, £8 16s., Net Profit, £92 14s. 2d. ; Credits—Gross Profit, £129 10s. 8d., Discounts Received, £3 4s. 6d.) ; Balance Sheet Totals : £1,986 4s. 2d. (Liabilities—Sundry Creditors, £579 10s., Capital, £1,406 14s. 2d. ; Assets—Furniture and Fittings, £267 12s., Stock, £1,243, Sundry Debtors, £211 10s. 8d., Bills Receivable, £104, Cash at Bank, £150 4s. 6d., Cash in Hand, £9 17s.).

Exercise 12.

G. Zero Date : 31st December ; Interest, £29 15s. 7d. (Products—Debit, 31st Jan., 37,200, 31st March, 126,000, 31st March, Balance of Products, 217,400 ; Credit, 28th Feb., 11,800, 14th March, 116,800, 31st March, Balance of Principal, 252,000) ; Balance due by Herring Bros., £2,829 15s. 7d. H. Zero Date : 31st December ; Interest, £40 15s. 4d. (Products—Debit, 7th Jan., 5,950, 25th May, 36,250, 30th June, Balance of Products, 297,600 ; Credit, 10th May, 195,000, 30th June, Balance of Principal, 144,800); Balance due by Jansenn & Co., £840 15s. 4d. J. Account Sales : Net Proceeds, £1,237 2s. 5d. ; Balance due by J. Saxby, £437 2s. 5d. (Debits—Gross Proceeds, £1,319 ; Credits—Warehousing, £12, Insurance, £1 15s., Landing Charge, £5 9s. 6d., Commission, £39 11s. 5d., Del Credere Commission, £23 1s. 8d., Bill Receivable, £800, Balance, £437 2s. 5d.). K. Account Sales : Net Proceeds, £2,263 12s. 6d. ; Consignment to Begum & Chattergee : Totals, £2,350. (Debits—Goods on Consignment, £1,600, Insurance, £11 10s., Freight, £46, Sundry Charges, £2 10s., Landing Charges, £8 10s., Insurance £1 10s., Commission, £76 7s. 6d., Net Profit, £603 12s. 6d. ; Credits—Gross Proceeds, £2,350). L. Account Sales : Net Proceeds, £737 12s. 6d. ; Consignment to A. Cain : Totals, £839 7s. 6d. (excluding Discount on Bill) (Debits—Goods on Consignment, £750, Freight, Insurance, etc., £32, Consignee's Expenses, £17 12s. 6d., Commission, £39 15s. ; Credits—Gross Proceeds, £795, Net Loss, £44 7s. 6d.).

Exercise 13.

E. Income and Expenditure Account Totals: £194 (Debits—Rent, £51, Sundry Expenses, £5, Advertising, £24, Printing Expenses, £22 10s., Surplus, £91 10s. ; Credits—Subscriptions, £34, Net Proceeds from Lectures, £10, Net Proceeds from Plays, £150). F. Income and Expenditure Account Totals : £720 (Debits—Boat House Rent, £200, Wages of Waterman, £240, Printing and Stationery, £54, Postages and Sundries, £12 4s., Depreciation of Furniture and Fixtures, £17 10s., Surplus, £196 6s. ; Credits—Subscriptions, £350, Entrance Fees, £150, Proceeds of Gala, £220). Balance Sheet Totals : £1,931 11s. (Liabilities—Capital £1,747, Income and Expenditure Account, £184 11s.; Assets—Club House, £1,500, Furniture and Fixtures, £157 10s., Cash at Bank, £274 1s.) G. Receipts and Payments Account Totals : £345 15s. 1d. (Debits—Entrance Fees, £42 2s., Subscriptions, £175 10s., Donations, £10 10s., Interest on Investments, £7 14s., Receipts from Canteen, £84 13s. 9d., Sale of Tennis Balls, etc., £15 15s. 6d., Closing Balance, £9 9s. 10d. ; Credits—Opening Balance, £15 7s. 11d., Upkeep of Grounds, £95 7s., Wages of Groundsman, £125, Printing and Stationery, £6 12s., Postages, etc., £3 2s. 7d., Stores for Canteen, £51 18s., Purchase of New Mower, £45, Bank Charges, £3 7s. 7d.). H. Trading Account Totals (Wines, Spirits and Cigars) : £672 6s. 7d.

(Debits—Opening Stock, £84, Purchases, £355 0s. 2d., Profit, £233 6s. 5d. ; Credits—
Sales, £581 16s. 7d., Closing Stock, £90 10s.) ; Income and Expenditure Account Totals :
£1,723 4s. 11d. (Debits—Salary of Secretary, £150, Wages of Caretakers, £352, Rent,
£200, Rates and Taxes, £70, Lighting and Heating, £100 10s., Printing and Stationery,
£79 17s. 2d., Newspapers, £27 8s., Sundry Expenses, £20 3s. 6d., Repairs, £70 10s.,
Decoration of Premises, £500, Depreciation of Furniture and Fixtures, £67 19s. 2d.,
Surplus, £84 17s. 1d. ; Credits—Subscriptions, £1,489 18s. 6d., Profit on Wines, Spirits
and Cigars, £233 6s. 5d.) ; Balance Sheet Totals : £2,049 2s. 8d. (Liabilities—Sundry
Creditors, £365 13s. 6d., Capital, £1,683 9s. 2d. ; Assets—Furniture and Fixtures,
£711 12s. 1d., Stock, £90 10s., Sundry Debtors, £146 2s. 10d., Cash at Bank, £640, Cash
in Hand, £60 17s. 9d., Decoration of Premises, £400).

Exercise 14.

F. Profit : £32 (Closing Surplus, £739, less Opening Surplus, £1,027, plus Drawings,
£320) ; Statement of Affairs Totals : £4,499 (Liabilities—Sundry Creditors, £2,014, Bank
Overdraft, £1,746, Capital, £739 ; Assets—Motor Van, £170, Fixtures and Fittings, £190,
Stock, £1,948, Sundry Debtors, £1,126, Bills Receivable, £1,006, Cash in Hand, £59).
G. Profit : £662 (Closing Surplus, £1,702, less Opening Surplus, £1,400, plus Drawings,
£360) ; Statement of Affairs Totals : £2,902 (Liabilities—Trade Creditors, £1,200,
Capital, £1,702 ; Assets—Horses and Carts, £180, Fixtures and Fittings, £92, Stock,
£1,500, Sundry Debtors, £760, Cash at Bank, £350, Cash in Hand, £20). H. Statement
of Affairs Totals : £8,974 14s. 6d. (Liabilities—Sundry Creditors, £1,171, Bills Payable,
£350, Bank Overdraft, £730 9s., Capital, £6,723 5s. 6d. ; Assets—Freehold Premises,
£4,500, Plant and Machinery, £1,148 3s. 6d., Fixtures and Fittings, £203 10s., Stock,
£1,030 7s. 6d., Sundry Debtors, £2,067 13s. 6d., Petty Cash, £25) ; Journal Totals :
£9,083 11s. (Debits—Freehold Premises, £4,500, Plant and Machinery, £1,148 3s. 6d.,
Fixtures and Fittings, £203 10s., Stock, £1,030 7s. 6d., Sundry Debtors, £2,176 10s.,
Petty Cash, £25 ; Credits—Provision for Bad Debts, £108 16s. 6d., Sundry Creditors,
£1,171, Bills Payable, £350, Bank Overdraft, £730 9s., Capital, £6,723 5s. 6d.). J.
Profit : £252 10s. (Closing Surplus, £1,905 10s.,less Opening Surplus, £1,853, plus Drawings,
£200) ; Statement of Affairs Totals : £4,155 10s. (Liabilities—Sundry Creditors, £2,100,
Bills Payable, £150, Capital, £1,905 10s. ; Assets—Plant and Machinery, £1,372 10s.,
Office Furniture, £123 10s., Stock, £1,425, Sundry Debtors, £959 10s., Bills Receivable,
£200, Cash at Bank, £60, Cash in Hand, £15) ; Journal Totals : £4,206 (Debits—Plant
and Machinery, £1,372 10s., Office Furniture, £123 10s., Stock, £1,425, Sundry Debtors,
£1,010, Bills Receivable, £200, Cash at Bank, £60, Cash in Hand, £15 ; Credits—Provision for Bad Debts, £50 10s., Sundry Creditors, £2,100, Bills Payable, £150, Capital,
£1,905 10s.).

INDEX

Printed in Great Britain by Butler & Tanner Ltd., Frome and London

OTHER VOLUMES PUBLISHED BY THE DONNINGTON PRESS

The works specified below have been written to provide that concise, up-to-date and authentic information which is required by those preparing for professional examinations. They will also be found of great practical assistance as works of reference to professional Accountants, Secretaries, and others. The prices quoted are net. Postage in each case is 9d. extra.

ARITHMETIC

ARITHMETIC. By D. A. Young, B.A. Hons. 9s. 6d.

AUDITING

ELEMENTS OF AUDITING. By R. Glynne Williams, F.C.A., F.T.I.I. 10s. 6d.

BOOK-KEEPING AND ACCOUNTANCY

PRINCIPLES AND PRACTICE OF BOOK-KEEPING AND ACCOUNTS. By B. G. Vickery, F.C.A. 15s.
PRINCIPLES OF ACCOUNTING. Edited by S. W. Rowland, LL.B., F.C.A. 17s. 6d.

EXECUTORSHIP

LAW AND ACCOUNTS OF EXECUTORS, ADMINISTRATORS AND TRUSTEES. By B. G. Vickery, F.C.A. 15s.

ENGLISH

ENGLISH GRAMMAR, COMPOSITION AND CORRESPONDENCE. By M. A. Pink, M.A., and S. E. Thomas, B.Com., Ph.D. 10s. 6d.

GEOGRAPHY

GEOGRAPHY. By T. M. Keeling, A.C.I.S., F.R.G.S., and W. R. H. Walters, B.Com.(Lond.). 12s. 6d.

INCOME TAX

ELEMENTS OF TAXATION. By R. Glynne Williams, F.C.A., F.T.I.I. 10s.
INCOME TAX, SUR TAX AND PROFITS TAX. By R. Glynne Williams, F.C.A., F.T.I.I. 15s.

LAW

ELEMENTS OF COMPANY LAW. By Harry Farrar, M.A., LL.B., Barrister-at-Law. 10s. 6d.
GENERAL PRINCIPLES OF ENGLISH LAW. By O. K. Metcalfe, M.A., LL.M., Barrister-at-Law. 10s. 6d.
PARTNERSHIP LAW. By O. Shepherd, M.A., LL.B., Barrister-at-Law. 10s. 6d.
PRINCIPLES OF MERCANTILE LAW. By E. W. Chance, O.B.E., LL.B., Barrister-at-Law. 21s.

All these volumes are obtainable through any bookseller, or direct from—
THE GREGG PUBLISHING CO., LTD., 51 RUSSELL SQUARE, LONDON, W.C.1

SPECIALISED

POSTAL TUITION

for the
Examinations of the

ACCOUNTANCY

SECRETARIAL

BANKING, LEGAL

AND INSURANCE

Professions, for the
External Degrees of the

UNIVERSITY OF LONDON

etc., etc.

Many intensely practical
(non-examination) Courses
in business subjects

For full particulars, send for free
prospectus, stating the examinations or
subjects in which you are interested,
to the Secretary,

METROPOLITAN COLLEGE

ST. ALBANS

D0311931